**HOW CORPORATE SALES PROFESSIONALS
GENERATE THE LEADS THEY NEED**

selling against the goal

KENDRA LEE

Wishing you a steady flow of top quality leads!
Kendra Lee

Dearborn™
Trade Publishing
A **Kaplan Professional** Company

This publication is designed to provide accurate and authoritative information in regard to the subject matter covered. It is sold with the understanding that the publisher is not engaged in rendering legal, accounting, or other professional service. If legal advice or other expert assistance is required, the services of a competent professional person should be sought.

President, Dearborn Publishing: Roy Lipner
Vice President and Publisher: Cynthia A. Zigmund
Senior Acquisitions Editor: Michael Cunningham
Interior Design: Lucy Jenkins
Cover Design: Design Literate
Typesetting: the dotted i

Published by Dearborn Trade Publishing
A Kaplan Professional Company

Printed in the United States of America

05   06   07   08   10 9 8 7 6 5 4 3 2 1

Library of Congress Cataloging-in-Publication Data

Lee, Kendra.
    Selling against the goal : how corporate sales professionals generate the leads they need / Kendra Lee.
       p.   cm.
    Includes index.
    ISBN 1-4195-0825-3 (6x9 pbk.)
    1. Selling. 2. Sales management. I. Title.
HF5438.25.L42 2005
658.8'1—dc22

                                                                2005009915

Dedication
To Bill, Bill, Michael, and Jeffrey
A special thanks to Paul Suter

PRAISE FOR *SELLING AGAINST THE GOAL*

"The most comprehensive book ever written to satisfy and exceed sales goals. *Selling Against the Goal* works for novices, experts, and everybody in between because it covers all aspects of a salesperson's job from A to Z. You can't be successful in sales if you aren't educated on the process—this book *is* the process and the information it contains is invaluable. Managers should make it a must-read for all new employees."

Lisa E. Shevy, President and CEO,
Women's Business Enterprise Council–West

"After reading only a few pages, it became readily apparent that this is not another sales process book. Rather, it contains a wealth of real-world tips, tools, and activities that will help sales professionals become more successful. *Selling Against the Goal* certainly does an exceptional job integrating sales and marketing activities to provide a practical, easy-to-read guide for sales (and marketing) professionals at any experience level."

Bob Kantin, President, SalesProposals.com

"In today's competitive sales environment, it's a must-read for sales professionals looking for sound, practical advice on how to generate leads and make things happen in their territory."

Tom McBride, Vice President of Sales, Jefferson Wells International

"Kendra has created a valuable resource for anyone looking to exceed in sales. *Selling Against the Goal* provides personal motivation tips, an excellent approach to differentiating personal income goals from corporate income goals and statistical sales approaches. These solutions are a must-have for any serious salesperson's tool kit for success!"

Donna L. Boreing, Vice President, Integration, Conversion,
Colorado & Nevada Operations, Anthem Blue Cross & Blue Shield

"*Selling Against the Goal* is destined to become the *de facto* reference for all sales professionals who are serious about achieving quota."

Michael J. Nick, Author of *ROI Selling,* and President, ROI4Sales.com

"Kendra Lee provides us with an invaluable resource for developing sales performance at all levels in today's competitive business environment. The breadth of this book encompasses more than improving individual sales performance, it's really an essential guide for all business owners. It is an enlightening read!"

Jodie Brown, MA, President, Summit Solutions, LLC

"Kendra Lee has developed a practical, how-to approach for generation and closing qualified sales prospects. She advocates tracking sales opportunities through the customer buying stages instead of traditional methods. Finally, someone willing to help you "win big"! A must-read primer for even the most experienced salesperson."

Patricia Gorman, Executive Vice President–Business Solutions,
The TriZetto Group, Inc.

"This is a must-read for any salesperson starting out or matured. Lee's step-by-step techniques guide you through success in sales with no smoke and mirrors, just straight talk from a strong-headed businesswoman who wanted to test herself and her lead-generating process in helping you plan for success!"

Rob Rose, Member Services Center Manager,
Denver Metro Chamber of Commerce

"This book should be required reading for anyone beginning a sales career. The basic skills explained are often overlooked by sales training programs. Identifying and managing partners to help generate leads is usually discovered only after years of sales experience. New in sales? Buy this book!"

Mike Addison, CEO, ExecuTrain

"SysTest Labs was very pleased to utilize the services of Kendra Lee, and I found this book to be an excellent and informative follow-up to the sessions we spent together. I recommend this book to all sales professionals and sales managers."

Tim Walker, Executive Vice President of Global Sales, SysTest Labs

"There are books that talk about how things should be done and then there are those that actually walk you through the process. Kendra's book doesn't just state that the word *leads* should be replaced with *opportunities* but also provides actual examples and guidelines for salespeople. My guess is that everyone, at some point, can use the 'how to organize an event for less than $350' information."

John Venator, President and CEO, CompTIA

Contents

P A R T   F O U R

Finding Activity Content and Lists

P A R T   F I V E

Creating a Territory Lead Generation Plan

Job Title: Sales Rep
Job Responsibilities: Generate Leads, Close Sales
How to Get the Job Done: It's up to you, my friend.

That's a pretty accurate depiction of how most sales reps enter the marketplace. They understand their title and their assignment, but nobody really ever tells them how to meet their sales goals and fulfill their responsibilities. This book provides sales reps with invaluable, tangible sales tips—the keys they need to unlock the door to success.

The first step, of course, for any sales rep is generating leads. Before leads become revenue, they must be found and cultivated. You must know how many leads you need, where to go to find them, who can help you get them, which activities will work for your target market, what to communicate to compel a response, how to follow up with those who don't respond to your message, what to do next with those who do respond, how to tweak your activities to get the highest response rates, what to report to your manager, and how to keep the leads flowing consistently.

The step-by-step process provided on the following pages will help you with lead generation efforts and assist in determining how many leads you need to meet your personal goals. It also includes activities you might execute as part of those efforts, with examples you can copy.

This book is designed so that you can begin at any point based on what your personal needs are at the time. If you need to put a plan in place to present to management, begin at the beginning. If you only need ideas on how to set up a lead generation campaign, start with Part Two. If you are looking for examples and sample templates to use in your lead generation activities, jump to the appendixes. Each section is self-contained and yet builds upon its predecessor. By the end of the book, you will have a complete territory plan.

So why are you reading this book? Because you want to outperform your fellow reps while generating the income you deserve. You want to be a success and you know in sales that starts with finding customers to whom you can sell. You don't want to sit back and wait for marketing to generate leads for your territory or for the phone to ring. You don't want to wonder if you will have enough leads to make your quota or if you'll lose your job. This book helps you to not only find the prospects you need but also to entice *them* to contact *you.*

You want to take control of your territory, your opportunities, and, ultimately, your income, just as I did for myself when I developed and mastered these techniques. You want to be the best sales rep you can be—taking control of your own success. I invite you to use this book as your planning and execution tool for lead generation and, ultimately, sales success in your territory. It *is* your plan for success. You are in charge.

When Kendra Lee began her sales career, she was set up to fail. Kendra was assigned to a territory in Denver, Colorado, that was, as she describes it, "dry as a bone." The territory had no real prospects, no strategy for finding prospects, and a $1 million sales quota that was due within ten months. It would have been a good time to quit.

But Kendra had put herself in this position because she wanted to become a successful rep. Prior to taking this leap of faith, she had a great job in IBM's finance department and was being groomed for success. But the job of juggling numbers no longer appealed to her, and she wanted a new challenge. At the time, IBM was restructuring and offering sales positions to members of its team with one important caveat: If you didn't succeed as a sales rep, you couldn't have your previous job back. Kendra, excited by the prospect of being a salesperson for IBM, decided to take the risk.

So she flew to Denver with only four months of sales training, little understanding of the market, and the question whether she had made the right decision—not exactly the best conditions for becoming a successful sales rep.

When Kendra arrived in Denver, it quickly became apparent that her decision may have been a foolish one. Her lead list included bowling alleys, movie theaters, insurance companies, and other small, professional service firms in Denver, all of which were highly unlikely buyers of computer equipment in the late 1980s. Rather than give up, Kendra dug in. She created her own system for generating leads and closing sales.

When Kendra took on her first sales challenge in Denver, she applied many of the techniques you will read about in this book. Steps such as analyzing her territory, targeting the very best opportunities, and generating significant numbers of leads helped her meet her $1 million quota and then surpass the same quota ten times within three years. She earned IBM's highest sales honor—Golden Circle—and was being asked by IBM managers across the nation to help them instill her process with their sales teams. Not surprisingly—at least for Kendra—she turned down their offers.

Kendra was looking for a new challenge and decided to take her techniques and ideas with her to a new company. She wanted to test herself and her system and prove that she could sell computer software. Not long after she made her decision, Kendra was selling for the second largest manufacturer of computer software—Sybase—with a goal of becoming the company's number one sales rep and closing a million-dollar deal within the year. It took her only four months, thanks in large part to the lead generation system she had created.

With customers basically coming to her, Kendra decided to take the next bold risk of her career—starting her own company, KLA Group. Since starting KLA Group in 1995, Kendra and her team of professional trainers now consult for Fortune 100 companies, small and medium-sized businesses, and individual sales reps on ways they can improve their sales results. Much of her company's work is based on the lead generation techniques that you'll read about in the following chapters.

If you're a sales rep who feels you've been set up to fail or simply aren't achieving the goals you have for yourself, read on. The information Kendra has to share is guaranteed to help reps meet their quotas and help companies reach their goals.

Good selling!

SETTING YOURSELF UP TO SUCCEED

Part One helps you define where you are going through your own vision and goals. It gives you the measurements you can use as guideposts on your path to success and helps you define how many leads you need to generate to achieve your vision.

1

SIX KEYS TO SUCCESS'S DOOR

Flo was a sales rep in a territory at TJ *Parker Ideas. She had worked with TJ Parker Ideas for two years and had only made her quota in the last month of the year for both years. She had higher goals than that but couldn't figure out how to meet them. She was intimidated by the fact that her competition and peers seemed "light years" ahead of her, but she didn't know what they were doing that was making them so much more successful. They seemed to have more opportunities than she did, yet she had a similar territory. Rather than simply getting on the phone and making cold calls from the phone book, she took a step back and looked at her challenges and began to develop a plan that would give her a road map toward success. She realized it might not be perfect or hold all of the answers, but at least it would give her initial direction and a foundation to build from.*

In my experience, I've come across hundreds of sales reps like Flo. They are people who are motivated to sell but just don't know how to begin. They know they are not as efficient as they could be yet don't know what to do differently. It's a difficult proposition to be sure but regardless of experience, territory, the company a rep works for, the solutions he or she sells, or his or her quota, there are six keys to being the best sales rep you can be, no matter what. If you can master these six keys, you will be an extremely successful sales rep, even if you don't have the seemingly innate talent of some of your peers. The following chapters help you to master these six keys to success. And it all begins with *a plan* and *lead generation*.

I. A VISION

You need a vision for your territory that you can get excited about, one you believe in. Even though it is important to understand your management's and your company's vision, you need your own as well.

To help assess your vision, ask yourself questions such as these: What do I plan to achieve? What do I plan to turn this territory into? Share your vision with others who can get excited with you. Make sure your team knows what your vision is so it can feel your excitement and share it. (If you don't think you have a team to share it with, then turn to Chapters 8, 9, and 10 on partners and define your own team.)

As you develop your vision, avoid listening to naysayers, but do address potential failure. There's no reason to acknowledge doubters, but it's important for you to know that failure will be part of the process. As a salesperson, it is inevitable that some people will say no and some lead generation campaigns will fail. When this happens, will you put those people who said no into your contact management database to call them back in six months to see if there is a new opportunity? Or will you forget about them and never call them again? Will you look at what failed in the lead generation campaign and learn how to do it differently next time, or will you give up on campaigns completely? How will you deal with failure?

Create your vision. Embrace it. Then communicate it and believe in your ability to be a success.

2. A PLAN

Once you have your vision for your territory, you need to develop a winning plan to achieve it. As hard as it is for a busy salesperson like yourself, you must take time out of your time-consuming schedule to do strategic planning. Executives recognize that strategic planning is a necessity for both long-term and day-to-day competition and so must you.

For a sales rep, this means preparing through account planning, opportunity planning, and territory planning. All the things a spontaneous sales rep hates but that are a necessary evil. It is not something you can do once a year and then forget about. Planning becomes a way of life. You must have the discipline to plan to succeed and then stick with the plan you create. Without a good plan and execution, you have little hope of achieving your goal. You *need* a lead generation plan.

Ask yourself: What are all the steps I need to take to achieve my vision? Think of every little step. Write them all down and organize them in the logical order you will take toward achieving your vision. Once you've written them down—start executing the steps. Odds are you will accomplish your goals long before you complete every step in your plan.

If you don't have a plan, you won't achieve your vision as easily or as quickly as you would if you do have a plan. Think of it as though you are driving to get to an appointment at 9:00 in the morning—an appointment with a new prospect in a new city in a different state. How will you get there without a plan? Your plan is your road map to success.

I had a vision of achieving IBM's highest sales award, Golden Circle, in a territory nobody thought would generate much revenue. To achieve Golden Circle, I had to sell 140 percent of my quota in that territory. I wrote a plan that included 178 steps. I had generated 100 percent of my annual revenue within five months after completing only 34 steps. I achieved Golden Circle by the tenth month, after completing 64 of those 178 steps. Planning works.

Prepare to win. Plan to win. And you *will* win. Be a die-hard planner.

3. DIE-HARD EXECUTION

To compete in today's market, you have to change the rules or at least find a way to get them to work in your favor. Die-hard, consistent execution is your key to changing the playing field. Many sales reps find the details involved in successful lead generation tedious and unnecessary. Once the leads begin to flow, they get busy and let other priorities replace the attention to detail that brought in the leads.

Execute in conformity with the plan you create, keeping your vision in mind. Leads will abound if you continue to execute according to the plans you put in place, involving critical resources and meeting your time frames. No matter how busy you get, execute with precision.

I take two days out of the territory every year to do my planning for the next year, so I know what I need to execute. Yes, it is a challenge to take that time away from customers, and I *hate* it. And yet this is the plan I work from for the rest of the year. It is my road map for achieving the goals I have set for myself, and I must execute against—that is, according to—it. Once the plan is complete, I schedule the key milestones on my calendar and then schedule my daily activities around them. This ensures I execute against my lead generation plan.

At midyear I take another day out of the territory to fine-tune my plan and schedule the key milestones for the balance of the year. I look to see what has worked over the previous six months and what has not. I make adjustments, then move forward with confidence in my execution strategy for the rest of the year.

Throughout the year I keep the plan close at hand, and each week I look at it to see what it is I need to accomplish. The plan tells me what I need to do in my weekly activities to get to my end goal. Without this planning and execution, I could never have achieved the levels of sales success I have over the past 16 years.

4. CONSTANT AND CONSISTENT LEAD GENERATION

If you don't practice constant lead generation, you will not have new opportunities flowing into your pipeline on a consistent basis. You also will not have your name in front of your customers and prospects to ensure they will think of you first when an opportunity does arise.

Many sales reps work a set of opportunities to closure, then begin the lead generation process over again. This leads to inconsistent commissions and a sales manager's questioning your selling abilities. Your goal should be to consistently generate leads so you have new opportunities constantly entering your pipeline.

The more opportunities you have flowing in, the less dependent you will be on closing specific deals. You can afford to lose one deal if you have five more opportunities behind it in your pipeline. Practice consistent lead generation.

5. FOLLOW UP! FOLLOW UP! FOLLOW UP!

A majority of all leads turn into a sale within one year for somebody. Why shouldn't they be your sales? It's not enough just to begin your lead generation tactics—follow up! Stay on top of the prospect until you know it is a real opportunity. Qualify that lead before discarding it. More sales reps disregard leads than you can imagine. If you work hard to get the lead, follow up on it. I have found that in today's market it takes nine calls to get a prospect to return your call. If you stop following up after three calls, it will take you a long time to fill your pipeline.

Following up means keeping your commitments. If you promise a customer or prospect an item by a certain date, you must meet that deadline. Don't call with excuses unless it is absolutely imperative. If you know you cannot meet a commitment, give as much advance warning as possible.

Call when you say you will call. Meet when you say you will meet. Get an answer by the date you say you will.

Following up also means staying in touch over time. The prospect who says he or she isn't going to do anything for 12 months will do something eventually. Stay in touch so you are there when the opportunity does arise.

It is amazing how many people don't keep their commitments. By keeping your own, you portray yourself as an organized, interested business partner, not just another salesperson. Keeping commitments begins with following up on leads from your lead generation activities. Set the standard that prospects can expect from you from the start.

Customers tell me all the time that they know they can count on me because I follow through on my promises. They don't hesitate to refer me within their organizations or to their peers. They are confident they can trust my professionalism simply because I follow up.

6. UNDERSTANDING AND CARING FOR YOUR CUSTOMERS AND PROSPECTS

This means that you take a real interest in your prospects and customers. "You don't do anything unethical," warns Phil Harris, VP of Sales for Akibia, "and you are honest." You listen first. You think about your response. Then you talk. Listen 80 percent of the time. Talk only 20 percent of the time.

Approach prospects and customers with ideas and recommendations of interest to them—even in the prospect stage of the sales cycle. Understand their business needs, not just in terms of how it affects your products or services. What are their business challenges? How can you help them meet those challenges? Show your value by the overall knowledge you have, not just your product knowledge.

Your lead generation activities should reflect the knowledge you have gained. Plan your activities to match the business needs of your target audience so they are of interest and importance to that audience. Not only will this improve your response rates, but it will also demonstrate the value you can bring to customers if they choose to purchase from you.

SUMMARY

Flo has many people telling her not to worry, assuring her she'll make her number. She always has. But Flo knows she needs to change the way she is running the business of her territory. After two years in the territory, she loves her customers and understands their needs. Now she needs to clarify her vision and set a plan to achieve it. Once she has the plan in place, she expects to stick with it throughout the year, even if she has tons of leads flowing in and is wildly successful. She has promised herself she will follow up on all her potential leads no matter how busy she gets. She has decided this is going to be her year and she is going to make it happen! Flo is going to use the following chapters to discover a plan that will match her vision and help her achieve the success she knows she is capable of achieving.

2

LEAD GENERATION BEGINS WITH YOUR GOALS

As Flo examined her mediocre success *of the previous two years, she decided it was time to approach her territory just as she had approached finding a career—by analyzing her goals so she could create a plan to achieve them. She started by looking at what she wanted to achieve in this territory and how to earn enough to buy the new car she had been eyeing recently without impacting her normal spending and saving and her other goals. It was a critical first step as she started down her new path to success.*

KNOW WHAT YOU WANT

All success in a career begins with knowing what you want from that career and why you are pursuing it. The same is true with selling and lead generation. You are in sales to achieve a set of personal goals. Those goals determine the number of sales you need to make in your territory, which in turn determines the number of leads you need in your funnel based on your closing ratio, which determines the frequency and number of lead generation plans you need to execute. This is illustrated in Figure 2.1.

FIGURE 2.1 Personal Goals Determine Your Lead Generation Plans

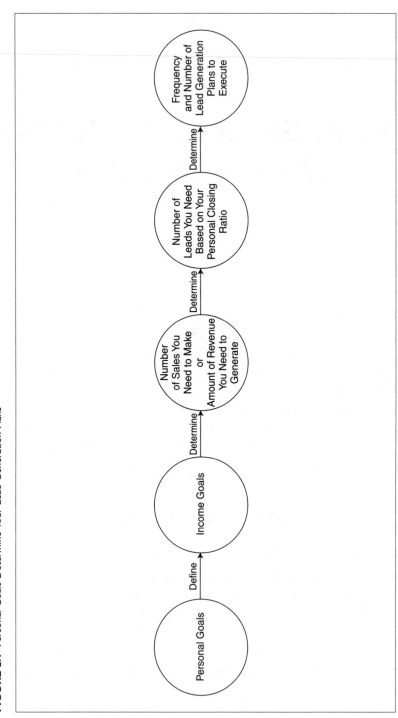

You must have a vision of what you want from your lead generation plans to achieve success. That vision and motivation start with your own goals. Your sales manager cannot provide the vision and motivation, only the stick by which you will be measured within the company. You must provide your own motivation.

SETTING YOUR GOALS THAT DRIVE LEAD GENERATION PLANS

What are your personal goals? Do you want to buy a house or car, take a trip, support a family member? How much income do you need to accomplish those goals?

What are your professional goals? Is there a promotion you want, an award for which you are striving? Do you want to achieve a certain share of market in your territory or a specific customer satisfaction rating? How much income do you need to accomplish these goals?

Consider how you will achieve these personal and professional goals through your sales territory. Do you need a raise to meet specific financial goals? Do you need to overachieve your quota by a certain percentage to qualify for a bonus that will get you that new car or trip?

These are important questions, and they can all be summarized by the following specific questions that will help you set your professional goals:

- What annual income do you need to support your lifestyle?
- What commissions do you need to earn to achieve your annual income?
- Is there a special award you would like to achieve?
- Is there a promotion you would like to receive?
- Do you want to grow your market share?
- Do you want to help your team be more successful?

WRITE DOWN YOUR GOALS

Once you have identified your goals, write them down. These are the goals that will motivate you to execute your lead generation plans. They will keep you going when you would rather stop writing e-mails at night or planning events on weekends. Figure 2.2 provides a handy format to use for documenting your goals.

To motivate yourself, set a deadline date for achievement. By what date is it reasonable to assume you can achieve each goal? Set realistic, but motivating, deadlines. For example, if you set a deadline ten months out, you will not be as motivated to begin an action plan as you would be if the deadline were only ten weeks away.

I currently have 15 goals with achievement deadlines all within the next 6 to 18 months. I tried to pare back, but these are goals I feel passionate about. I also have 7 goals I term my "ceaseless goals," goals I want to stay focused on but that will never end.

Each of my goals is quantified with a number I can measure, so I will know when I have achieved it. Each goal also has an assigned month, day, and year achievement deadline.

Identify Your Income Goal

Your first goal should be your income goal. It is the one that will allow you the financial freedom to accomplish all the others. Your income goal will include:

- Your base salary, if you have one
- Commissions

FIGURE 2.2 Goals to Focus On

Goals to Focus On As of _____ (today's date)		
Goal	**Priority**	**Deadline**
Your Income Goal:		

- Anticipated bonuses
- Any other income sources

Your manager's goals won't motivate you the same way your own goals will. Use your manager's goals as a starting point to calculate your personal income goals. Then think about what you really need to earn to support the lifestyle you want. Perhaps you need to earn more commissions to support it, or you need a promotion. It seems my own goals are always much higher than any manager could set for me, and they are stronger motivators even than keeping a job because they are personal to me. Don't rely on your manager's revenue quota goal for you to be your personal motivator. Take control and determine your own motivators.

Determine Your Real Quota

Your manager may have assigned you a sales quota or target. This may be the manager's or the company's target for you to achieve. But your real target is the amount you need to sell to achieve your income goal.

Using your income goal, you want to determine how much you need to sell under your current commission plan to meet that goal. Analyze your commission plan to calculate what revenue number you need to

T *i p s*

- Be careful to list only as many goals as you can reasonably accomplish.
- If you have a goal that has an achievement deadline of more than one year, set interim goals that you can achieve within the next 12 months to move you closer to the end goal. This will keep you focused and motivated, while moving you closer to your final goal.
- To improve your chances of achieving your goals, you must have an attitude that you can achieve them. If you can't see yourself achieving a goal, change it. Clearly, it is not a motivating goal, and you won't devote the effort you need to achieve it. Choose a goal you are passionate about and determined to achieve.

sell to meet your income goal. This will now become the quota or target you need to achieve in your territory. This is the quota you want to assign to yourself.

By tying your quota or target to your income goals, you have a personal stake in succeeding to achieve that quota. This new quota is a meaningful number to you. It is a number you can get excited about because it is tied to your vision, not just your manager's vision or your company's vision.

Give yourself some time to think about your personal and professional goals and the income you need to achieve them. These are the goals you are working toward when you put your lead generation plan in place.

SUMMARY

Flo knows she wants to make her quota number before the last month of the year. Now she needs to determine what that specifically means to her. She decides her deadline for achievement is September 30. If she can make her quota by September 30, she will feel she has achieved success. But now she realizes the quota her manager gave her isn't her real quota. She wants that new car without its impacting her current spending and maybe even a special vacation to celebrate if she achieves the success she'd like to this year. This means she really needs to sell more than her quota. When Flo figures out the number, she feels a bit of panic. It looks great on paper, but how will she achieve it? After all, in the past two years she's just barely squeaked by in the last month of the year with the quota she's been assigned. Now she's raised her own quota!

3

KNOW
YOUR STATISTICS

Flo jumped right into the year, eager to
make the quota she had assigned herself. But she found herself working 12 hours
a day, generating leads and following up with people. She always thought she was
putting in an honest day's work and felt very proud of her efforts. The problem
was, based on her results, she was barely making minimum wage. She certainly
wasn't close to achieving the income goal she set for herself. She couldn't understand why she wasn't more successful with all the work she was putting in. She
had a plan. Why wasn't it working? Although spending time crunching numbers
was not her favorite thing to do anymore, Flo knew she needed to analyze the effort she was putting into the job and determine where to make a change. Maybe
the products she was selling just weren't as good as she thought they were. Perhaps
she needed to quit and find a better sales job.

Once you have defined your goals, it's time to do the math and determine how many leads you need to achieve your sales goals and what
activities will give you the highest return. Those numbers help you track
results and find out if your goals are within reach.

WHAT'S YOUR HOURLY RATE?

Reps have more tasks to perform than there are hours in a day. The choice of where to spend your time is not always as obvious as you might like. One way to make it easier to choose what you should or shouldn't do on a daily basis is to consider your hourly rate, just like a consultant. Then for tasks you aren't sure of, you can ask yourself if this is the wisest use of your time.

Figure 3.1 shows my calculation of Flo's hourly rate, who, in this example, earns a total of $60,000 per year in base salary and commissions. She works nine hours in a typical day, receives three weeks vacation, takes an average of two sick days per year, and is given eight company holidays. Plugging in this information, we quickly learn Flo is earning only $28.37 per hour. It's easy to see why she is frustrated and contemplating changing jobs.

FIGURE 3.1 Calculating Your Hourly Rate

	Calculation
Hours of holiday, vacation, and sick time taken in an average year	
1. Number of holiday days taken	8 days
2. Number of vacation days taken	15 days
3. Number of sick days taken	2 days
4. Equals total number of holiday, vacation, and sick days	25 days
5. Multiply by the average number of hours you work per day	9 hours
6. Equals the average number of hours taken for holiday, vacation, and sick days	225 hours
Hours worked per year	
7. Average number of hours you work per week	45 hours
8. Multiply by 52 weeks per year	52 weeks
9. Equals average total hours worked	2,340 hours
10. Subtract the average number of hours holiday, vacation, and sick time taken per year (the number calculated in row 7)	225 hours
11. Equals the total hours you worked last year	2,115 hours
Hourly Rate	
12. Income you earned last year	$60,000.00
13. Divided by the total hours you worked last year (the number calculated in row 11 above)	2,115 hours
14. Equals your hourly rate	$ 28.37

At this hourly rate, Flo should be careful to invest time only in activities that will help improve her overall earnings. She can't afford to spend time on wasteful activities.

Use the same chart shown in Figure 3.1 as an example to quickly calculate your own hourly rate.

WHAT'S YOUR CLOSING RATIO?

Identifying the number of leads you need to generate to achieve your goals begins with understanding your closing ratio. Your closing ratio is the number of qualified opportunities you need to work in order to close just one opportunity.

How do you define a qualified opportunity? Begin by considering what characteristics you look for in a new prospect before you are willing to spend your valuable time on that prospect. For example, was it necessary to meet the prospect in person and discuss your services, or could an e-mail conversation constitute a qualified opportunity in your company? How much of an interest should the prospect have expressed in your products or services before you consider it qualified?

Most sales reps will not recognize a prospect as qualified until the prospect has answered some specific questions. The questions depend on the industry and company in and for which the sales reps are working. Some examples might include:

- Does the prospect, and the prospect's company, match the profile of a good fit for the sales rep's solutions?
- Does the prospect have a need the sales rep's solutions can address effectively?
- Does the sales rep's company have a solution that is a fit to meet the prospect's needs?
- Does the contact have the ability and openness to make a change in a reasonable time frame?
- Is the prospect in a position to significantly influence, recommend, or make decisions?
- Does the sales rep know the decision maker and the decision-making process?

- Does the prospect have the budget or access to a budget for a solution to the defined need?

Ask yourself what questions you need a prospect to answer before you consider him or her a qualified lead. These are the ideal characteristics you look for in a qualified opportunity. Create a list of these characteristics and post it on your wall to remind yourself. It is easy to be swayed by a prospect who says he or she *might* buy when the two of you are on the phone. But if that prospect doesn't meet your ideal characteristics, your closing ratio will be impacted.

To determine your closing ratio, consider how many qualified opportunities you need to work at once to close one opportunity. If you work ten opportunities and close two of every ten, your closing ratio is one out of five, or 20 percent.

What is *your* closing ratio?

WHAT'S YOUR AVERAGE SALE AMOUNT?

The next step in calculating how many leads you need to generate in order to achieve your goals is identifying the dollar value of your average sale. Your average sale is just that, an average of your total sales. Yes, every sales rep has the exceptional megasale and minute sale. But there is a middle range into which the majority of your sales typically fall.

To determine your average sale, add the total dollar amount of your sales for the previous year and divide by the number of sales you had. If this is your first year selling or you are new to your company, ask other reps in your company what the middle range of their average sale is and use that number for yourself. Once you have worked for the company for a while, you can adjust your average sale calculation based on your own sales.

If you close some sales that are higher than the average you use, you will need fewer qualified leads than you determined. If you close some sales that are lower than the average sale you use, you will need more qualified leads than you determined.

What is your average sale range?

The dollar amount you need to sell to achieve your personal goals is the dollar amount you determined you needed when you set your personal goals earlier. It may be equal to or more than the quota you have been given depending on the goals you have set for yourself. See Figure 3.2 for some quick sales formulas to remember.

ARE YOUR STATISTICS BASED ON THE COMPANY YOU ARE SELLING FOR?

You might wonder if your statistics are based on your own selling skills, the company and solutions you are selling, or the territory you are assigned. Interestingly, I have found that no matter what company you sell for, if you have a viable solution, your statistics are more dependent on you than on your company or your solution.

Now that can be good news or bad news. The good news is that you are in control of your selling destiny. The bad news is that you have nobody to blame if you aren't successful. Your selling style is reflected in your closing ratio and your average sale. If you typically sell deals 25 percent greater than your peer reps, you'll probably sell proportionally larger deals for any company. If your closing ratio is typically 1 out of 4, your closing ratio will probably remain 1 out of 4 with any company.

SUMMARY

Flo recalculated her hourly rate and, yes, it is poor. But now she realizes it is impacted by both her closing ratio and her average sale. She believes her company's

FIGURE 3.2 Some Quick Sales Formulas to Remember

Closing Ratio	=	Number of qualified leads you need to close one opportunity
Average Sale	=	Total dollar amount you sold last year divided by total number of sales Or Average sale of a typical rep in your company
Dollar Amount You Need to Sell	=	Dollar amount you set as your personal income goal

products are good, and she likes her job, so she really doesn't want to quit. Perhaps the answer is for her to improve her closing ratio and increase her average sale. Flo decides she is going to recommend additional services on every proposal to see if she can increase her average sale. Even if only 25 percent of her prospects purchase the additional services, she will still increase her average sale.

As for her closing ratio, Flo decides she needs more information on how she can impact it. She feels she's a pretty good salesperson. Perhaps she needs to find better leads to work—ones that are more likely to close? She makes a note to analyze the customer groups she is targeting. Maybe there are better ones she can focus on—ones more likely to be interested in what she is selling. But first she wants to see how many leads she needs to generate to make her quota now that she knows her closing ratio and average sale size.

4

HOW MANY LEADS ARE ENOUGH?

A *sales rep needs to calculate the number of leads she'll need to generate before she can reach her goals. Flo had a problem—she was chasing every opportunity that came her way in hopes of closing more deals yet she wasn't winning the number she needed to achieve her income goals. Flo wasn't qualifying the less than ideal opportunities because she was afraid she might not get other leads to replace them. As a result, Flo's closing ratio was worse than those of other reps in her company, and she was working harder than they were.*

CALCULATING YOUR DESIRED NUMBER OF QUALIFIED LEADS

Once you know your closing ratio and your average sale, you can now calculate how many leads you need to generate to achieve your personal goals. You want to know the number of leads you need so you can determine how many lead generation plans to implement throughout the year.

Figure 4.1 guides you through the process of calculating the number of qualified leads you need to generate. In this example, you have a

FIGURE 4.1 Calculating Your Desired Number of Qualified Leads

	Calculations
1. Note the number of qualified opportunities you need to close one sale (your average closing ratio from the previous chapter)	5 qualified opportunities
2. Note your average dollar amount for one sale	$ 25,000.00
3. The dollar amount you need to sell per year to achieve your personal quota goal	$1,200,000.00
4. Divide by 12 months	12
5. Equals the dollar amount you need to sell per month to achieve your personal goals	$ 100,000.00
6. Divide by the average dollar amount of one sale (from row 2)	$ 25,000.00
7. Equals the total number of sales you need per month to achieve your personal quota goal	4
8. Multiply by the number of qualified opportunities you need to close one sale (from row 1)	5
9. Equals the total number of qualified opportunities you need in your funnel **per month** to achieve your personal goals	20 leads per month
10. Divide the total number of qualified opportunities you need in your funnel per month by 21 selling days per month	21
11. Equals the number of qualified opportunities you need to generate **per day** to achieve your personal goals	0.95 leads per day
12. Multiply the number you got from row 9 by 12 months	12
13. Equals the number of qualified opportunities you need to generate **per year** to achieve your personal goals	240 leads per year

closing ratio of 1 of every 5 qualified opportunities as calculated in Chapter 3, and an average sale of $25,000 as determined in Chapter 3. You need to sell $1.2M to achieve the personal goals you set for yourself using the techniques in Chapter 2.

With an average of 21 selling days per month, you need to generate about 1 qualified lead per day, 20 qualified leads per month, or 240 qualified leads per year. You are feeling exhausted at the thought of trying to generate 20 qualified leads per month and want to find a way to reduce that number.

INFLUENCING THE NUMBER OF LEADS YOU NEED

The number of qualified leads you need to generate may seem insurmountable. However, you can influence that number as you formulate your plan.

The two primary variables in the calculation are your *closing ratio* and your *average sale size*. If you can improve your closing ratio and/or increase your average sale size, the number of leads you need to generate will be reduced. So if you are feeling overwhelmed by the number of leads you calculated, consider how you can improve your closing ratio or your average sale size.

Improving Your Closing Ratio

To improve your closing ratio, look first at how effectively you are qualifying new opportunities. Have you defined the ideal characteristics of a qualified lead? Are you using those characteristics to qualify which leads you will work and which ones you will let go? You want to work only well-qualified, best-odds opportunities to improve your chance of closing them.

Next look at your sales process to see how you can improve it. Examine at what point in the sales process you typically lose an opportunity. Ask yourself what it is that happens in the sales process at those points. What could you do differently at each point? Are there new activities you need to perform? Are there things you could anticipate and execute earlier to avoid losing the sale at that point? Are there people you could engage to help you win? Do you need to expand your contact base in the account? Do you need to adjust your style at that particular point in the process?

If you can improve your closing ratio from 5:1 in Figure 4.1 to 4:1, you can considerably reduce the number of qualified opportunities that you need to generate, as shown in Figure 4.2.

How can you improve your selling skills in your trouble phases of the sales process to positively impact your closing ratio?

FIGURE 4.2 Impact of Improving Your Closing Ratio

	Calculations
1. Note the number of qualified opportunities you need to close one sale (your average closing ratio from the previous chapter)	4 qualified opportunities
2. Note your average dollar amount for one sale	$ 25,000.00
3. The dollar amount you need to sell per year to achieve your personal quota goal	$1,200,000.00
4. Divide by 12 months	12
5. Equals the dollar amount you need to sell per month to achieve your personal goals	$ 100,000.00
6. Divide by the average dollar amount of one sale (from row 2)	$ 25,000.00
7. Equals the total number of sales you need per month to achieve your personal quota goal	4
8. Multiply by the number of qualified opportunities you need to close one sale (from row 1)	4
9. Equals the total number of qualified opportunities you need in your funnel **per month** to achieve your personal goals	16 leads per month
10. Divide the total number of qualified opportunities you need in your funnel per month by 21 selling days per month	21
11. Equals the number of qualified opportunities you need to generate **per day** to achieve your personal goals	0.76 leads per day
12. Multiply the number you got from row 9 by 12 months	12
13. Equals the number of qualified opportunities you need to generate **per year** to achieve your personal goals	192 leads per year

Increasing Your Average Sale

To improve the size of your average sale, look first at the size of op-portunities you go after. It may be possible to work larger opportunities, but you have passed up those opportunities because they take longer to close. If the length of the sales cycle in a large opportunity concerns you, work a mixture of large, medium, and small opportunities simultane-ously. Small and medium opportunities keep your revenue flowing while you also pursue the larger opportunities that will reduce the total number of leads you need. Diversification in your sales opportunity portfolio is just as important as it is in your stock portfolio. Consider how you can pursue opportunities of varying sizes in conjunction with one another.

There may also be additional services you can add on to your current opportunities that will increase the size of your average sale. With each new sale, think about the additional services your company offers. Are there any you can include that will drive your average sale up by even the smallest amount while still providing value to your customer? Examples might be maintenance or subscription services, training, additional features, or user-group memberships.

In our business, mentor coaching is a small additional cost yet provides sustained value to our clients. Our clients don't think to ask for it because it is not a commonly offered service, so unless we recommend it, it goes unsold. Every little sale adds to your overall average sale and helps reduce the total number of new leads you need to generate to meet your income goal.

Consider how you can increase the size of the opportunities you are working. Even a 15 percent increase in the size of the opportunity can have an impact, as seen in Figure 4.3. If you can increase your total sale by 15 percent, or $3,750, you can also reduce the number of qualified opportunities you need to generate in Figure 4.1.

Improving Both Your Closing Ratio and Your Average Sale

If you can improve both your closing ratio and your average sale, you can have a significant impact on the number of leads you need to generate as shown in Figure 4.4.

The Smallest Numbers Add Up

Because you are dealing with a large number of leads, even the smallest improvement can have an impact on the number of leads you need to generate and the plans you need to implement in order to generate them. As a result, any improvement in your overall sales skills will be an improvement in your lead generation.

FIGURE 4.3 Impact of Improving Your Average Sale

	Calculations
1. Note the number of qualified opportunities you need to close one sale (your average closing ratio from the previous chapter)	5 qualified opportunities
2. Note your average dollar amount for one sale	$ 28,750.00
3. The dollar amount you need to sell per year to achieve your personal quota goal	$1,200,000.00
4. Divide by 12 months	12
5. Equals the dollar amount you need to sell per month to achieve your personal goals	$ 100,000.00
6. Divide by the average dollar amount of one sale (from row 2)	$ 28,750.00
7. Equals the total number of sales you need per month to achieve your personal quota goal	3.48
8. Multiply by the number of qualified opportunities you need to close one sale (from row 1)	5
9. Equals the total number of qualified opportunities you need in your funnel **per month** to achieve your personal goals	17.39 leads per month
10. Divide the total number of qualified opportunities you need in your funnel per month by 21 selling days per month	21
11. Equals the number of qualified opportunities you need to generate **per day** to achieve your personal goals	0.83 leads per day
12. Multiply the number you got from row 9 by 12 months	12
13. Equals the number of qualified opportunities you need to generate **per year** to achieve your personal goals	208.68 leads per year

Examine how you can improve your own sales process and thereby improve your closing ratio. With each new sale, think about the additional services your company offers. Are there any you can include that will drive your average sale up by even the smallest amount? Work a combination of large, medium, and small opportunities simultaneously to improve the size of your average sale.

FIGURE 4.4 Impact of Improving Your Average Sale and Your Closing Ratio

	Calculations
1. Note the number of qualified opportunities you need to close one sale (your average closing ratio from the previous chapter)	4 qualified opportunities
2. Note your average dollar amount for one sale	$ 28,750.00
3. The dollar amount you need to sell per year to achieve your personal quota goal	$1,200,000.00
4. Divide by 12 months	12
5. Equals the dollar amount you need to sell per month to achieve your personal goals	$ 100,000.00
6. Divide by the average dollar amount of one sale (from row 2)	$ 28,750.00
7. Equals the total number of sales you need per month to achieve your personal quota goal	3.48
8. Multiply by the number of qualified opportunities you need to close one sale (from row 1)	4
9. Equals the total number of qualified opportunities you need in your funnel **per month** to achieve your personal goals	13.91 leads per month
10. Divide the total number of qualified opportunities you need in your funnel per month by 21 selling days per month	21
11. Equals the number of qualified opportunities you need to generate **per day** to achieve your personal goals	0.66 leads per day
12. Multiply the number you got from row 9 by 12 months	12
13. Equals the number of qualified opportunities you need to generate **per year** to achieve your personal goals	166.92 leads per year

CALCULATING THE DESIRED DOLLAR SIZE OF YOUR FUNNEL

You want to determine both the number of leads you need in your funnel and also the average dollar size you need to maintain. Frequently, you have a few opportunities that are much larger than your average sale and, likewise, a few that are much smaller. But overall you need a certain

FIGURE 4.5 Calculating the Desired Size of Your Funnel

	Calculations
1. The dollar amount you need to sell per year to achieve your personal quota goal	$1,200,000.00
2. Multiply by the number of qualified opportunities you need to close one sale	5
3. Total you need in qualified opportunities for one year	$6,000,000.00
4. Divide by 12 months in the year	12
5. Equals the total dollar amount you need to maintain in your funnel per month	$ 500,000.00

dollar amount to be sure you can achieve your personal goals based on your closing ratio. For this reason, you want to know the total dollar amount you need to maintain in opportunities in your funnel.

The calculations we just completed for you assume an average sale of $25,000. But we know you will have some sales that are greater than $25,000 and some that are less than $25,000. Your ultimate goal is to sell $1.2 million. Figure 4.5 calculates what dollar amount you must maintain in your funnel at all times to achieve your $1.2 million goal.

As with the number of qualified opportunities you need to generate, this number can be reduced by improving your closing ratio. Likewise, if you do not achieve your personal quota for one or more months, you will want to recalculate the number and maintain a higher dollar amount in your funnel.

SUMMARY

Flo used her closing ratio and average sale to calculate the number of leads she needs to generate to make her quota this year. The results were not what she had hoped. After analyzing the numbers in all sorts of manners, Flo realizes she must improve both her closing ratio and her average sale this year and add that to her personal goals list. But even though she'd like to do both, she recognizes she cannot assume she will accomplish them soon enough to impact the number of leads she needs to generate this year. Flo decides she had better focus on generating 1 qualified lead per day, 20 qualified leads per month, and 240 qualified leads this year to achieve the vision she has set for herself.

5

FOCUS ON YOUR FUNNEL

Sammy had it made. TJ Parker Ideas's *products and services basically sold themselves in his territory, so he spent all his time closing deals and neglected spending time on generating new leads. In his mind, it wasn't necessary as new leads were a dime a dozen. And because he didn't like cold calling or lead generation planning, it seemed a horrible way to spend his time. He and Flo talked a lot, and he saw how much time she spent doing territory planning. It wasn't paying off for her, so why should he do it? Besides, he had every reason to believe marketing would maintain a flow of leads into his territory as they had done in the past. Flo was envious of Sammy and how easy his territory seemed. Maybe Sammy was right that planning was a waste of time.*

But when the market took a tumble, their company was forced to cut its marketing budget, choosing to focus on only three target markets, none of which was in Sammy's territory. Suddenly, Sammy was on his own, with no leads coming in, no leads in place, and nowhere to turn for help. Like the story of the ant and the grasshopper, Sammy was weeks behind where he needed to be and "winter" was closing in fast. He had to spend weeks and months generating new leads with no commissions flowing to catch up with the time he had let slip away. It wreaked havoc on his personal budget, as well as on his relationships with current customers. Sammy learned the hard way that he needed leads, not just for the here and now, but for the weeks and months ahead.

THE FUNNEL ON THE WALL APPROACH

Whereas knowing how many leads you need in order to generate a sale is ultimately important, you also need an easy way to keep your eye on where your leads are coming from and the number of new opportunities you are working. You want to be sure you have sufficient opportunities to meet your goals based on your closing ratio. You also want to be sure you have opportunities spread throughout your year so you are closing sales steadily and maintaining a consistent income stream.

To avoid the common trap Sammy fell into, you must maintain a consistent flow of leads throughout the sales year, using a system that will allow you to track the number of opportunities you are working, the dollar value of those opportunities, and their stage in the sales cycle. This will allow you to maintain a consistent closing rate and earn consistent commission checks.

One approach I especially like is called the Funnel on the Wall. We've been using this approach in our company for ten years and have found it keeps each sales rep focused on their funnels on a daily basis—not just monthly when the Excel forecast is due to management. And it's fun!

In the Funnel on the Wall approach you track sales opportunities through the customer's buying process. Rather than focusing on the sales process, putting focus on the customer's buying process allows you to see from the customer's perspective where the opportunity is. It helps you determine your sales strategy while also concentrating on lead consistency.

The Concept

The Funnel on the Wall is a poster board with an inverted pyramid sales funnel divided into the stages of the customer's buying process drawn on it and explained in this chapter. Each time a rep finds a new qualified opportunity, he or she writes the opportunity on a sticky note pad, such as a 3M Post-it Note, and places the sticky note on the funnel. As the opportunity progresses through the customer's buying process, the rep moves the sticky note down the funnel. When the rep closes the sale, the sticky note moves to the bottom of the funnel and stays there for the year.

Each rep has his or her own funnel in an easily accessible place.

The Sticky Note

Each sticky note (see the sample sticky note in Figure 5.1) documents five components:

1. **The opportunity name.** Use the name of the problem, project, or possible solution or some other name that will easily help you identify the opportunity.
2. **The company and/or person with whom you are working.** Note your key contact for this particular opportunity. It may be the person making the decision, or it may be a manager under that person. Name whoever you are primarily working with on the opportunity. That way, when you look at your funnel, you can quickly think about your specific strategy with your key contact. For companies you have merely identified as suspect prospects, you may not have a contact name. Put these company names on sticky notes so you don't forget them, but put them at the very top of your funnel until you break in and get a contact name.
3. **The anticipated dollar value of the solution to your company**. Early in the sales process you won't necessarily know the solution value; however, you probably have some idea what it costs to solve the problem you have identified or to deliver the solution the customer is considering. Note that number even if it is only an estimate. This will help you when you want to quickly analyze your funnel to determine if you have enough opportunity in it.
4. **The anticipated date of service or installation on which you actually get paid a commission.** Noting the implementation date is a quick reminder where your sales activities are in relation to the date the customer in fact wants to begin work. No opportunity should move down into your funnel until you know the implementation date. Without the date the opportunity is not qualified enough to move. My favorite question to ask to pin a prospect to a desired implementation date: "By what date would you like to have solved this problem or at least have begun addressing it?" This gives me the implementation date I need for my funnel—and for my sales strategy.
5. **Your odds of winning the opportunity.** The odds tell you how hard you need to work to win the opportunity. They are your fore-

castable chance of winning the opportunity. If the odds are low as you move down the funnel, you may choose to let the opportunity go, thanking the prospect politely but withdrawing yourself. If you don't think you can win an opportunity, it makes more sense to withdraw and focus your efforts on opportunities you can win. Let the prospect know you would welcome another opportunity, and provide the reasons why you don't believe this is the best opportunity for the two of you to work together. Examples might include a poor solution fit where the prospect can find a better fit with another provider, an unsecured or too low budget, or an inability to get the attention of key people involved in the decision. Use a percentage to indicate what you think your odds of winning might be. Early in the funnel your odds of winning should always be low because you haven't learned enough about the prospect or the opportunity to be certain of a win. As you progress through the sales process, you will have a good feeling for what you think your chances are that you will win an opportunity. Watch the prospect for key indicators, such as keeping meeting dates, providing access to the right people, engaging in detailed conversations with you, and asking for additional information. If the key indicators are present, your odds of winning are good. Be conservative with your odds so you never become too comfortable in how you follow up on the opportunity. I want very strong indicators before I give an opportunity 90 percent odds. In fact, the customer has to have *told* me he or she is going to move forward with me before I'll go as high as 90 percent. I recognize there are too many factors out of my control to confidently forecast high odds consistently.

Early in the sales process you may be missing some information for a sticky note as the opportunity may not yet be fully qualified. For example, you may not know the potential solution value. If you cannot estimate the missing information, place the sticky note on the funnel without it. This ensures you will not forget about the opportunity or the missing information.

You may find that you have multiple opportunities within one account. Each opportunity should have its own sticky note, as each one will

FIGURE 5.1 Sample Sticky Note

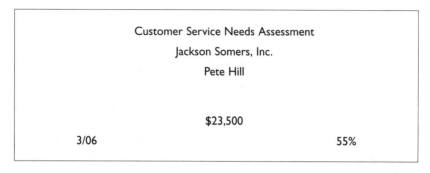

move through its own buying process. You want to be able to analyze each opportunity individually.

Use Colors

To maintain a balance between existing customers and prospective new accounts, use two different colored sticky notes. Yellow may denote customers and green prospects. In this way you can quickly see if you are balancing your time between customer and prospect accounts and adjust your daily activities appropriately.

If you have several large enterprise customers, you may choose to use a different color sticky note for opportunities in each enterprise. This allows you to quickly see how many opportunities you have with any one company.

You can also use different color sticky notes for different services you provide. If you are paid differently for selling different products or services, you may choose to use colors that distinguish between them.

I like to keep my funnel relatively simple and use only three colors. I use bright blue for new prospects, yellow for existing customers, and bright pink for the two largest enterprise customers I oversee. I have tried using more colors but found it made my funnel too complex. I wasn't able to quickly analyze it and required a color-coded key to remember what each color stood for! When I found myself losing time as I read my funnel, I decided it was counterproductive and went back to using only three colors.

Update Your Sticky Notes

If you don't mind working in pencil, I recommend writing your sticky notes in pencil. As you move through the sales process, you will update the solution value, implementation date, and odds. As you gather more information, you will be able to refine your sticky notes. Do this so you always have accurate information visually available to you. Your funnel is a quick analytical tool, helping you determine your sales and lead generation strategy. Without accurate, current information, it loses its value to you.

After each prospect meeting or at the end of the day, look at your sticky notes to see what updates you need to make based on your work that day. Making changes on a daily basis helps you stay on top of information changes, keeping your funnel accurate. Even better, you feel a sense of accomplishment as you refine each opportunity.

CREATING YOUR OWN FUNNEL ON THE WALL

To create a Funnel on the Wall, begin with a poster board. We've tried using $8\frac{1}{2}'' \times 11''$ pages and ministicky notes, but there just isn't space to fit all your opportunities on it. And you want to be able to put every opportunity in your Funnel on the Wall.

You will be looking at your funnel every day, so choose a color and make it fun. I typically choose a green poster board as green signifies money!

Draw a funnel across the whole poster board, giving the funnel as much space as possible. A yardstick and a pencil are great tools for ensuring your lines are straight before marking them with a permanent pen. Add the different stages of the buying process inside the funnel. Figure 5.2 gives you an example of what it should look like.

You can dress up your funnel by adding your income goal, target average sale, target number of leads you'd like to maintain in it, or your revenue goal. My funnel has had each of these written on it at different times depending on what I was focusing on for my own personal development. I write it in the upper left corner, the first place your eye will go

FIGURE 5.2 Example of a Funnel on the Wall

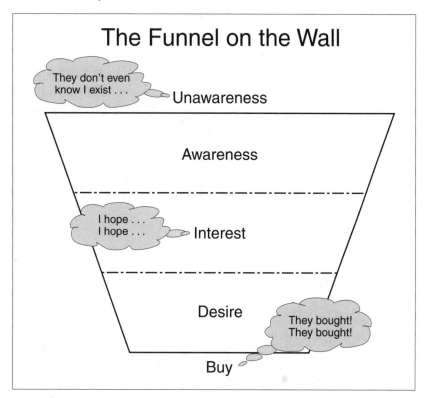

each time you look at it. This is also a spot that is least likely to be covered by a sticky note as the leads start flowing in! My very first funnel also had a couple of pictures I was working toward from my goals list: a luxury car and my first son. I now have too many leads to do that, but it was a motivating reminder each time I worked with my funnel!

Once you have created your funnel, hang it on the wall and begin adding sticky note opportunities to it!

THE STAGES OF THE FUNNEL

As you add your opportunities to your Funnel on the Wall poster board, you want to place the sticky notes on the funnel according to each opportunity's status in the customer's buying process. Your prospects and customers go through a buying process when they are making a buying decision just as you move through a process when you are selling to them.

The buying process portrays the customer's perception of the opportunity rather than your optimistic sales perception. It helps you determine your sales strategy with each opportunity and your territory lead generation needs. There are lead generation activities you can execute at each stage of the customer buying process to help you move sales along while also generating new leads. At all times you want sales opportunities spread equally across the stages of the buying process. This helps you maintain the steady flow of sales expected by your manager and is necessary for a steady income stream.

There are five stages in the customer buying process as described in the following sections:

I. Unawareness

Unawareness is the first stage of the buying process. In this stage the prospects or customers do not know about either your company or the service you are targeting to sell them. They are not yet a lead because they don't know they need you. They may not even realize they have a problem that needs to be solved. Companies you are targeting with your initial lead generation activities fall in this stage until they respond to an overture from you to indicate some level of interest in learning more about your company.

Here your lead generation activities should focus on creating awareness for yourself, your company, and your solutions. This is the phase where many sales reps employ cold calling, although "warm-up" activities are much more effective. Use direct mail, e-mailings, public speaking, and events such as executive breakfasts to create awareness with a broad set of your target prospects *before* you attempt to get in the door through cold calling. Prospects will be more receptive to your call if they are aware of who you are and what you might offer.

Put referrals, references, new prospects, and companies you would like to break into above your funnel in this phase. Also put customer contacts who are not familiar with your solutions or have not yet met you in this stage.

2. Awareness

In this second stage of the buying process, prospects or customers are aware they have a problem that *might* need solving and know you could assist with solving it. They have not decided to solve the problem. They are not yet sure the problem warrants solving. In this stage, prospects need to decide if they want to investigate solving the problem or let it be.

Effective lead generation activities in the *Awareness phase* include such events as association meetings or Webcasts, articles, speaking engagements, brief case studies, e-mailings, referrals, and cold calling. Ideally, the activity should be focused on the type of problem a prospect has and on making the prospect want to solve it. In Chapter 6 I talk about how to segment your territory into target markets so you can execute lead generation activities to groups of people who might have similar business problems or objectives. If your prospect is a large account you would like to break into, use these same lead generation activities with very specific messages and language focused only on that account.

Companies in this phase are not yet qualified. They will meet your ideal characteristics for a potential prospect, but because you have not yet created a need, they cannot be qualified. At this stage, you are involved in initial phone conversations to qualify if you should move forward with an opportunity.

Put leads who have responded to your lead generation activities and you are following up with in this phase on your Funnel on the Wall.

3. Interest

Prospects in the *Interest phase* of the customer buying process have decided a business problem warrants investigation and are interested in determining how they might solve it. You have asked initial probing questions during the Awareness phase, had one or two phone meetings, and believe this is a good opportunity worth your time to pursue. In this stage, you qualify that your company's solutions may be a good fit for the prospect's problem.

To find leads already in the Interest phase, use such events as demonstrations or Webcasts, e-mailings, telemarketing, and cold calling. Most reps seek out leads already in the Interest phase because they recognize those prospects have qualified themselves. The challenge here is that you want to find prospects at the *beginning* of their Interest phase when they are embarking on their investigation. This allows you to guide and influence their investigation as part of your sales process.

Because it is hard to always find leads at the beginning of the Interest phase, I recommend targeting your lead generation activities to prospects in both the Awareness and the Interest phases. You can use your lead generation activities, such as brief case studies, Webcasts, speaking engagements, and articles, to move a prospect from Awareness into Interest with minimal effort. Combined with periodic touch-base phone calls, you can guide these prospects into the Interest phase with little time investment and already be engaged when they are ready to begin their problem-solving investigation.

Keep opportunities in this phase of your Funnel on the Wall until they are well qualified. Hold meetings to continue questioning for their business needs and to determine the appropriate match to your solutions. Establish if they have the budget, ability to make a decision, sense of urgency to make and implement a decision, and desire to pursue you as a possible provider of the solution they are seeking. Talk with many people within the customer's organization. Determine if you have solutions that can meet their business needs profitably. Once you have qualified these points, you are ready to move your opportunity sticky note to the Desire phase.

I find that the Interest phase in your Funnel on the Wall is where your opportunity sticky note stays the longest. This is an investigative phase, and prospects do their due diligence here. A lot of meetings and conversations must occur before prospects are ready to say they definitely want to fix their problem. Once they make that decision, you can move your opportunity sticky note to the Desire phase.

4. Desire

In the *Desire phase* of your funnel, you have opportunities who are truly qualified. These prospects have decided it makes sense to solve the problem and are interested in finding the best-fit solution. You are working hard to handle all objections, demonstrate your capabilities, outsell your competition, present a compelling proposal, and close the sale. The prospects are talking with competitors and looking at multiple options to solving their problem.

You want to stay focused on these opportunities because they are the ones that will close once you have done your job. Follow-up is critical in this phase. You should be talking to as many people in the customer organization as possible. Lead generation activities focused on your capabilities and varied solution offerings are excellent selling tools in this phase. Use white papers, articles, speaking engagements, events, e-mailings, and cold calling as ways to engage key people who have not yet met you.

Focusing on this phase helps to improve your closing ratio. The better you can address objections, demonstrate your company's capabilities, and match your solution to prospects' needs, the better your chances of winning. If you can handle the Desire phase with ease, you will close more opportunities.

You do not want to move an opportunity out of the Desire phase, however, until a decision has been made and the paperwork is ready to be signed. Your customer or prospect must make a commitment. Opportunities should remain in this phase while the paperwork is being signed and any financing secured. Something could happen to reverse the decision: the market could take a downturn, leadership could change, or budgets could be revised. You want to wait to celebrate the final phase of winning the opportunity until you have reached a point at which your company can bill the customer and you can count the opportunity as completely sold.

5. Buy/Sold

You've done it! Your customer has made a buying decision in your favor. You've closed the deal, and the installation has occurred or the work is being performed. Now you can celebrate the opportunity as completed and move it out of Desire.

This phase is below your funnel. It is the stage at which you generally receive your commission check or credit against your quota for the opportunity. Your sales work on this opportunity is done and your follow-up work now begins. Congratulations on your sale!

Although you definitely want to celebrate, you also have lead generation opportunities here. Use this win to create a new case study, plan an event, or write a new direct mailing to other companies that might have similar problems to solve. Ask for referrals and references, and use references and testimonials in your new lead generation activities.

Also look at how you can generate additional leads in this company. If it is a large company, there may be other organizations you can penetrate to seek out new leads. Use the case study you created from this win to share with those organizations. Send e-mails outlining the business problem and how you solved it, mentioning additional capabilities your firm has. Offer to speak at team meetings about the work you are doing in the account. Hold executive briefings. Leave voice mail updates on the progress of your implementation, and ask for a meeting to see where else you might work together. These are all effective lead generation activities to penetrate large accounts and keep your Funnel on the Wall full.

Let all your sticky note sold opportunities pile up in this phase throughout the year on your poster board funnel to make you feel good about the hard work you have done!

MOVING OPPORTUNITIES THROUGH YOUR FUNNEL ON THE WALL

After each prospect meeting or at the end of the day, update the information on your sticky notes. At the same time, you may want to adjust the position of the sticky in your funnel if the opportunity has moved. Even though you hope the opportunity is moving forward in the customer buying process, there are times it will move backward.

Not all your opportunities will move through the buying process. Some opportunities will fall out; some will be lost; others will come to no decision. Some opportunities will move up and down in your funnel as they move through the buying process.

Flo's key contact in an insurance firm is Dennis. He told her he wanted to move forward right away on implementing a new hire training program. Dennis wanted Flo's company to help design the program and use several of Dennis's trainers to assist in the development. Flo is very excited. This is a new prospect she has never worked with and it is a highly visible project. Dennis has the budget to do the project as well as executive level support. Flo clearly understands Dennis's needs. She designed a solution based on his needs at a very reasonable price, reviewed the proposal with him, and moved the opportunity into Desire in his funnel based on his sense of urgency to begin.

Flo's plan was to close the opportunity when they met a week later. However, in that meeting, Dennis disclosed that his trainers weren't as available as he had hoped, so he had decided to wait another month or so before moving forward. In fact, there was the possibility that the trainers wouldn't be available at all, and Dennis didn't want to move forward if they couldn't participate in the development process. Disappointed, Flo returned to the office and moved the opportunity back to Interest in her funnel, reducing the odds and changing the implementation date on the opportunity sticky note.

For each opportunity, you decide where it should be in the funnel based on the customer buying process. You will have opportunities that move out to six months or a year. With these opportunities, you may choose to take them off your funnel, log them in your contact manager for follow-up in six months or a year, and throw the sticky note completely away. When an opportunity implementation date moves out beyond six months, I recommend removing it from your funnel but definitely logging it for follow-up in four to five months. If the company is a new prospect, put it back into your lead generation target market (which I define in Chapter 6) to receive lead generation activities. The prospect may receive a lead generation e-mail or event invitation that excites it and puts it back into your funnel again earlier than the time frame originally suggested to you.

I feel a sense of accomplishment each time I move an opportunity down my funnel. There is something about picking it up off the funnel and actually placing it in a new, better position that truly makes me feel good about the work I am doing in the account. The conversation with the prospect puts a smile on my face, but this goes beyond the smile. Enjoy that feeling as you move your opportunities through your funnel. You are moving closer to your goals and toward success!

USING YOUR FUNNEL ON THE WALL TO ANALYZE YOUR LEAD GENERATION POSITION

The customer buying process is focused on the customer's perception of where an opportunity is in its selection process. Even though your Funnel on the Wall reflects this perception, it is also a sales strategy tool for you.

The Funnel on the Wall allows you to quickly analyze the number of opportunities you have in your funnel. Do you have enough at each stage? Are there gaps in some stages that you need to address? Do you need to do some lead generation? Are there opportunities you need to close? Are there opportunities that have stalled and require your attention? Perhaps you have focused only on large opportunities and find the funnel needs a greater number of leads based on your closing ratio.

While analyzing the number of opportunities, also analyze the dollar size of your funnel. Even if you have the right number of opportunities in your funnel, do you have the right revenue size opportunities? You may be most comfortable with medium and small opportunities. Your funnel may be full of stickies, but when you add up the revenue potential, it could still be short of your necessary dollar amount. Can you find a way to increase the opportunity sizes? Or do you need to do lead generation for larger opportunities?

If you use colored sticky notes to distinguish customer opportunities from prospect opportunities, you can quickly analyze whether you have a strong balance that provides diversification in your territory. It is not unusual to find your funnel heavy on the customer opportunity side. That is where many reps are most comfortable, but that is, however, not a healthy funnel. You want to be sure you have new prospects flowing into your territory at all times. Mergers and acquisitions, industry downturns, and employee changes occur all the time, causing great opportunities to be put on hold across entire companies. Working with new prospects unwaveringly reduces your risk if these negative actions should occur in any of your customer accounts.

I like to maintain a funnel of at least one-third new prospect opportunities and two-thirds customer opportunities. My favorite part of selling is generating new business. I love selling to new companies, meeting new people within their organizations, and learning about their businesses.

If new business generation is a struggle for you, set your goal to be a balance of one-quarter new prospect opportunities and three-quarters existing customer opportunities.

Frequently, my new prospect opportunities at the top of the funnel are different companies because I am just beginning to penetrate an account and have not yet found additional opportunities. As a new prospect opportunity moves down the funnel, more opportunities often pop up because I have begun broadening my reach of contacts within the account.

When analyzing individual opportunities, look at customer opportunities to be sure you are not too heavily invested in any one company or any one division within an enterprise. Investing your time too heavily in one area is extremely risky, especially if you don't have a broad base of contacts within the account. If you find yourself in this position, you want to do lead generation in two areas. First, you want to leverage the work you have already done within one division to gain access to other divisions within the enterprise. This strategy reduces your risk should a significant change occur in the one division that causes your opportunities to be placed on hold. Second, you want to broaden your base of contacts within the division you are already working. This strategy helps you avoid the risks associated with your key contact leaving the company or changing positions, causing you to begin your sales process from the get-in-the-door stage.

Finally, don't forget to analyze the *Buy/Sold phase* for opportunities you have sold year to date. This phase quickly shows where you stand against the annual quota you have set for yourself. You can look at the Desire phase of your funnel to see what is about to close, combined with the Buy/Sold phase to determine if you have enough opportunities deep in your funnel. If not, you can determine what you can do to move opportunities out of Interest and into Desire. Also, you want to examine the Buy/Sold phase to identify companies for which you might be able to do additional lead generation activities to drive repeat business. See Figure 5.3 for more points to analyze in your funnel.

CELEBRATE YOUR SUCCESSES

Keep your closed opportunity sticky notes on your funnel at the very bottom all year. Have fun with them! Watch them pile up and take time

FIGURE 5.3 Points to Analyze in Your Funnel

Use your funnel to analyze your territorial strategy. Some points to analyze include:

1. Total number of opportunities relative to the total number of opportunities you need to maintain in your funnel at all times, as calculated in Chapter 4. Do you have enough opportunities in your funnel, or do you need to execute more lead generation activities?
2. The number of opportunities you have in each stage of the customer buying cycle in your funnel. What lead generation activities can you execute to both increase the number of leads you have in each stage and move opportunities forward in the buying process?
3. The total dollar value of opportunities in your funnel against your goal, as calculated in Chapter 4. Is the total size of opportunities sufficient to meet your goals, as defined in Chapter 2? Do you need to do lead generation for more opportunities or for bigger opportunities? Do you need to consider ways to increase the size of the opportunities you already have in the funnel?
4. Time frames for closing the opportunities. Is everything happening in June and nothing in May or July? Is a dry spell coming? Are your leads flowing consistently? What can you do to maintain consistency in all phases of your funnel? Do you need to execute lead generation campaigns targeting prospects in a specific phase?
5. The percentage of prospect opportunities versus existing customer opportunities. Do you need to do more lead generation in customer accounts or prospects to diversify your funnel and reduce your risk? Do you have too many opportunities in any one customer account? Should you have more opportunities in some accounts?
6. The number of successes you have had in relation to the number and amount you need to close to achieve your goals, as calculated in Chapter 2. Analyze your success to identify those techniques you used that led to the win. Consider how to repeat those techniques to speed your time to close and improve your closing ratio. Are there wins you have had that can be leveraged to generate leads in other organizations within that same company? Can you leverage the knowledge of the business problems you helped solve into lead generation activities targeting other companies with those same problems?

out to celebrate your successes. Be sure to mark them with some noticeable action or reward—some reps ring a bell to mark the close of a deal; others have a ritual dance. Feel good about your sales successes!

In addition to the opportunities you have closed, celebrate the small successes you have along the way to your big success of closing the sale. Every time you move the opportunity further along with each phone call, fax, visit, and proposal, recognize your accomplishment!

KEEP YOUR FUNNEL ON THE WALL TO YOURSELF

The Funnel on the Wall is different from your forecast. Your forecast includes all the opportunities you have qualified and believe you can close. To be effective, the Funnel on the Wall should include *all* opportunities, pre- and postqualified. It is not designed to be your sales forecast. Rather, it is a tool to determine if you are working enough opportunities to get the necessary number of qualified opportunities to meet your personal goals. It allows you to stay on top of all the opportunities: big and small, high or low odds through qualification.

Because your Funnel on the Wall is not your sales forecast, be careful how you display it. Don't display your funnel if your manager will hold you accountable for every opportunity you have on it. In this case you may want to keep it on a letter-size paper and store it on top in a drawer or carry it with you. Sticky notes come in small sizes as well as larger sizes and can be used on smaller paper too.

Your Funnel on the Wall does not replace your sales forecast. Continue using the sales forecast to report on your qualified opportunities and your sales strategy to close those opportunities. Both are critical tools in your path to success.

SUMMARY

Flo created her Funnel on the Wall so she could quickly determine if she had enough leads flowing through it to make her quota. She wants a good mix of new prospect and customer opportunities, and is using different colored stickies to represent new prospects versus customers. As an added benefit, she realizes she will be able to quickly identify any potential dry spells in her commissions that will need her attention.

As she looks at her funnel, Flo feels great. She has a visual that shows the progress she makes every day. She knows this will help keep her focused on her goals.

BREAKING DOWN YOUR TERRITORY

Part Two helps you determine where your best-odds opportunities are and how you find them. It helps you break your territory into manageable chunks for executing your lead generation campaigns. In it you identify who you are going to work with to get the leads you need and how you will work with those people.

6

SEGMENTING YOUR TERRITORY INTO TARGET MARKETS THAT WORK FOR YOU

*"**M**y territory? I'll just look through the Yellow Pages and begin dialing for dollars from A through Z! I'm sure to find a bunch of leads if I just call everybody!" Infamous last words for Fred, a sales rep who made the dire mistake of neglecting to do the necessary research and legwork before he started calling on potential customers. Fred had no idea who he was calling or why they would want to talk with him. Flo wasn't surprised when, ill prepared, Fred found himself six months into his year at 30 percent of quota with few leads to work. He couldn't get any prospects to talk with him. And now his manager was requiring daily meetings to review his activity levels. He had to do some*thing. *Flo sat back and watched. She was not going to make the same mistakes Fred was making.*

WHAT IS A TARGET MARKET?

Target markets are areas you choose to concentrate on in your territory. You need a strategy to break your territory into manageable groups, analyze it, and then execute lead generation campaigns. As a rep, you want to target those markets where you have the best opportunity to get business in the door. You cannot afford to waste time pursuing all the companies in your territory. Rather, you want to try to identify the groups of companies that will require the least amount of time and money to get the highest return for lead generation activities. I call those your "best-odds" target markets. This chapter helps you identify your best-odds target markets so you don't find yourself in Fred's situation.

Typically, territories can be divided into industry target markets; however, they can also be grouped by geography, number of employees, dollar revenues, or any other type of commonality. Dividing territories into target markets, as illustrated in Figure 6.1, is referred to as *segmenting*.

"The most important thing a sales rep can do to be successful at lead generation is to profile target markets," says Phil Harris, vice president of sales at Akibia. "Identify what companies you are going after and what title you are going to call on."

Your time is valuable and you do not want to waste it. Based on the number of leads you know you need to generate (from Chapter 4) and your personal hourly rate (from Chapter 3), you need to focus only on those target markets that can give a high return. A well-chosen target market is one where you have the greatest opportunity to close business.

Once you have identified the best-odds target markets, you can plan lead generation activities for them and begin pulling in the leads.

WHO ARE YOUR TARGET MARKETS?

Your company may have identified companywide target markets on which to focus its marketing efforts. There may be a large budget set aside for marketing efforts, including direct mailing, advertising, trade shows, executive events, case study development, Web site content, white papers, and new product development.

These target markets may or may not be within your territory, meaning you may not be able to take advantage of those marketing efforts to help drive leads in your territory. Unfortunately, this does not change your company's expectations for your personal performance in your assigned territory. It is expected that you will achieve your sales goals with or without the marketing department's assistance. And, of course, you have a personal goal you want to achieve.

Now that you know your statistics from Chapter 3, including how many leads you need to generate in your territory, you want to identify

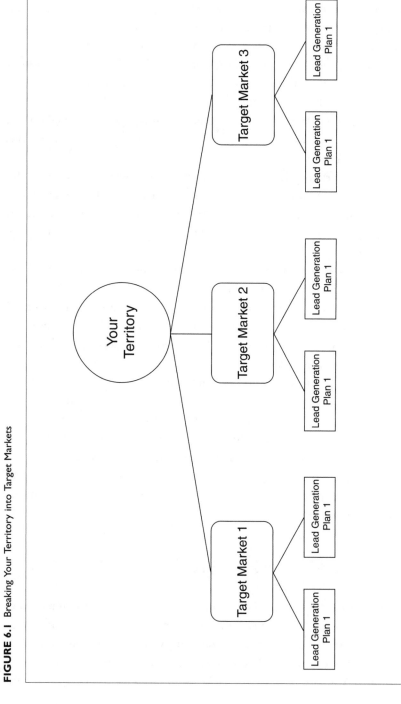

FIGURE 6.1 Breaking Your Territory into Target Markets

who your best target markets are. Even if your company is focusing marketing efforts in your territory, you still want to define your target markets so you can focus your personal lead generation activities on those "best odds of penetrating and winning" segments in the territory.

There are three main scenarios under which you may find yourself as you analyze your territory to define your target markets:

1. **You have been in your territory for more than one year.** You can use your own historical data to help you uncover your best-odds target markets.

2. **The territory is new to you,** but was previously assigned to another rep. You can look at that rep's historical data, as available, to help you make preliminary target market determinations. If historical data are unavailable to you, use scenario number three below.

3. **The territory is newly created.** You can use a combination of any historical data that fit pieces of the new territory and use your best judgment to make a very preliminary target market determination. Look at historical data for companies the same size as those in your territory and located in the same geographical area, or for industries similar to the ones you cover. For example, there are big differences between manufacturing and distribution, but there are significant similarities as well. You want to interview the manufacturing rep's customers to identify possible similarities to your distribution territory. After a few months of working in the territory, you want to assess your target markets again to see if they are producing the leads you had hoped for. If not, you want to analyze what you have learned about your territory and choose new target markets.

ASSESSING HISTORICAL DATA

In assessing historical data, look at your own past sales and past sales made in the territory before you were there. "We want to know what companies typically buy from us and who within those companies buy from us," advises Harris. "Those are the companies and contacts we want to target." You also want to know what solutions customers typically purchased, the average size of a sale, and typical business problems your company's solutions helped solve.

Ask yourself the following questions to see if there are any similarities between the sales made over the past one to two years that you can use to group your territory into target markets:

- **Are they in the same industry?** Industry is a very obvious target market and one used by many companies. If you have a geographic territory or a territory consisting of several industries, you may need to take your analysis to a lower market segmentation. Some industries are too broad to market to without deeper segmentation. For example, if you have manufacturers, were past sales primarily to clothing manufacturers, auto parts manufacturers, or some other type of manufacturer? Your lead generation messages and effectiveness of activities may be very different in each of these segments.

- **Do all the customers appear to be companies of approximately the same size?** In this instance, your solution may be a good fit for a specific size of company, which can be a target market or deeper segmentation of another target market. For example, the majority of your customers may have revenues of $500 million to $1 billion. But they may also be in the manufacturing industry. Your target market may become manufacturing companies with revenues of $500 million to $1 billion.

- **Are all the customers in the same geographical location?** Is this of significance or is it a coincidence? In some cases, your solution may suit a geographical area particularly well. An example of this is your company's having exclusivity of a product or service in this area, which is common in the cable and telecommunications industries. It may just mean that you have had a growth year in the area, but there is nothing else in common about the customers. Or it may mean you have a concentration of resources available in that region and are therefore better able to support customers located there.

- **Are all the customers using the same solution?** Are they all using the same product to do the same thing? Is the solution solving the same basic business need? If so, determine what the similarity is between those customers, and that similarity could then define the target market. You may find the similarity is revenue size, number of employees, industry, or geography, but beginning with the solution is an easy way to deduce this.

The more defined you can be in your target market segmentation, the easier it will be for you to create lead generation activities with high response rates. Market segmentation definitions allow you to use focused messages, target very specific business needs, and offer relevant solutions based on the parameters of the definition. Definitions allow you to create lead generation messages that appear very personalized, grabbing the attention of prospects and increasing your response rates before having an initial prospecting conversation.

If you are selling only one or two products or services, you may think that you have a very narrow market. What you want to consider is how customers are using that product or service today. They may not all use it the same way. If this is the case, you can create target markets within your niche market based on how customers use your solutions.

An easy way to determine how customers use your company's solutions is to call a group of 10 to 15 customers in your territory and interview them. Ask customers how they are using the solution. What does it help them accomplish? What do they like about it? Why do they find it of value? What would they tell other customers the value is? What would they tell other customers the solution can help them do? Not only will this information help you define target markets, it will also provide beneficial input for the key messages you want to use when approaching new prospects in those target markets. Your lead generation activities will become specific to the niche target markets in their messaging and offers.

It is easier to attract and win prospects whose characteristics are similar to those of existing satisfied customers. Historical data analysis helps uncover those similarities and segment a territory appropriately into best-odds target markets. You can use past sales records, contact manager data as well as customer, sales rep, and manager interviews to gather historical information.

If you know there have been unsuccessful reps in your territory before, you may want to try a new strategy, different from the company's product positioning. Consider what excites you about the solutions you are selling. What can you enthusiastically sell? Who would want to buy those solutions? Why would they buy them? What business value do the solutions bring to them? If you can answer these questions and support them with strong business value to the customer, you should make this your target market.

As you work in a territory over a period of several years, you can track your own historical performance by target market. This information can be plotted to show territory growth against a personal quota, quota attainment, and target markets. You can use it to identify trends and further refine target markets.

North American Standard Industry Classification Codes

To deepen your market segmentation, use the U.S. Standard Industrial Classification (SIC) codes or the North American Industry Classification System (NAICS) codes. In 1997 the SIC codes were replaced by the NAICS codes. Under the NAICS, every company is assigned a six-digit industry code. The NAICS not only categorizes companies into industry categories based on this code but it also organizes the categories on a production-/process-oriented basis. This system was originally designed as the index for statistical reporting of all economic activities of the United States, Canada, and Mexico, but salespeople can use it easily for target market segmentation.

The NAICS codes are used by the U.S. government as well as by research and database companies to classify the primary industry in which a company is engaged. If your organization classifies its list of companies by SIC or NAICS codes, you can easily generate very granular lists of potential prospects. Typically, if you purchase a database or list of prospects, you either define it by the NAICS codes when you order the list or the NAICS codes will be included in the information you receive about each company. To learn more or to order the NAICS codes, search the Web under "North American Industry Classification System."

USING CUSTOMER DATA TO DETERMINE TARGET MARKETS

When historical sales data are not available, which is the case with many companies, you can request a list of customers from customer service, accounts receivable, or ordering departments. You can then use this list to analyze the customers in the same manner as you analyzed the historical data. Look at maintenance records or service calls to get customer names. Also check with your company's help desk or read the history sections in your electronic contact manager; you might choose to talk to the sales manager over the customers you find. You can also call the customers directly and interview them as described in the "Assessing Historical Data" section earlier in this chapter.

You may want to call the customers you uncovered to better understand how they are using the company's solutions. If you find even one customer who is excited about the solutions, consider this a preliminary target market and do a limited number of opportunity generation activities to see if there are other companies with similar business needs and interests. Use the information gathered from the customer interview to determine what the message to the preliminary target market should be. Ask customers if they will allow you to use their company name or will supply a testimonial. The customers may even give you some referrals.

TESTING POTENTIAL TARGET MARKETS

Opportunity generation activities are preliminary lead generation activities you do to test a target market and ascertain the level of interest. These activities help you validate whether a target market will be a best-odds target market for you.

In opportunity generation activities, you choose a random subset of a potential target market to run a lead generation activity or set of activities. These activities highlight how customers are currently using your solutions, what business needs the solutions met, and the results those customers have achieved as a result of implementing your solutions and using your services. You track the number of companies that respond to your activities. Based on the number of the responses and the resulting potential opportunity size, you determine if this is a target market to pursue or to pass on at this time.

Fred had hundreds of potential companies in his territory. He chose to cold call them all, resulting in his selling only 30 percent of his quota. Neither his target market nor his lead generation strategy was effective. He needed to reevaluate. Fred may receive 100 responses from a lead generation activity, with only 2 resulting in qualified leads. Depending on the quality of the leads and the size of the 2 opportunities, he may be very pleased with these results or may choose to pursue a different target market.

The content for your opportunity generation tactics comes from interviews and conversations with current customers, ideally from the potential target market you are testing. This content is created in the same manner as the content for your typical lead generation activities. To learn more about creating the content, see Chapter 20, "Where to Find Good Content."

CHOOSING TARGET MARKETS WITH NO HISTORICAL OR CUSTOMER BASE

In some instances you may find yourself starting with no historical data and no customer base. In this case, consider how your company feels its solutions can be positioned. If you are the first person to attempt to penetrate this territory, talk with marketing, your sales manager, other sales reps, customer service, professional services, implementation, repair, and any other people who have a direct interface with the customer. Often these people can give you a good idea of where your solutions are the best fit and what types of companies would find the greatest value in them. You may choose to hold a 90-minute planning session, inviting some of these people and asking them to share their recommendations in an open forum.

Other excellent sources of information are your company's products and services positioning from marketing and the company Web site. After all, the company designed them, so it should understand who would be most likely to use the information. The company had a target audience in mind, broader than just a few target markets, and this is what you want to learn about.

Interview marketing, product marketing, customer service, technical support people, managers, and executives to gain their perspective on the following topics:

- **What business needs and challenges a solution solves.** What types of companies have those needs? Which companies in your terri-

tory have those needs and who are they? Can they be grouped
into a target market?

- **In what industries they typically see those needs and challenges.**
  Are any of those industries similar to industries in your territory?
- **Unusual ways customers have implemented solutions.** This may
  help you identify niche market opportunities.
- **What business needs and challenges companies in your territory
  most likely have that your solutions can solve.** Often this group
  of people has had some experience it can share with you to help
  you determine how best to position solutions in your territory
  with prospects and who would be the best groups or segments of
  companies to target.
- **Why customers in your territory need your solutions for their
  business success.** Work to identify financial business results customers have realized. Once you understand the business results
  customers have experienced, you may be able to identify groups
  of customers within your territory to whom those same results are
  priorities. You can also use this information in your lead generation content.
- **Who the best contacts are for you to speak with about solutions
  in a typical company in your territory.** A word of caution here:
  don't let them tell you, "Why, the president or CEO of course!"
  In many instances the CEO or president *may* be a good contact,
  but there is sometimes another executive with direct responsibility for resolving the challenges your solutions address. That is the
  contact or set of contacts you want to uncover to target with your
  lead generation activities.
- **What solutions are the best fit for typical companies in your territory.** Your company may have hundreds of solutions. Just as your
  lead generation activities focus on a subset of your territory, so
  should your lead generation activities focus on the business problems a subset of all your solutions addresses. All you want to do
  with your activities is to grab attention and begin a conversation.
  Once you are in the door with a new prospect, you can determine
  which solutions your company offers that might be the best fit for
  the prospect's situation.
- **Why the company decided to target this territory.** Who did they
  see as the potential customers in it? Clearly your company sees an

opportunity in this new territory. You want to understand what types of companies it thinks have the greatest opportunities, why, and who in the companies it believes you should be approaching. Ideally, this would be your top target market and an excellent place to begin your lead generation activities.

You may also choose to speak with existing customers from another rep's territory to gain their perspective on the value of your company's solutions and how those solutions might work for companies in your territory. This can be especially valuable if the companies from that territory have similar characteristics to the companies in your territory. But even if they don't have similar characteristics, the information they provide can often be refined to fit companies with different characteristics. If you find yourself in possession of good data from companies unlike the ones in your territory and you don't know how to apply the data to your own potential best-odds target markets, go to marketing or your manager to see if they can help you apply it.

Questions you might ask companies from another territory are similar to the ones you would ask your customer-facing teams, including the following:

- What business needs and challenges did this solution help you address?
- Specifically how did this solution help you address your business needs and challenges?
- Describe the types of companies in your territory. How do you think companies such as these might use this solution in their own organizations? What business issues do you think it would help them solve? The person you are speaking with might not be able to answer this but may have a business perspective or experience broad enough to give you some good points to consider. You never know what experience or background a person has, so don't assume he or she can't answer before you ask the question.
- What did you like best about this solution? What would you have done differently? Why?
- Having already described the types of companies in your territory, you can ask who this person would recommend you talk with in an organization about this solution.

Wherever possible, identify three or more target contacts you might approach so you can vary your lead generation activities and pursue multiple contacts at one time. Secure different titles as well as different business organizations, such as marketing, operations, and logistics. All you need is one contact to respond and the sales process in a prospective new account is launched.

Use the data you collected from your interviews to form preliminary target markets, and then use opportunity generation activities to test them.

SOLUTION-ALIGNED TARGET MARKETING

You want to sell something you can get excited about. Your enthusiasm will come across in communications with prospects, making them want to meet with you. You will sell more effectively and ultimately close more opportunities, which will improve your closing ratio and in turn bring you closer to your personal quota goals.

If your company has a wide and varied set of solutions, you need to choose which ones to focus on in your lead generation activities. You can absolutely sell any of these solutions. Your objective in lead generation is to first get in the door so that you can later have a conversation that allows you to pull from that larger, complete set of solutions. However, if you can't get the first appointment to begin the sales process, it doesn't matter how varied and rich your set of offerings.

In choosing which products to focus on, consider any obvious market superiority that your company may have. Find out what products have major enhancements that excite you. Some questions to ask yourself include these:

> Your objective with lead generation activities is to gain access into an account with a contact who has decision-making authority or whose recommendations are valued. Once you are in the door, you can apply your selling skills to guide the prospect to the best solutions for his or her needs.

- What exciting new products or services will be coming out that could be grouped together and sold into a targeted set of companies or accounts?
- How do all my company's products or services fit together to this target market's advantage?
- What solutions meet a similar set of business needs that can be grouped together for lead generation efforts?

Solution-aligned target marketing is particularly effective in existing customer accounts. In these accounts, execute lead generation activities and educate existing customers on the company's breadth of offerings. However, keep in mind that any lead generation activities cannot be too general or they will cause you to appear as though you don't understand your target audience's businesses or needs. In this situation, run lead generation programs around new solutions or solutions new to that account.

SAMPLE TERRITORY TARGET MARKET SEGMENTATIONS

There are many different segmentations that could be devised for a territory. Figure 6.2 lists some of the more common segmentations you might consider.

As you refine your territory target markets, you may find yourself combining and further segmenting groups to create more defined target markets.

Fred knew Flo had segmented her territory and asked her to help him analyze his territory. He was not going to fall into the trap of trying to

Always make sure that the solutions you are focusing on are profitable to your company and will help you achieve your vision for your territory. Profitable solutions are ones your company can implement with the products, skills, and capabilities on hand. They are typically not one-off solutions your company has never implemented before.

FIGURE 6.2 Sample Territory Target Market Segmentations

1. Geographic, targeting companies in a defined geographic region
2. Industry based, targeting companies by the NAICS industry classification
3. Solution aligned, targeting companies most likely to purchase a specific set of offerings
4. Focused on a specific customer line of business, such as manufacturing, accounting, human resources, sales, marketing, logistics, distribution, customer service, and so on
5. Size of prospect company, targeting companies based on:
   - The number of employees in the company; for example, targeting companies with fewer than 500 employees
   - The number of employees in the departments that would utilize your solutions; for example, companies with 60 to 250 inbound customer service employees
   - The number of office locations; for example, companies with four or more remote locations and two headquarter locations in North America
   - The company's annual revenue; for example, companies with between $750 million and $1 billion in annual revenue
   - Annual expenditures in your solution market; for example, companies that typically spend more than $350,000 per year in maintenance services
   - Fortune 50, 100, or 500 companies, based on publicized lists of these companies
6. Year-to-year revenue growth; for example, fast-growth or slow-growth companies
7. Based on last purchase from your company. If you sell in the PC or auto business, you know that customers tend to purchase every two to three years. Using this information, you could create a target market of past customers who are likely to buy within the next 12 months and plan lead generation campaigns to them.
8. Based on total amount spent with your company. You may choose to analyze your territory by spending history and categorize it by obvious groupings you see emerge from your analysis. For example, companies that spend $5,000–15,000, $15,001–30,000, $30,000–60,000, and more than $60,000 each year.

target too broad a set of accounts again. He had 70 percent of his quota to achieve in less than six months. He had to work smart, and Flo's method sounded like a good one. Flo helped Fred analyze his territory's historical data. He then held a planning session with six people across his organization who had direct interface with the customers to get their input on where he should be targeting his lead generation activities. Using the information he had gathered, Fred then interviewed seven customers in his territory to learn how they use his company's solutions and the value the solutions have brought to their business. After scrutinizing all the data together, Fred and Flo concluded Fred's top target market was financial services companies selling leasing services through large office equipment manufacturers. Fred further determined his target companies should be regional financial services companies with three to eight offices and 10 to 30 sales reps. Fred had come a long way from focusing on A to Z in the Yellow Pages.

BEST-ODDS OPPORTUNITY CHARACTERISTICS

It is just as important to understand where you do *not* have a good market fit as it is to understand where you *do* have a good fit. Salespeople often neglect to define their best-odds opportunities and their poor-fit opportunities. Knowing these characteristics makes it simple to qualify leads as they come in the door. It also makes it easy to quickly identify poor-fit target markets.

Characteristics may include those not appropriate to your solutions, company size, attitude or culture of the organization, location of the company, number of employees, industry, or competitive alignment.

Figure 6.3 shows a profile of best-odds and poor-fit opportunities for a product company based on our previous example of what Fred learned about his top target market. Notice the gap between the best-odds characteristics and the poor-fit characteristics. The best-odds characteristics are the ideal ones you would like to see in an opportunity, but you won't necessarily walk away from an opportunity that does not fit these characteristics, even if it is not as ideal as it could be. You *would*, on the other hand, walk away from an opportunity that falls within the poor-fit characteristics because you cannot afford to waste your time pursing it.

Take a moment to note the characteristics of a best-odds opportunity and a poor-fit opportunity in your territory.

DOCUMENTING YOUR TARGET MARKETS

Once you have completed your analyses of your territory, list your top five best-odds target markets according to priority. Make sure you choose manageable-sized target markets, defining them using multiple segmentations. For each target market you will create lead generation

FIGURE 6.3 Profile of Opportunity Characteristics for a Product Company

Poor-Fit Characteristics	Best-Odds Characteristics
Financial services companies focused on selling services other than leasing	Regional financial services companies selling leasing services through large office equipment manufacturers
International or large enterprise companies with more than eight offices; small companies with fewer than three offices	Regional with three to eight offices
Fewer than 10 or more than 40 sales reps	10 to 30 sales reps
In financial difficulty	Financially strong
Reps with full-service offerings; very experienced, independent sales reps who do not value assistance in their selling activities	Sales reps who value offering additional solutions to their clients; reps who value assistance in their selling activities
Downsizing	Growing
Heavy turnover at the executive level	Experienced executive team
Already working closely with another provider	Working with several providers but no loyalty to one provider; possibly companies that aren't working with any providers

plans that you will execute over the next 6 to 12 months. If your target markets are too large, you will find it difficult to execute your plans and follow up on leads.

Many sales reps choose manufacturing as a best-odds target market without further segmentation. If you look up manufacturing in the NACIS codes, there are 8,643 matches. Those matches are not the number of companies but rather the number of *segments* within the manufacturing industry. Companies are then classified under each segment. Imagine how difficult it would be to execute a highly focused lead generation plan to 8,643 different types of manufacturers. Consider how to refine your target markets into small, manageable segments. At first it may feel as though you are limiting your opportunities, but it is really just the opposite. With a well-defined target market, your messages can be very specific. You will be able to devote more time and money to the defined lead generation activities because you would be getting a higher return on your invested efforts. Ultimately, you will garner a higher response rate and better-quality leads from the smaller group size.

If you have a large target market you don't feel you can further segment, you want to divide it into a manageable size of no more than 300 companies for each lead generation activity. For example, you can divide the companies simply based on the letter of the alphabet, with the first activity focused on all companies that begin with *R* through *Z,* and then repeat that activity two weeks later for all companies that begin with *L* through *Q* and so on. As another option, you may choose to divide the segment into geographic locations by zip code, city, or county. Find a logical way to divide your large target market and then execute the lead generation activity over a period of time. This allows you to comfortably follow up with leads from the activity. Keep this in mind as you choose your target markets.

YOUR SIX-MONTH FOCUS

After you have identified your top five best-odds target markets, narrow them to the top two. These will be the first two you use to develop lead generation plans for the next six months. As a sales rep, you do not have time to focus on all five best-odds target markets. You need to generate leads, work opportunities, close sales, and possibly assist with implementation. You cannot do all these tasks successfully while also creating and following up on lead generation activities in five different target markets.

Begin with your top two target markets. Plan and execute lead generation plans for those two target markets for six months. Get the leads flowing in and the lead generation plans in full motion. Once you have successfully launched the lead generation plans in both target markets, you are ready to consider creating a plan for your third target market.

Your objective is to balance your funnel with leads coming in and new opportunities closing. To do this, in the beginning you need to target your lead generation activities by focusing only on your top two target markets.

SUMMARY

Flo is thrilled. She analyzed her historical results for the past two years, talked with customer service people working within her current customers, and even spoke with some of the customers herself. She feels she fully understands the business problems her customers had and the value they found in her company's solutions. Using this information, she was able to choose two target markets where she has the greatest number of prospects who might have similar business problems and need the same value her customers received.

7

GENERATING LEADS IN NAMED ACCOUNTS

Flo had been selling to her largest account since she started working for TJ Parker Ideas but had only one point of contact. It was a large company too, with nearly 1,000 employees. What Flo failed to realize was that of those 1,000 employees, there were probably 25 across the company she should be setting up appointments with and begin selling them on Parker services. She knew she should be doing more in this account, but she just wasn't sure how she could generate leads effectively in a large account. It felt as though all she could do was dial for dollars and pray for results.

TOP TEN STRATEGIC CUSTOMERS AND PROSPECTS

Even though you want to focus your lead generation activities on your top target markets, you simultaneously want to focus on the largest opportunities within your territory, whether they are part of your top target markets or not. Know who the top customers and prospects are within your territory so they are not forgotten in your lead generation activities. These customers or prospects may or may not have an immediate sales opportunity for the current year, but they do have the potential to purchase large amounts of your company's solutions. They may require a resource investment to realize their full potential over the next several years, and you want to have a plan to make this investment as part of your overall lead generation activities.

THE VALUE OF A CUSTOMER

It is especially important during lead generation planning to remain focused on your largest customers that fall outside your target markets or they will get ignored. You know it is much cheaper and easier to find new opportunities in existing customers than it is to find new prospects willing to buy. While not all customers have immediate opportunities, you do not want to neglect today those who will most likely have opportunities in the long term. Use lead generation activities to stay foremost in top customers' and prospects' minds

To avoid losing focus on high potential customers, create a list naming the top ten customers in your territory using a format such as that shown in Figure 7.1. To identify these top ten, first request from accounting a

FIGURE 7.1 Top Ten Customers List

TERRITORY PROFILE: NAMED CUSTOMERS	
Top Named Customers	**Customer's Target Market(s)**
1.	
2.	
3.	
4.	
5.	
6.	
7.	
8.	
9.	
10.	

historical analysis of those customers who have purchased the greatest amount based on total sales revenue over the previous two years. Then review the top 15 customers and consider the revenue potential you believe exists in those accounts. Using these two data points, choose the top ten customer accounts that have the greatest revenue potential over the next *two* years. Do not limit your choice to the customers with the greatest revenue potential in the current year because account penetration could take some time and you don't want to overlook any significant future opportunities.

As you list your top ten customers, note their target markets. You will be able to include top customers falling within your target markets in pieces of your lead generation programs, especially for solution-aligned or new announcement-related programs, such as the announcement of a new product, division, company executive, or merger or acquisition. Customers falling outside your top two target markets will need their own lead generation plan.

TARGETING TOP PROSPECTS

Your territory may include a number of very large companies that are not doing business with you but fit the profile of an ideal customer with the potential to become large revenue-generating customers. However, they may not fit the profile of your top two target markets and therefore will fall outside your lead generation activities without a lead generation plan just for them. For example, you may have the headquarters of a large telecommunications or biomedical firm located in your territory. You know they purchase large amounts of your company's types of solutions but aren't purchasing currently from you. This is a company you would want to target even though it is not in your top target market.

To stay focused on your top prospects, create a list of your top ten prospects similar to your top ten customers list using a format such as that shown in Figure 7.2.

Identifying the top ten prospects may not be the simple analysis it is to identify the top ten customers. You might want to think about your territory and who are the largest prospects that you should have on the list. This, however, is very subjective. What if you don't realize there is a

FIGURE 7.2 Top Ten Prospects List

TERRITORY PROFILE: NAMED PROSPECTS	
Top Ten Named Prospects	**Prospect's Target Market(s)**
1.	
2.	
3.	
4.	
5.	
6.	
7.	
8.	
9.	
10.	

potentially large prospect in your territory because it is not a highly visible company? To avoid this occurrence, speak with your manager and peers. You may also choose to speak with service delivery people from your company who work within your territory. Compile a list of the companies these people feel are the top prospects in your territory—those companies with the greatest revenue potential for purchasing your company's services.

If you have access to business information search engines, such as Hoover's, Dun & Bradstreet, or others, you have the option of running a report showing the top companies by revenue in your territory. This can

Regardless of the target markets you have chosen for overall territory focus, you want to identify the top ten customers and top ten prospects where you think you have additional revenue opportunity. You want a lead generation plan to maintain and grow your customers—especially the top ten—and a plan to penetrate your top ten prospects.

be an easy or a difficult task depending on how the territory is defined—by geography, industry, or some other delineation. Look at your own territory to determine how best you can identify your own top prospects.

BALANCING YOUR LEAD GENERATION EFFORTS

You want to limit your lists of your top ten customers and top ten prospects to no more than ten accounts each so you don't become distracted from your target markets. Just as in identifying the top two target markets so you can focus your attention on them, the same is true here. Lead generation requires careful balancing between your top two target markets, top ten customers, and top ten prospects to ensure leads are flowing equally from all three areas. Don't forget you also need to balance your overall lead generation execution with follow-up sales activities and closing!

I have found that there are years I can only focus on the top three customers and top two prospects that fall outside my target market. This is okay as long as it is a well-thought-out strategy.

CREATING PLANS FOR CUSTOMERS AND PROSPECTS COMBINED

Suddenly you have two top target markets, ten top customers, and ten top prospects for which you want to execute lead generation activities—and you can't possibly figure out when you will have the time to do it all. After all, you have to *close* some opportunities too!

Once you have decided on whom you want to focus, you can now reexamine each one and determine if you can group or segment them in such a way that would allow you to use one lead generation plan for multiple target markets, customers, or prospects.

For example, in large companies there may be many similarities even if they are not in the same industry. At KLA we focus on helping companies improve their sales results. We work with many different industries and many different organizations within each company. Although their business drivers are different, in large companies we find their needs

> If you choose to reduce the number of top customers and prospects to fewer than five to ten accounts each, make sure you take time to review your decision six months into the year. Ask yourself if this strategy still makes sense or if you need to adjust it based on the results you are seeing in your lead generation and sales activities.

are often similar. Customer service has to be more responsive, questions answered correctly the first time, time on the phone reduced, and at the same time new opportunities also being sought out. Support and services people should be professionally representing the company, looking for new sales leads, holding initial conversations about new solutions, and closing add-on sales. Sales should be generating more leads, broadening their account penetration, and selling consultatively at the executive level. Managers should be working more closely with their people, helping them to grow and develop. The needs are similar enough that a KLA sales rep can create one lead generation program based on a set of needs and then easily tweak it to fit all 20 top customers and prospects.

Figure 7.3 suggests some possible segmentations you might consider for grouping your largest customers and prospects. Each of these segments could be used to create a unique lead generation campaign that fits a set of companies that appear to have nothing in common at first glance.

FIGURE 7.3 Sample Top Customer and Top Prospect Segmentations

1. Individual titles, such as VP of Sales, CIO, Customer Service Director
2. Organizations or lines of business, such as manufacturing, finance, human resources
3. New company solutions your company is announcing
4. New solutions for this customer or prospect
5. Similar business needs
6. Similar business challenges or problems
7. Similar business drivers or objectives
8. Similar business objectives
9. Associations they belong to
10. Charities they support

Look for unusual similarities between your top customers and prospects to see how you might share lead generation programs and activities across the different companies and leverage your efforts. Once you do this, the mountain of lead generation activities you need to execute won't look so insurmountable.

SUMMARY

Flo is delighted! She's identified her top two target markets, top ten target customers, and top ten target prospects. She is pleased to think she can use lead generation activities beyond cold calling to better penetrate her top prospects and customers. She sets a new goal for herself. In her top customer of nearly 1,000 employees, she wants to expand her account penetration from 1 to 10 contacts by September 30, and next year she would like to grow it to 25 contacts. She plans to use lead generation activities to warm up her entrance and to stay in touch with all those people.

As Flo thinks about her territory and her income goals, she knows she needs to get 240 leads a year from these target markets, customers, and prospects— nearly 1 per day. Now who should she work with to help her get those leads?

8

IDENTIFYING PARTNERS
WHO CAN HELP YOU

Flo had just completed a full day of appointments with two existing customers and three new leads. Overall, she was pleased. One customer had requested a proposal for another project. The other had given her three contacts to call to discuss a new opportunity. The leads looked good and she had begun gathering information about their needs, setting next appointments with each. It had been a full day to say the least.

Upon returning to her office at 6:00 that evening, Flo looked at her Funnel on the Wall and realized that she needed to run some more lead generation activities. At nearly one lead per day, Flo knows her lead generation planning has to be highly effective, but it's killing her. She should draft a direct mail letter for an event that marketing is running, but she has to respond to all the e-mail replies that had come in from an e-mailing campaign she'd launched in one of her top ten customers before she left the office that morning. When would she have time to send the new leads the information she had promised and write the proposal her customer had requested this morning? She was feeling overwhelmed. Was this the path to success?

In one sense, Flo is very successful. She has calculated the number of leads she needs to maintain in her funnel. She has identified her top target markets, customers, and prospects. She has begun running lead generation campaigns in her territory—and prospects are responding! But she's feeling overwhelmed because she is trying to do it all herself rather than leveraging other people who might help her.

LEVERAGE! DON'T TRY TO DO IT ALL

You don't want to try to do everything by yourself. You want to enlist assistance in the form of partners. Leverage resources available to you and let other people sell in your territory for you or, at the very least, help you to sell more effectively.

"I don't try to do it all by myself," says VP Alliances and Business Development Cheryl Gilinsky of SimPath Learning.com. "I use external partners because they increase my feet on the street. They are already in customer accounts. They have many salespeople in the territory. They bring me leads."

This is especially important when you are launching a new territory or are new to the territory yourself. Sure, you could run an event or send out a few direct mail letters and e-mailings by yourself. You could probably even follow up on the leads you got from them. But to be your most effective in generating leads, you have to follow the steps and do it right: Plan a multiactivity campaign, secure good lists, write content, launch and follow up on each activity, update the lists, follow up with the leads, measure the results from each activity, make adjustments to your campaign plan based on the measurement results, and then start the process over. And that takes time. Time you most likely won't have once the campaigns begin producing leads.

So what are your options? When the leads begin to flow, do you stop lead generation activities? You want a consistent flow of leads into your funnel, so you don't want to stop lead generation activities. Should you cut back on them? If you have set high goals for yourself, that may not be the answer. Your best option is to leverage other people who have similar goals and will benefit from working with you, just as you will benefit from working with them.

WHAT IS A PARTNER?

A partner is anybody who can help you achieve your goals. "A partner is an individual or company that sees your vision, understands and supports it profitability," says Holly Simon, Global Alliance Manager for KLA Group. "It must be a win-win for both sides." In selling, we often think of partners in terms of those people who can help us meet our quota goals, but you don't need to limit your thinking to only that group of people.

A partner can be a formal business partner of your company where there is a contractual arrangement between your company and his or her company. These partners typically have an incentive from the contractual agreement to work with you. They are the easiest partners to work with because they are motivated by the partnership compensation plan. You don't need to sell them on the value of teaming to launch and follow up on lead generation programs. It is not unusual to find that your two companies have created joint marketing materials you can use in lead generation. Sometimes the partnership may extend to cobranding of products. In addition, their firms often make resources—such as lists, data analysis, telemarketing, conference room space, and equipment—and funds available to sales reps to run lead generation activities with you. Combining their resources and funds with your own gives you the ability to run more frequent and higher-quality, more targeted campaigns.

A partner may be someone with offerings complementary to your own. Here you are both selling to the same target market and possibly the same target contacts. Just as with the contractual partner, these partners are motivated to work with you because you can share resources, and maybe even funds, to sell into the same organizations. Although these partners should be motivated to work with you, you need to find sales reps with a vision similar to your own. You want to work with reps who understand the value of partnering in lead generation activities and how to be a good partner, as I talk about in Chapter 10.

A partner can also be a person who has goals similar to yours and thereby obtains success in the same manner as you. Even though no contractual agreement exists, this type of partner is motivated to work with you because you are focused on similar goals. These partners may be people you network with in leads groups, associations, clubs, or other networks to which you belong. Typically, they are salespeople too. They usually sell into the same target market you do but to different people or organizations. They can bring you information about prospective companies you have targeted, but they may not be able to make introductions for you. To assist you, they need to understand the business value your offerings bring, your profile of an ideal prospective company, and the contacts you typically target. They keep their eyes and ears open and pass you leads, just as you do for them.

People within your organization also make good partners. Peers; salespeople selling other product lines; support staff; and implementation, customer service, technical support, help desk, accounting, and product development people are all potential partners for you. These people are motivated to be successful in the same company you work for. Often they have customer-facing roles, working directly with customers just as you do. Because you want leads in customer accounts as much as you want them in new accounts, these people are an excellent source of leads in your customer accounts. Typically, they are motivated to work with you because they are paid bonuses or commissions on the basis of customer satisfaction, repeat sales, team quota, or profit sharing. If you are successful in the account, so are they.

"Partners have their own customer lists and their services complement ours," explains SimPath's Gilinsky. "I want to work with them whenever and wherever I can to find new opportunities. Plus, they may have needs in their own companies that we can serve. That makes them potential leads to us as well."

When I worked for IBM, those of us in Sales knew that the people who performed maintenance on customers' hardware or installed new cabling were excellent sources of customer information. Of course, the consultants working in customer accounts were another more obvious source. Combined, the information they provided frequently led to new opportunities in those accounts. Look inside your own company to uncover your customer-facing people, from customer service to consulting services. Get to know them and establish a partnership with them.

I make sure all my partners know what my vision is for my territory each year. They are involved in my annual planning sessions and midyear updates. They have an opportunity to provide input each time. I value and encourage their input because I know that combined with them, my territory is stronger because of our partnership.

As you look around, you find there are many people who could be your partners. Together you can both be successful. "Partners have their own customer lists and their services complement ours," explains Gilinsky. "I want to work with them whenever and wherever I can to find new opportunities for both of us."

PARTNER VERSUS RESOURCE: MAKE THE DISTINCTION

A partner is not just a resource. A resource is someone you can call on to help you get your job done and better manage your time. Examples of resources you can engage might be an administrative person who processes your orders or telemarketing, education, and marketing people, executives, or managers. Resources play an important role in your territory as they are your tactical support system. They are people you can count on to assist you with a specific activity.

Resources attend lead generation planning meetings and listen to understand how they can assist you in your programs. They accept action items within their roles and work to complete them in your time frames, making recommendations to improve on your ideas and direction. Resources help you by answering your questions, guiding you based on their expertise, and alerting you to possible problems.

When a project is complete, resources continue on with their role and wait to be engaged again. They are not people with whom you need to maintain ongoing communication other than to be social.

Resources are motivated to help you because you are engaging them to perform activities that fall within their job responsibilities. For example, a marketing associate would be happy to put together a list of contact names in his or her target market if asked and might even assist in drafting a direct mail letter. Taking advantage of available resources helps you use your time more wisely and, when leveraged appropriately, enhances your end deliverable.

PROFILING YOUR NETWORK OF PARTNERS

Outside Your Company

Outside your company are numerous partners you can call on. Your company does not need to have a formal agreement with other companies for you to consider them a partner. Often these people are very much interested in "partnering" or "aligning" with you because they, too, have something to gain in the relationship.

Sources to find potential *partners* outside your company might be:

- Formal business partners with contractual alliance agreements with your company
- Companies with complementary products or services
- Referenceable customers with something to gain if you or your company succeeds
- Prospects with something to gain if you or your company succeeds
- Customer insiders with something to gain if you or your company succeeds
- Key members of professional associations within your target markets
- Key members of professional associations within your industry
- Key members of formal network groups
- Leads groups

Sources to find potential *resources* outside your company would be anybody who can supply you with key information about, or access into, your target markets and your top ten prospects or customers, including:

- Professional associations within your target markets
- Professional associations within your industry
- Online membership organizations, such as institutes, publications, and networks
- Chamber of commerce leaders, employees, and members
- Colleges and universities
- Database companies

In considering partnering with people outside your company, think outside the boundaries you have previously used. Think of all the different people you are selling to as well as their support staff.

For example, let's say you sell CIOs, vice presidents of information systems, and data processing managers in one of your top target markets. You can consider partnering with sales reps from other industries selling to the same contacts. To find these partners, think about what business needs these contacts have and what they typically purchase to meet those needs. You can then partner with sales reps providing offerings that meet these same business needs. You might also consider partnering with sales reps who sell software, financial leasing services, training, wiring, building and equipment, mobile phone services, pager services, consulting, and moving and storage. In thinking broader, you realize these contacts also have personal needs. With this in mind, you could partner with attorneys, accountants, professional business coaches, car salesmen, home contractors, and more.

For out-of-box resources, think beyond the people you work with and become active in associations your contacts participate in. Attend conferences your contacts attend, meet them in breakout sessions, and get to know them personally during social activities. Read the same publications they read and even write articles for them.

Don't hesitate in considering all your potential partners and resources. Ask yourself the following questions and stretch your thinking to identify some new potential partners and resources who can help you achieve your goals and contribute to your funnel:

- Who else has something to gain if your product is installed or your service is utilized?
- Who else can sell something that complements your solutions?
- Who else is trying to gain access into the same target market, accounts, and contacts?
- Who has information you need to penetrate your target market and accounts?
- Who would be willing to help you penetrate your target market and accounts?
- Who knows the group of contacts you want to access?
- Who has something to gain by assisting you?

Inside Your Company

There are people within your company as well who will partner with you to help achieve your territory goals. They want to help because in many instances it means that they will achieve their own goals too. For example, an inside sales rep whose role it is to support a salesperson in moving customers through the sales process to closure has an interest in your success. An administrative assistant who is measured by the number of renewals he or she processes wants to see you succeed in closing those renewals.

Within your company consider asking the following people to partner with you in your territory:

Your Manager	Customer Engineers
Your Peers	Service Technicians
Executives	Account Executives
Product Specialists	Sales Reps from other districts
Services Specialists	Alliances
Technical Staff	Marketing
Customer Service	Telemarketing
Financial Analysts	Inside Sales
Consultants	Education and Training Department
Accounting	Education Coordinator
Proposal Preparers	Manufacturing
Legal Department	Procurement

Depending on their own compensation plans, measurement objectives, and professional goals, these same people could be either partners or resources to you. Some of them might prefer to act as resources rather than your partners. They may not be interested in spending time planning with you or executing your lead generation campaigns. Rather, they may simply prefer to be available to provide input to you and assist you with specific activities as necessary. This is fine as long as you recognize it and allow them to work within the role they want to play.

Your company is full of resources to consider engaging in your lead generation plan. Give careful consideration to how you will engage people in your territory. Determine specifically what you want people to do to help in your lead generation activities, and then ask for their support. You cannot assume someone will support you as a resource simply because it is that person's job. Treat all people with respect; listen to their opinions. Provide enough lead time that they can complete your requests without undue stress. Thank them for their efforts, no matter how small.

Ask yourself the following two questions to help distinguish persons who will make better resources or better partners in your lead generation and territory plan:

> Don't push people into a partner role with you if they don't want it. Their actions won't support you and ultimately will hinder your progress.

1. **Will they help me be more efficient in what I do?** Will their activities help me to execute faster? Do they want to help only with specific activities? Is it most suitable to engage them only in specific programs? If so, these people will make good resources.
2. **Will they help me be more effective at achieving my territory and lead generation goals?** Will they help me strategize and refine my plans? Do we have common goals and objectives? Do they want to engage long term with me? Do I want to maintain a long-term relationship with them? Can I reciprocate for them? If so, these people will make good partners. If a person helps you be more effective and efficient, latch on to that person and build that relationship! Such people make your very best partners.

PARTNERS AVAILABLE TO YOU

You already have partners and resources working with you even if you don't think of them in those terms. Consider who they are and where you can work together. Figure 8.1 provides a helpful format to brainstorm a list of people you are already working with to determine if they are partners or resources and how you might best work together.

Notice that this format asks for your partner's or resource's name rather than his or her company name. This is an important distinction. Companies cannot help in your lead generation and selling activities. People can. You need to build relationships with the people who work for the companies.

FIGURE 8.1 Partners and Resources Available to You

Contact Name	Company / Organization Contact Works For	Does contact help me execute faster? (Resource)	Does contact help me be more effective? (Partner)	What activities can we do together?	Are we already working together?	What target markets can we work on together?

Once you have captured the names of all the people you are work-ing with, brainstorm a second list of other people you are not currently working with but perhaps should be. These are people or organizations you want to begin building relationships with to expand your capabilities.

SUMMARY—A PARTNERING SUCCESS STORY FOR FLO

Let's look at Flo's story once again and see how she can get through her to-do list when she begins leveraging partners:

- *Draft a direct mail letter for an event Flo and a partner plan to run in her top target market. Her partner had a marketing assistant writing the let-ter. She expected to receive a draft by the end of the week for her review. The preplanning activities for the event were right on schedule.*

- *Respond to all the e-mail replies that had come in from an e-mailing cam-paign she'd launched before she left the office that morning. Flo had a wonderful sales assistant working with her. Because of the success of her territory, she had lobbied her manager for a part-time assistant to help with activities such as this and won. Flo had directed her sales assistant to read the e-mails and reply to ones she could directly from Flo's e-mail, leaving only the ones she was uncertain of for Flo. She noticed her sales assistant had flagged 3 and answered 21. Not bad. Based on Flo's direction, her sales assistant had also updated their contact management software with the replies and next steps. Prior to her sales assistant coming on board, Flo had scheduled a day in the office, keeping her meetings to a minimum, to allow herself time to answer the e-mail replies herself.*

- *Send the new leads she met with today the information she had promised. Flo would do this herself. New leads need special care and handling. She wanted her communications to reflect the level of knowledge and informa-tion she had gained in speaking with each one. As she better understands their requirements, she will engage one of her partners to broaden the sale.*

- *Write a proposal her customer had requested this morning. Flo will work with her technical resources to sketch out the best solution, including part-ner services where there is a good fit. She has a good idea what the solu-tion should be, but her technical resources could do an even better job.*

Using their information, she would pull together a proposal in time to meet the client's deadline next week.

Yes, it had been a good day. As Flo expected, her territory was running smoothly because she was using her partners to help her strategically and resources to assist tactically. She wrote her sales assistant a quick thank-you e-mail and decided to go home and celebrate a successful day.

9

QUOTA'ING YOUR PARTNERS

arol has always been "over the top" in her promises to Flo. This time it has gone too far. As a partner, Carol has always wanted to set her numbers high so she looks like a star, but her unrealistic promises have cost Flo, because she hasn't been able to live up to them. At the start of the year, Carol stated she could bring 50 leads to Flo, and she included this number in her quota. Flo planned her lead generation activities counting on Carol's 50 leads. Now it's August, and the actual number of leads is only 3 with just a couple of months left to sell. As Flo gears up to launch numerous lead generation campaigns too late in the quota year, she finds herself asking what she could have done differently to avoid this situation.

YOU ARE THE GENERAL MANAGER

You are the general manager of your territory. It is your business, and you want to run it as one. You know the revenue (quota) you need to generate (sell) to achieve your goals from Chapter 2. You know your closing ratio and average sale from Chapter 3. In Chapter 4 you calculated how many leads you need in your sales funnel and the desired dollar size of your funnel.

As with any good general manager, you know you cannot run the business alone. You cannot easily generate all the leads and maintain the revenue level you need to maintain in your sales funnel without some help. This is your primary reason for engaging partners. You cannot hire employees, but you can leverage others to work with you.

DETERMINING THE QUOTA MEASURE

Selling is a numbers game. To meet your quota, you want to know how much your partners can contribute to your lead generation efforts and how many leads you need to generate on your own. Part Three covers in more detail the activities to use to drive leads. Chapter 11 tells you how to calculate the number of lead generation activities you should run based on how many leads you need to drive.

The best way to determine how many leads partners might contribute to your territory is to assign them a portion of your lead generation quota, gain their buy-in to that portion, and then plan how to attain their quota portion together.

Of course, we aren't talking about a real quota. The reality is you do not have that level of authority over your partners. Rather, we're talking about an agreement between you, as general manager of your territory, and your individual partners regarding what revenue amount of your solutions they think they can drive or sell. For example, a computer hardware sales rep might partner with a software sales rep. When the computer hardware sales rep finds a new opportunity, he or she can call the software rep to partner, and together they can sell the opportunity.

If a partner cannot resell your solutions, you want to consider another form of quota measure, perhaps something such as shared leads or joint lead generation activities. For example, a consulting firm may partner with its public relations firm. Although they don't sell each other's solutions, they do both sell to the same clients and contacts. They can watch for opportunities for each other's solutions, share lead generation campaign ideas, act as referrals, and even recommend one another. In this situation, they could agree to the number of referrals they might pass or introductions they might make for each other in a given year.

I like using shared leads as my quota measure for partners. That way I am not counting on them actually closing business. Rather, I am counting on them to provide me with leads that I can then close myself. I feel more in control this way, and if I don't see the leads coming in, I can quickly respond, either increasing my lead generation activities, increasing lead generation activities with another partner, or engaging more closely with this partner to help her run more effective lead generation activities. Regardless, I know early in the sales process if there is a potential problem that requires my attention.

> You want to use a quota that will measure the success of the partnership on both sides: yours and your partner's. Encourage your partner to measure you against your commitment to him or her. This reinforces the value you feel in the relationship.

If I use sales as my quota measure with partners, I must be in constant communication with my partners, understanding what opportunities they are working and if they feel the opportunities will close. I won't know until late in the sales process if they have lost the opportunity they were sure would close. This delays my ability to respond with more lead generation activities. So although revenue from my partners definitely is important, the leads that result in revenue are the most important activity measure to me.

There are many things you may choose to measure. The most common would be:

- **Number of leads generated.** My preferred measure as it can be used with many different types of partners. You could also measure the number of referrals or recommendations they provide.
- **Number of sales.** Some reps are measured by units of sales, such as new client accounts or projects sold, rather than by total revenue.
- **Number of new clients sold.** If you are paid on the number of new client accounts, you may choose to measure partners on the number of new clients they bring to you each year. Clearly this will be a smaller number than the number of shared leads.
- **Revenue amount sold.** A good measure for determining how close you are to achieving your quota.

SETTING THE QUOTA

To calculate partner quotas, look at past performance and future potential of each individual partner in your territory. Review your sales for the past two years and see where the partners have assisted or where the leads were supplied by the partners. Using this information, you can then calculate two target numbers:

1. Assign a quota you would like to see the partner strive to achieve based on the data. This is the number you will share with the partner in your "Quota Conversation."
2. Assign a second, more conservative quota based on what you believe the partner can realistically achieve given the information the partner has and his or her experience in the territory.

To motivate your partners, you want to choose a quota number that is neither too large to be unrealistic nor too small to be demotivating. Choose a number you feel is attainable and realistic given your experience with the partner. If you don't know the partner well, start with a low number to avoid disappointment if the partner's results are not what the partner promised.

It is not unusual to have a partner who believes he or she can deliver more than you believe is possible. Let's look at how Flo could use information she has about Carol and two additional partners to set quotas for them.

> *Carol believes in setting her objectives slightly higher than may be attainable to motivate herself. Flo has worked with her for a year and learned Carol can talk a good story but doesn't always deliver. Carol has told Flo she feels she can easily bring her 50 leads this year based on the lead generation plans she has in mind! Upon consideration, Flo believes 20 is probably a more realistic number. After all, Carol didn't bring in too many leads last year. Flo doesn't want to discourage her, but she needs to be realistic. Flo's average sale from Carol's leads is $8,000.*
>
> *Patrick is more cautious in his promises than Carol is yet is also a strong salesperson. He is well thought of by his clients, runs well-planned and executed lead generation programs, and has high response rates. Flo*

believes that if she can run just two *campaigns with Patrick, she will get 30 good leads, but she would be happy with 15. Patrick doesn't feel comfortable committing to 30 leads and has agreed to 10. Flo's average sale from the types of leads Patrick provides is $15,000.*

Flo has never worked with Dave but has had some excellent initial conversations about how they might work together this year. Flo believes Dave would be comfortable targeting ten shared leads, but because they have never worked together, Flo doesn't know if he will bring even one. Flo will talk with him in a month to see if he will agree to the ten leads and will then begin planning some joint lead generation activities. History tells Flo that the average sale she could expect from Dave's types of leads is $12,000. She is basing this assumption on the choice of her offerings and the types of companies Dave has said he will target with his lead generation activities. This is sufficient data for her to estimate her average sale of a lead from Dave.

After careful consideration, Flo can use the information she gathered from her conversations with Carol, Patrick, and Dave to assign each of them quotas. She should choose quotas she feels will be realistic and achievable for them without being too risky for her. Figure 9.1 demon-

FIGURE 9.1 Partner Quota Worksheet: Total Number of Leads

Partner Contact Name	Target Markets / Accounts to Use With	Annual Number of Leads You'd Like	Annual Number of Leads Jointly Agreed Upon	Realistic Number of Leads Annually	Deadline for Buy-in	Realistic Total Revenue Contribution to Your Sales Funnel
Carol	Health Care	50	50	20	Complete	20 leads × $8,000 = $160,000
Patrick	Financial Services	30	10	15	Complete	10 leads × $15,000 = $150,000
Dave	Financial Services	10	To be determined	0	Jan. 31	0
Total partner quota		90	60	35		$310,000

strates how Flo can track the quotas she has assigned to Carol, Patrick, and Dave by:

- The annual number of leads Flo would ideally like each partner to generate
- The annual number of leads Flo and the partner have agreed on in conversation
- The realistic number of leads Flo thinks she will get from each partner for the year

Quota'ing Partners without Historical Partner Performance

If you have never used partners before, you may not have any historical data you can review to determine what the right number of leads might be for a quota. In this case, have a conversation with the partner and discuss what you think is a realistic number of leads for the partner to pass to you this year. Use this number as the annual number of leads you jointly agreed on. If you would really like to see the partner pass more leads and you plan to work to make that happen, assign a higher number for the column of annual number of leads you would like each partner to generate. After your conversation with the partner, consider what number of leads you think the partner realistically can generate given that this is the first time you will have worked together. Use this number in the realistic number of leads annually column. This is the method Flo used to calculate the number of leads Dave might contribute.

Calculating Total Revenue Contribution

Once Flo has the quota information, she can project what her total revenue contribution to her sales funnel could be from each partner at the end of the year. As general manager of her territory, Flo wants to be conservative when relying on others to generate revenue for her rather than being overly optimistic. Therefore, she should use the smaller of the "Agreed Upon" or "Realistic Number" columns from Figure 9.1 when performing the Realistic Total Revenue Contribution calculation.

FIGURE 9.2 The Model: Determining the Number of Leads You Need to Generate on Your Own

	Best-Case Scenario	**Worst-Case Scenario**
Annual Number of Partner Leads Jointly Agreed Upon	60	60 × 50% = 30
Total Number of Qualified Opportunities You Need	−240	240 × 1.25% = − 300
Overage / Underage	= (180)	= (270)

USING THE CALCULATED QUOTA DATA

After determining her partners' quotas, Flo wants to calculate what impact that has on the number of leads she needs to generate on her own to meet her goals. She uses this information in Chapter 11 to determine how many lead generation activities she needs to execute.

In Chapter 4, Figure 4.1, we determined that Flo needed 240 leads per year to sell $1.2M. This would allow her to attain her personal quota goal. Figure 9.3 uses this information combined with the partners' total Annual Number of Leads Jointly Agreed Upon from Figure 9.2 to estimate how many leads Flo will now need to generate. It shows a best-case scenario where the partners generate 100 percent of the leads they com-

FIGURE 9.3 Determining the Dollar Size to Maintain in Your Funnel per Month

	Best-Case Scenario	**Worst-Case Scenario**
Realistic Total Revenue Contribution to Your Sales Funnel	$310,000/12 months = 25,833	$25,833 × 50% = $12,917
Total Dollar Amount You Need to Maintain in Your Funnel Per Year	−500,000	500,000 × 1.25% = −625,000
Overage / Underage	= (474,167)	= ($612,083)

mitted to. If all the partners provide the number of leads they commit to, this calculation tells you how many leads you need to generate. But we know it is unlikely all partners will meet their quota because of all the variables. Their territory may change, resulting in their no longer being a good partnering fit for you. Their company may announce a new offering, pulling their attention away from your territory. Or they may simply have a bad year.

To adjust for all these possibilities, the model also provides a worst-case scenario. In this scenario, the partners generate only 50 percent of the leads they committed to, and thus Flo needs to generate 25 percent more leads than she originally calculated. This allows for a margin of error on both Flo's partners and Flo's side. We purposely make the model aggressively negative so you can see a true worst-case scenario with the confidence of knowing things really should not get any worse than this!

In both scenarios in Figure 9.2, Flo is still short the number of leads she needs in her sales funnel to meet her quota goal based on her closing ratio calculated in Chapter 3. When you do your own calculations in the model, ideally you would like to have assigned all or more of your own quota to partners who will help you generate leads. If you are able to assign all of your quota, you can spend your time assisting your partners in executing their lead generation activities and in following up on the resulting leads. In this case, Flo was unable to assign all of her quota to the three partners she is working with. The results tell Flo that she will want to execute enough lead generation activities to drive between 180 and 270 leads. To reduce this number, Flo may also choose to engage more partners.

If you prefer to track revenue rather than leads, you can. Figure 9.3 uses these same best-case and worst-case scenario calculations to determine how much revenue Flo needs in her funnel. Flo has calculated the total dollar amount she needs to maintain in her funnel per year in Chapter 4, Figure 4.5.

Overassign Quota

To reduce her risk when partners do not deliver as anticipated, Flo will overassign total partner quotas. Ideally, your objective is to have enough partners working with you that you are able to maintain a minimum of two times the amount of leads or revenue you want generated by partners in your funnel at all times.

In our example, Flo was working with only three partners. I recommend working with a manageable number of partners large enough to help you significantly off-load some of your lead generation activities. I have done this successfully with as many as 15 and as few as 6. Use the models in this chapter to help you determine how many partners you *should* be working with. Then apply common sense to see how many partners you can *realistically* work with given the demands of supporting a partnership. I discuss those demands in more detail in Chapter 10.

> Assign large enough quotas to be able to maintain a minimum of two times the amount of leads or revenue you want to attain. This helps you manage the risk associated with partners who do not achieve their lead generation quotas in your territory.

THE QUOTA CONVERSATION

Once Flo has determined what quota she would like to present to each of her partners, she is ready to have the Quota Conversation. The quota you choose should be one you and your partner can agree to strive for throughout the year. It should serve as a measure of the success of your joint efforts. Throughout the year, it will help you determine if adjustments in your joint plans need to be made.

This is not a quota you are going to use for calling your partner to say, "Dave, I've 'quota'ed you with bringing me ten leads this year. I'm sure you can do it. Just let me know if you need any help." That conversation won't get you anything. Rather, this is the opportunity for a conversation about what you can achieve together.

When Flo calls Dave, her new partner, her conversation may sound something like this to demonstrate her commitment to the partnership: "Dave, I think we can generate ten leads together in the financial services market this year. I'm very excited and looking forward to working together. What do you think? Is this a reasonable number, or do you think it should be higher?"

Dave replies: "We've been talking about how to work together for a while now. I see the synergy in what we do. I actually think that if we execute the lead generation plans we've discussed, especially the e-mailing and executive event, we can generate closer to 12 leads this year. Frankly, I'd rather see the number at 15, but I don't want to be overly optimistic."

The exciting thing for Flo, besides having partner buy-in, is that once the partner agrees, she has, in effect, given away a piece of her lead generation quota. In this example, Dave has agreed to help Flo generate 12 to 15 new leads this year against her original objective for him of 10 leads.

WATCH YOUR PARTNER'S PERFORMANCE

To catch Carol's poor lead generation performance earlier, Flo should have been watching her own funnel and the number of leads from Carol, measuring them each quarter. When she saw the leads were not materializing, Flo should have insisted on a meeting to review the plans behind each lead generation activity as well as to review the activity content.

Your partners cannot be left on their own to produce against the quotas you have assigned. You know your target audience, your offerings, and the key messages to use better than do your partners. They need your guidance and recommendations to successfully deliver leads to you. Quota'ing is not abdication of responsibility. It is assignment of responsibility. Your partners cannot be a success without your guidance and continued involvement.

YOU CANNOT QUOTA EVERYONE

Be aware that you will not be able to quota all your partners and resources, internal or external to your company. A librarian may be a key resource in getting you the information you need to target your markets and get new opportunities, but the librarian probably will not accept responsibility for actual lead generation activities in your territory.

A customer may be a key partner for references and referrals, but the most you can probably quota the customer with is a set number of referrals or references for the year. This is still an important quota that you want to track as leads fill your funnel, and ultimately some do turn into revenue. However, it would be difficult to have a Quota Conversation with this customer.

Most significant to you as a sales rep is the partnership with the salesperson from another company who can be responsible for lead generation in your territory because that person has just as much of an interest in selling as you do.

SUMMARY

Quota'ing partners is perhaps the hardest concept in this book, yet if Flo can grasp it, it will be the foundation of her lead generation planning. Flo now knows with confidence how many leads she can expect her partners to target, and she has their commitment from the Quota Conversation. Using this number, she is ready to determine how many lead generation activities she will need to execute on her own as will be discussed in Chapter 11. With all this information, Flo can determine at the start of the year what her success will be at the end of the year!

10

GROWING YOUR PARTNERSHIPS

*F*lo devised a plan to touch base with *each of her partners once a month, maintaining strong relationships with each one. She created standing appointments to connect on their joint lead generation plans. During these meetings, she also wanted to know what her partners were focused on to see if there were additional areas where they should be engaged together, or new types of opportunities she should be looking for on their behalf.*

In spite of all this, Flo missed the signs with Carol and found herself short 47 of Carol's promised leads. This situation would not be so alarming if Flo had had more than three partners.

HOW MANY PARTNERS SHOULD YOU HAVE?

As a rule, you want to work with at least ten partners from outside your company and as many people within your company as you can manage, while also executing your lead generation plans and selling. Another guideline we discussed earlier noted that you want to have enough partners to help you maintain two times your funnel measurement. You may be able to do this with fewer partners, but having ten partners helps you offset the risk when several partners are not performing up to your expectations.

GROWING YOUR PARTNER BASE

You may not have ten outside partners to work with today. In that case, you want to add an action item of gaining additional partners through lead generation activities to your territory plan. Once you know the profile of the partners you need, you can quickly build your network.

In Chapter 8 you identified a list of potential partners, activities you could do together with them, and the target markets they could help you serve. Now you want to consider the relationship from your potential partners' perspective. What do they have to gain by working with you? You need to bring something to the partners in return for their support.

You might bring leads, which your sales partners will appreciate. You might engage them in your lead generation activities, providing them the opportunity to meet new prospects directly. You might also bring referrals to other, new partners. You could help your partners expand their own networks, introducing them to salespeople who sell other complementary products.

Once you have determined who the partners are you need, where to find them, and what you offer them as a partner, you want to create action items in your territory plan to get those partners engaged with you based on what is important to *them*. Just as you sell to customers, you want to sell your partners on working with you.

STRENGTHENING A PARTNERSHIP

Partnerships require work. To drive people to work with you, share your territory objectives and lead generation strategies. Invite partners to your strategy meetings and talk about the role they can play in your lead generation campaign plans. Together create plans centered on joint successes. Be open to input from your partners to your plans. As the leads begin to flow, work the opportunities together, or split them between you. Update each other on your sales progress. Communicate frequently.

"Partnerships take a long time. They need to be nurtured. You have to develop [and] then train them," confides Cheryl Gilinsky of SimPath.

For partners to be successful in supporting you, "they must have a clear understanding of your solutions," advises KLA Group's Holly Simon. "They are looking for leads for you, just as you are looking for leads for them as you both are out doing business." To build a successful partnership, you must train your partners in your offerings, sharing information that helps them to better position your company with their prospects. Make it easy for them to learn about your company because they won't have the time to train themselves. As you train them, have your partners train you about their offerings as well so you can accurately represent them.

"Be sure you have a good understanding of your partners' skills and capabilities so you can articulate them clearly in your lead generation activities, and you can recognize opportunities for them when they arise," continues Simon. "Use your combined skills to be more successful in both your efforts." There is strength in your partnership, but you must clearly understand each other's capabilities to transform those capabilities into sales.

Sharing knowledge is success. The more you share with each other, the better positioned you are to represent each other's offerings effectively.

As you begin to work with your partners, you can build trust, openness, and credibility by working with each one to define how they will do business together. (See Figure 10.1.) Consider when you and a partner are working together on a new opportunity, what will you do if the

FIGURE 10.1 Three Key Elements to Partnering Success

1. *Trust.* Your partners must trust you. Build trust through communication, prompt response, and good follow-up.
2. *Openness.* Do not keep or hide information from your partners. Build openness by being open with your partners. Foster open and frequent communication, share risks and rewards, and practice joint decision making on both the easy and difficult decisions.
3. *Credibility.* Prove that you mean what you say and will follow through on your own promises. Build credibility by keeping your promises; not over-promising; making each other look good with customers, partners, peers, and managers; supporting each other; being honest; and sharing knowledge.

prospect wants to pursue only your partner's side of the solution? There may be situations when you choose to walk away from the opportunity as a team. There may be other situations when you tell your partner to pursue it on his or her own. Define how you will handle difficult selling situations yet preserve the partnership. Defining such situations in advance helps you to handle the challenges with confidence based on the verbal agreement in place and with less stress on the relationship.

Managing to Quota

In Chapter 9 you learned how to work with each partner and together agree on lead generation quotas. Unless you manage your partners, nothing will happen and those quota targets will be missed. Make it a point to touch base with your partners frequently on their progress with your lead generation activities, updating them on your progress as well. Involve them in adjustments you may make to your lead generation strategy, such as a change in your target market focus or the promotion of a new solution.

Use leads as the results to monitor and validate that you are spending your time with the right partners doing the right activities. Make your efforts count by spending time where you are seeing returns on the time invested.

THE PARTNER'S ROLE

Although a partner helps share the load in a business relationship, a key partner does more than that as well. There are eight things ideal partners do for you, simply because you are partners and they believe in your team:

1. **Listen to your vision for your territory and work with you to achieve it.** Your key partners attend your planning sessions, brainstorming and making recommendations based on their own experiences.
2. **Help set a strategy for success.** After listening to your vision, your ideal partners help set your strategy, defining how you will achieve your objectives.

3. **Help build a plan based on the strategy to realize your vision.** Strong partners often assist you in creating the components of your territory plan where you are partnering. Together you define your joint lead generation strategy and the plans in support of it.

4. **Work your territory plan with you and help share the lead generation workload.** Your top partners share your to-do list for lead generation where you are working jointly, bringing their own resources to augment your resources.

5. **Share partners' visions and goals, asking that you help achieve them.** At the same time you share your strategy, your key partners also share their own. When a partner is open with you, you willingly brainstorm and plan with the partner, helping the partner define his or her own territory strategy. You can see the opportunity for both of you in your partner's vision as well as your own. Together you plan lead generation activities your partner will manage and with which you will assist.

6. **Work with you on a long-term basis.** This should be at least six months but is generally much longer and beyond the boundaries of the companies you are both currently working for. As you work with the partners over time, you feel a joint commitment in your partnering relationship. This is one of the foundations of your partnering success. In many ways, partnership is like a marriage. The first few months are blissful and fun, but without the long-term commitment to the partnership, it's just a date. Once you begin long-range planning, you begin to reap the rewards. The leads don't begin flowing the day after you and a partner agree to work together. Rather, there must be a time investment and a commitment to making the partnership work. Work the lead generation plans you have agreed to, even when you are both too busy. If you each stick with your joint plan, the leads will come and the partnership will flourish. If you let the plan slide for whatever reason, the partnership will become dormant—and the leads will stop flowing.

7. **Play a role in your sales process.** Top partners don't stop their participation and assistance with sharing lead generation activities. They work opportunities throughout the sales process, participating in joint sales calls, proposal writing, closings, and more.

Your best partners know enough about your offerings to represent them in their own sales opportunities, and you want to do the same for them. And even though you are both capable of working separately to find opportunities, you know when it is important to engage each other.

8. **Maintain ongoing communication aimed at achieving long-term goals for both of you.** Your ideal partners recognize the value of the partnership and work to stay in touch with you just as you do with them. They keep you informed of activities related to your joint lead generation programs. They communicate leads as they receive them, opportunities they see, and challenges they are experiencing in executing their plans.

Not every partner you work with will do all these things. Out of your ten partners, there will be two or three who support you in this ideal manner. Some partners do it intuitively because it is their style or they recognize the value of partnering. Other partners can learn to do it if you provide an example, a model through your actions. Examine your partner relationships and identify those you believe have the potential to be ideal partners even if they aren't today. Begin to work with them as if they were a top partner. If the potential is there, those partners will respond to your interest and involvement, reciprocating and growing the partnership.

GAINING PARTNER BUY-IN TO YOUR VISION

If you are excited about your target markets and lead generation plans, your excitement is evident in all your communications. It conveys the attitude that you are someone your partners want to work with to achieve their goals. In most cases your partners have goals similar to your own. They are generally other salespeople who also have quotas to meet. Invite them to your territory planning sessions or share your vision in a personal meeting to show these partners how they can achieve their own goals by working with you.

The partners you work with within your company also have goals similar to your own. They many not be compensated in the same way as you are, but if in working together you can help satisfy both your goals, these internal partners will be willing to partner with you. Product and marketing managers typically focus on getting salespeople to sell more of their products. You could support a product manager in your lead generation activities by focusing an activity on one of that manager's products. After the campaign, that product manager could communicate the results back to other sales reps, increasing his product's exposure with those reps. You would receive lead generation assistance while the product manager would get the opportunity for more product sales.

As you work closely with the product manager, you may find the relationship beneficial in other ways. If extra product is available or if product is tight, the product manager is more likely to work with you than with other reps. If the product manager feels there is value in your relationship, you might gain access to special discounts or constrained product.

MAINTAINING PARTNER COMMUNICATION

Flo couldn't understand where she went wrong with Carol. To her credit, Flo was speaking with Carol each month. They had a standing appointment to discuss Carol's lead generation plans and where they should be engaged together. Carol was very excited about her lead generation activities and was working hard and fast on them. She didn't want to waste Flo's valuable time so just updated Flo on her activities via voice mail or e-mail. She promised to engage Flo when the time was right. Carol talked like a star, and because she was indeed busy, Flo went along with her.

Consider different ways you might stay in touch with your partners. Perhaps you could have a monthly meeting, invite partners to events you are hosting to continue their learning about your solutions, or send out a monthly update e-mail. "We are creating a newsletter for our partners," says Simon. "We want them to know what events we have coming up and the types of things we are doing with other partners so they will be excited about working with us."

Where partners carry a large piece of your lead generation quota, you want to maintain frequent contact with them—voice-to-voice or face-to-face. As many reps discover, e-mail and voice mail aren't enough to be certain your partners have the support they need to succeed. Meetings are your opportunity to see where your partners need additional information, if they are doing the activities they committed to, and how their lead generation funnel is looking. It is your opportunity to share the same information with them.

Between regular meetings, you want to determine when to e-mail versus when to call your partners. Some topics are better discussed by phone so your partner can hear the tone of your voice. When you have a new lead you would like the partner to be involved with, call; this gives the partner the opportunity to gather all the details and ask questions. Whenever the partner might have questions or the topic can be misinterpreted, plan to call rather than e-mail.

Some topics are fine to communicate by e-mail. Setting meetings, providing information updates, and forwarding other e-mails are great uses for e-mail. Other topics should be documented in an e-mail or a letter, such as target markets, tasks, and dates you have each agreed to. This gives you both something to refer back to and confirm. E-mail presents a challenge because you can't be sure what the intention is behind the written words. You can't ask questions to clarify, and you can't observe facial expressions or body language. When you send an e-mail, review it to be sure it is clear. Look for typical misspellings and grammatical errors as well as misused or dropped words that can be misinterpreted. Take the extra few minutes to communicate clearly and in the manner that will most accurately carry your message.

BE A GOOD PARTNER

Trust, openness, and credibility are the foundation of a strong partnership. Examine your different partnerships, considering the differences between your partner relationships. Are there certain partners you are more effective with? Do you treat them differently from the way you treat other partners? How do you treat them differently? Why do you do so? What do you think would happen if you improved the way you work with them? Do these partners have the potential to become top partners to you if you improve the level of support you offer? Participate in partner training sessions, learning about their company and solutions, so you are comfortable recommending them. Seek out opportunities for your partners' offerings. Pass leads to your top partners, asking them to follow up and trusting they will recommend your company's solutions. Working with partners in this way will strengthen the partnerships you have.

SUMMARY

Flo is quite relieved to have determined how to engage more partners in her territory. She has put a strategy in place to increase the number of partners she is working with. She knows that over time this will not only increase the number of leads she has coming in from partners but it will also help her avoid being too dependent on any one partner in her lead generation plans.

Flo feels confident she can be a good partner and has devised a plan to provide consistent communication to all her partners, building trust, openness, and confidence with each one. She is focused on helping her partners achieve their goals while strengthening their joint partnership. She's even thinking of expanding her communication plan to some of her key resources. Her support team is shaping up nicely.

ACTIVITIES YOU CAN DO

Part Three helps you determine how many lead generation activities you need to execute to achieve your goal and what activities are most appropriate for your target market given the resources available to you. In it you learn about the different types of activities, where to get the content to include in your activities, and how to combine activities to improve your overall lead generation response rates.

11

WHAT ARE ACTIVITIES?

After spending an entire day dialing for dollars, as Flo termed her cold calling, she was annoyed. She had not found one qualified lead but had placed over 125 calls. Flo knew it was time to try something different. She had a goal to achieve and this was not the way to do it!

Until now Flo had always relied on cold calling for lead generation, but it seemed to get harder and harder to find the leads she needed. She knew some of her peers and partners were using other activities to find their leads. Maybe now it was time for her to think about changing her own methods.

Flo started by brainstorming a list of different lead generation activities she could do besides cold calling:

- Send a direct mailing.
- Hold a seminar.
- Send an e-mailing.
- Get referrals.

The list wasn't long, but maybe it would be enough. Now all she needed to do was talk with some of her peers and partners to see how they made these activities work for them.

LEAD GENERATION ACTIVITIES

Activities are the lead generation approaches or actions you employ throughout a year to meet your lead generation goals. They drive the leads you need. Cold calling is the most common activity. Others include direct mail, e-mail, telemarketing, events, public relations activities, referrals, and networking.

Activities can pertain to generating leads in a target market or with your top ten customers and prospects. When implemented, these activities should complement your overall territory strategy. You have identified your top two target markets, top ten customers, and top ten prospects. You want your lead generation activities to fit in as many target markets and top accounts as possible so you can leverage your efforts across the maximum portion of your territory. With planning, this is not a difficult task.

Let's say you decide to execute a direct mailing. Once you have planned how you're going to execute the direct mailing as a project, it is a simple task to tweak the actual letter you are sending to fit different target markets or accounts. Although the writing of the letter may take an hour or so, the real work is in the planning: identifying the resources available to assist you, securing funding, getting and cleaning the mailing list, researching what marketing material you may be able to leverage in your writing, figuring out what solutions you want to target, identifying and securing the offer, determining the call to action, and scheduling your follow-up activities. Once these planning pieces are in place, you need only tweak the business message—and perhaps the solution positioning—for each target market.

To fully leverage your lead generation activities, you will not only use similar activities across your territory but also group them together in a campaign or program. When activities are grouped together, you are able to reach, or *touch* as they say in marketing, your target market or accounts consistently over a period of time, rather than reach them with one activity at a single point in time. Grouping activities keeps your name in front of your target market and accounts, ensuring you are in front of them when a need arises. This is an excellent way to penetrate your target market and accounts with minimal time investment. Grouping activities frees you up to focus your selling activities on contacts who are further along in their buying process. We'll talk more about group activities in Chapter 19.

WHY DO YOU WANT TO DO YOUR OWN DIRECT MARKETING?

Very often your most effective lead generation activities fit within what marketing refers to as direct marketing. But wait a minute! Doesn't your company have an organization that does marketing for you? Can't you call someone to demand they run lead generation activities for your territory so you don't have to do it all yourself?

Typically your company has a marketing organization, an outside agency or an in-house department, that focuses on direct marketing activities for the company and the company's highest focus target markets. This organization runs events, sends direct mailings, advertises, telemarkets, publishes articles, and more, all aimed at penetrating those target markets. Even though you want to take advantage of what your company is already doing and leverage those activities with your lead generation activities, you must keep in mind that the marketing organization's goal is to create exposure for the company and thereby bring in more leads to the company.

Marketing's goal is not the success of your personal territory. Its goal is the success of your company. Therefore, you want to implement your own direct marketing activities to ensure a steady flow of qualified leads for your own territory. Any leads that come to you from marketing should be considered a bonus but not be relied on as part of your own territory plan unless marketing is specifically focused on target markets within your territory.

If you are lucky enough that marketing is focused on your territory, partner with it to create your lead generation plans. Look upon the lead person focused on marketing with your territory as a partner. Do joint planning sessions with that person just as I discussed in Chapters 8, 9, and 10. Working together, you could schedule your cold calling activities to follow closely on a collateral piece the marketing organization is sending to your target market. These types of combined efforts increase your effectiveness and your marketing partner's response rates.

You can use direct marketing to quickly touch a large number of people just as your marketing organization does. By using direct marketing activities to warm up a lead, you allow your target prospects to qualify if they have an interest in your company's solutions. If they are interested, they will respond to one of your lead generation activities, making it easier for you to find and focus on prospects further along in their buying process. Because marketing is not your primary job but lead generation is, you want to focus on direct marketing methods that provide the highest return with the least amount of effort and expenditure on your part.

THE CASE FOR MOVING BEYOND COLD CALLING

While interviewing salespeople for this book, I found it interesting that their primary means of lead generation was cold calling—or waiting for marketing to send the leads. The challenge with cold calling is that only those prospects who realize they have a need they want to solve take your calls. Those prospects who are not yet aware they have a problem, or have not yet decided they want to address a problem, will not take your calls. This narrows your effectiveness considerably.

Another challenge with cold calling is that it targets only one person at a time. You cannot leverage your time to touch a larger audience. Rather, cold calling is limited to the amount of time you can devote to it on a daily basis. If you are too busy to make those calls, no lead generation is occurring in your territory.

Direct marketing activities are designed to touch many people at one time, entice a response that prequalifies their interest in your solution, and then give you the opportunity to follow up with those people who did not respond. These lead generation activities do require some preparation and planning on your part. And the first time, they are very time consuming. However, when you decide to do a direct mailing, it can be leveraged across your target market with minor adjustments. Once you have used a specific direct marketing activity and done the planning behind it, you have created a time-saving model you can follow in any of your target markets.

I strongly recommend direct marketing for lead generation. I don't have time to make cold calls every day. No matter how many times I schedule them into my calendar, they too frequently get scheduled over for something more important. With direct marketing, the letter, e-mail, or event I plan and execute happens and the responses come in. I have to follow up on them because these are qualified prospects and I can clear my calendar to do that. What's more, the leads are better qualified because the prospects *told me* to call them. I'm not surprising them with a cold call. I'll use direct marketing lead generation over cold calling any day!

Focus on direct marketing methods that give you the highest return with the least amount of effort and expenditure on your part.

INCLUDE A CALL TO ACTION

Every lead generation activity you use should include a call to action. The call to action is the request you make of the prospect to do something. Examples of a call to action might be to call or e-mail you, return a business reply card or tear sheet, enroll to attend an event, accept your call, request a copy of a white paper, or refer you to the appropriate person. Even a holiday greeting has an implied call to action: Please take my call the next time I call you because I took the time to send you a nice card. Use a call to action to tell prospects exactly what you want them to do.

In lead generation, a call to action is the way you help the prospect prequalify himself. If the prospect replies, he is interested. If he does not reply, you need to find another way to reach him.

Without the call to action, you have wasted your opportunity to generate a lead. You will also increase your lead generation workload unnecessarily as now you need another lead generation activity to try to get the prospect to respond.

TIPS FOR USING LEAD GENERATION ACTIVITIES EFFECTIVELY AS A REP

Leverage your marketing organization's activities. As mentioned earlier, your marketing organization is probably running a significant number of activities, typically aimed at creating awareness and driving leads into the company. Meet with marketing to understand what campaigns they are running that you might leverage. If marketing is printing 10,000 postcards announcing a new service, perhaps they can give 200 to you for use in your top accounts and target markets. If they are printing a

As part of your planning with your partner, be sure to discuss and agree upon who will pay for what, who will provide content, who will do the writing, who will handle creation and implementation, who will provide the list, and how follow-up of leads will occur.

newsletter for a trade show, perhaps they can print 50 extras for you to send to your top ten customers and top ten prospects. Find out what marketing is doing that might fit within your territory.

Key things to look for are a match with your target markets in the business messaging and solution positioning. If there is a match, you can use their materials as printed. Marketing might even address them and pay your postage as part of their campaign! For more ways to leverage your marketing organization, see Chapter 20.

Consider doing activities jointly with your partners. Just as your marketing organization is running marketing campaigns to generate leads, so are your partner companies. Find a way to take advantage of their activities in your target markets and top accounts. You know your partners are using other methods of lead generation. Now all you need to do is to explore what they are doing and see if you can leverage them.

If you have complementary products and services, join forces to do lead generation with your partners. Work together to find out what *their* marketing organizations are doing that you can latch onto together.

If their marketing organizations are not running campaigns you can use, plan your own joint lead generation campaigns. Share the workload in planning and preparation. Use each other's resources.

Use partners to follow up. If your lead generation campaign integrates with a partner's offering at all, consider sharing the follow-up with them. Even if you have done all the preplanning and execution, you may need assistance in following up with the leads.

> *Flo decides she wants to run a direct mail campaign into 150 accounts in her top target market. She is extremely busy as a number of her efforts in her existing accounts have paid off. She is concerned that she won't have time to place follow-up calls into the accounts that do not respond to her call to action. Now she has a choice to make. She could wait until things calm down a bit to run the campaign, or she could ask*

someone to help her with the follow-up calls. If she waits, Flo is con-
cerned she won't have any new leads to work when things do finally slow
down. If she asks someone to follow up, how can she be sure that person
has the sales skills to represent her well? The business problem Flo wants
to use in her campaign is one that would be solved using a partner so-
lution combined with her own, so she does have options there.

In this situation, using a partner could be a win-win for Flo and the
partner. The solution Flo is targeting would be a joint solution, so the
partner would be brought into the sales process anyway. Because it is a
partner solution, her partner sales rep should understand it just as well
as Flo, meaning the partner could position and sell it effectively. If the
partner is busy as well, Flo can divide the calls between the two of them
so they can share the workload, and both reap the rewards. Involving the
partner also strengthens the partnership as the partner feels more engaged in Flo's lead generation activities.

Make an offer. Marketing firms know that including an offer in a
campaign increases their response ratio. This trick can work for sales
reps doing lead generation as well. You don't have to offer a trinket,
such as a hat, or anything expensive, like the opportunity to win an iPod
or a trip. People like free information and other offers as well, so long
as they perceive it as having value. When prospects request free information, it gives you the opportunity to follow up with them.

Figure 11.1 lists a number of offers you can extend to your prospects
on a low-cost budget and with relatively little time investment. Notice
that all these offers are business related. Keep your offers business related so you know that when a prospect responds, there is an initial qualified interest. With the opportunity to win a trip or an iPod, you won't

Put a plan in place on how you will pass leads to one another and how you
will keep each other informed on the status of them. As part of your planning
phase, preset meetings to communicate regularly during the follow-up stage
to ensure you have set aside time to share new information and plan the next
steps. You want to be able to respond to new sales opportunities quickly.

FIGURE 11.1 Low-Cost Budget Offers

- Send a brochure
- Perform a free analysis
- Set up a personal visit to better understand their requirements
- Send a technical white paper
- Send a tip sheet, such as *12 Ways to Save $ in a Hospital Environment*
- Send a case study
- Send a press announcement
- Send a manual
- Extend an invitation to a free Webcast or event
- Send a CD or video
- Send a recently published article

be certain how many of the respondents want to win the prize versus read the company information you have enclosed with it.

An offer leads to an automatic call to action. You are asking the prospect to return something or go somewhere to accept the offer. These are very easy calls to action. Be sure to also include the option to call or e-mail you directly in the event the prospect has an immediate need. Don't stop with a Web address to simply request the free offer. That would be another lost opportunity for possible new leads!

Log the results in your contact manager. Maintaining a good contact manager database is key to successful follow-up and management of your sales process. With every lead generation campaign you do, log the responses in your contact manager. Whether positive or negative, make a note of who responded, what they said, and the date. Update the contact information gathered at the bottom of an e-mail, on a fax cover sheet, or during a phone call. If appropriate based on the response, schedule your next follow-up activity.

The contact manager history log gives you a trail of your activities and conversations with prospects. Over time this allows you to personalize your lead generation and follow-up activities to a greater extent with them. I have one target market that I have been working with for over seven years. It is a small target market of approximately 300 companies. All the people in that target market know Kendra Lee and KLA Group. Because of the amount of work I have done in it, I am able to use highly targeted messaging, talking about very specific business problems they are experiencing, upcoming conferences I know they will attend, and new directions their customers are taking. They read my direct marketing activities, and because I personalize every one with a name and personal comment, they don't even realize I am contacting them as part of a direct marketing activity. My response rates are often over 60 percent. Without my contact manager history, I would not have this capability.

Using a contact manager allows you to quickly retrieve the history of your conversations with someone you may not have spoken with for a long time. It is impressive when you are able to say to a contact finally responding to one of your many lead generation activities, "Hi Jerry! We spoke 14 months ago about some of your needs. At that time you were . . ." This ability builds your credibility and demonstrates both your knowledge of the prospect and your attention to detail, possibly propelling your sales process forward considerably.

WORK WITHIN THE GUIDELINES OF YOUR COMPANY

Keep in mind as you develop your lead generation and relationship building campaigns, you want to work within the guidelines of your company, such as:

- Using the correct company logo and colors
- Using the correct company language
- Not doing anything that goes against the goals and objectives of your company

Your marketing department will help to ensure you are in compliance with any company guidelines. This is important because marketing is working to build awareness for your company brand based on these standards. If you adhere to them, it increases the odds that your prospects will recognize your company logo and perhaps read whatever you are sending.

WHAT ARE THE ACTIVITIES TO USE?

Part Three helps you plan, design, and track direct marketing tactics for your territory. The next six chapters detail specific types of lead generation activities you can execute with minimal time investment as a sales rep. Each chapter includes:

- What the activity is
- Why use the activity
- How to use the activity effectively as a sales rep
- Following up with nonresponders
- Variations of the activity you can use
- When not to use the activity

HOW MANY ACTIVITIES DO I NEED TO EXECUTE?

In Chapter 9 we saw how partners can contribute to your lead generation efforts and that you can actually "quota" your partners for leads. Even though leveraging partners is an excellent way to reduce the amount of effort you need to put into lead generation, a partner's strategy alone will typically not drive enough leads to meet all your territory needs. We saw at the end of Chapter 9 how the difference between what your partners can contribute and your quota tells you how many leads you need to generate on your own. The resulting number helps you determine how many lead generation campaigns you need to plan and execute to drive the number of leads you must contribute on your own.

Response Rates

The number of leads you need is based on lead generation activity response rates—the percentage of people who typically respond to one of your lead generation activities. In marketing, the response rate rule of thumb is anywhere from below 1 percent to 1 percent.

The more granularly defined the audience and targeted the message in the activity, the higher your response rate will be. Marketing companies often celebrate when they have response rates of 1 percent or better. As a sales rep, you can't afford such low response rates; that means for every 100 people you touch with a campaign, you receive only one lead. This is much too low a return on your time investment, and you can set your goals higher.

There are two tricks I have learned for increasing your response rate: (1) address small audiences with very targeted business messages and

(2) string multiple activities together into a long-term campaign. I'll talk about this second trick in Chapter 18.

As a sales rep, you want to minimize the number of people you attempt to reach with any one lead generation activity so you have time to follow up on them and can refine your message. Both of these strategies will increase your response rate. My recommendation is to target 100 to 125 people at a time. If you have a larger audience, divide your list into groups of no more than 100 to 125 people. Sometimes I use groups of only 30, because I don't have time to properly follow up on a larger group.

With such a small target audience, you can now use business messages very specific to that audience. I mentioned my one target market of approximately 300 companies earlier. Because this is such a small target market, I am able to use highly targeted business messaging relating to the specific business problems that market is experiencing. This increases my response rate. You want to do the same with your lead generation activities.

Because your efforts will be specific to your target audience, you can expect response rates higher than marketing would typically receive. Chapter 20 guides you through creating a well-thought-out message specific to your target audience's business. Your message should include references to business issues or needs your target audience holds top of mind. Target audience members will likely respond to you if they have a need, even if they are not familiar with your company. As such, you can expect a minimum of a 5 to 10 percent response rate from any one lead generation activity you run. This means that out of 100 contacts touched, 5 to 10 will respond. If you combine lead generation activities into a long-term campaign, you will realize an increased response rate after the first three activities.

I find that my highly refined messages frequently earn a response rate well over 40 percent. You may find you are able to do the same as you master matching your lead generation content to your target audience's top-of-mind business needs and issues.

Calculating the Number of Activities to Execute

To calculate the number of activities you need to execute, you want to know your response rate. If you have never executed lead generation activities before, you can ask peers in your office to get a feel for their response rates. Because they are selling and promoting the same general solutions you are, they are your best comparison. If there are no peers to compare to, use the 5 to 10 percent rule of thumb.

As you execute activities, track your response rate. After you have run several lead generation activities, analyze your results to determine what your response rate is. To do this, add together all the response rates from each lead generation activity. Divide the total response rate number by the total number of lead generation activities you executed and measured. The result is your average response rate. Use this new rate to calculate the number of campaigns you need to run to get the leads you need. But until you have this information, use 5 to 10 percent as your response rate.

Once you have your response rate, you are ready to calculate the total number of lead generation activities you need to run to meet your goals. In Chapter 9, Flo calculated that she needed 270 leads after her partners' contributions in her worst-case scenario. Using 5 percent as her response ratio to be conservative in her calculations, in Figure 11.2 we calculate Flo needs to execute 44 lead generation activities this year.

Flo can improve this number either by improving her closing ratio and/or her average sales from Chapter 3, or by increasing the number of leads generated by partners from Chapter 9.

FIGURE 11.2 Calculating the Number of Lead Generation Campaigns

Flo's Goal:	270 Leads
Flo's Response Rate:	5%
Prospects Required:	5,400 270 leads ÷ 5% yield
Prospects per Activity:	125 Flo's target number per activity
Number of Activities Required:	43.2 5,400 prospects ÷ 125 prospects per activity

Activities = Goal (leads) ÷ Response Rate % ÷ Prospects Touched per Activity
43.2 = 270 ÷ .05 ÷ 125

SUMMARY

After talking with some of her peers, partners, and marketing, Flo realizes there is more to successful lead generation than just running an event or two or sending out a few direct mailings. Lead generation is more involved than just dialing for dollars, but if she does the proper planning, Flo realizes the return will be higher. Direct marketing activities appear to offer more potential for a successful return on her lead generation efforts than does cold calling. Now she wants to talk with people who are successful at different types of activities and learn how to execute them.

12

DIRECT MAIL ACTIVITIES

George was excellent at executing direct mail campaigns in his territory. He spent hours finalizing all the details from securing the list to matching the right offer to his audience to writing the letter. He had a process he used consistently and it seemed to Flo that he sent out a new batch of envelopes every week. His Funnel on the Wall certainly seemed to be full.

Flo had tried only once to do a direct mailing. Unfortunately, she was in such a hurry she didn't proofread the letter, and some of the people who read it were quick to point out her poor punctuation, grammar, and misspelled words. Needless to say, those leads were lost. In spite of Flo's poor experience, though, George was able to make direct mail work for him. So, Flo decided to meet with George to learn some of his tricks.

WHAT IS DIRECT MAIL?

Direct mail is one of the direct marketing activities you as a sales rep can easily employ if you have access to lists with contact names and addresses or have a contact database you maintain for your territory. It is also highly effective and can result in response rates higher than 5 percent, depending on how well targeted it is. Direct mail includes sending letters, newsletters, cards, brochures—anything you might send to a client through the mail.

WHY USE DIRECT MAILING?

With the popularity of e-mail and Web-based marketing, fewer companies seem to be using direct mail for initial lead generation. A well-written, well-researched, and personalized letter may actually be opened and read by the intended recipient. A professionally addressed letter can create awareness for your company name, even if it is not opened, when the prospect sees your company name in the return address section. Even if prospects have never before heard of your company, when they read the return address to decide whether to open it, you begin to create that awareness. If you include your own name in the return address, prospects read it, and you begin to create awareness for yourself as well.

Few business-to-business sales reps use direct mail to touch their prospects, and therefore it can be very effective for you, especially when combined with other lead generation activities.

Direct mailing is not limited to sending lead generation letters. It can also be used to send a newsletter, an invitation to an event, a recently published article, or a holiday greeting. Each of these can be used as direct mail lead generation activities.

HOW TO USE DIRECT MAILING EFFECTIVELY AS A REP

Limit the Number You Mail

The number one rule of direct mailing for sales reps is to mail only as many letters as you can follow up on.

Your response rate increases considerably if you use some form of follow-up rather than relying on prospects to contact you. You might be able to follow up on only 20 letters each week, or you might choose to set aside a lead generation day on your calendar and follow up on as many as 125. The method of follow-up you choose dictates the size of your mailing. For more information on getting lists and setting up contact groups in your contact manager, see Chapter 22, "Where to Find Good Lists for Campaigns."

Of course, your follow-up capabilities also depend on the method of follow-up you choose to use. If you have a telemarketing team following up, you can probably mail 300 letters and have telemarketing call everybody in a matter of a few days. But if the telemarketing team receives 40 leads from their calls, are you prepared to follow up on all those leads within several days? If, on the other hand, you are calling everybody personally, 300 may be too large a number for you to handle. If you are e-mailing to follow up, mail to only as many people as you can e-mail and then respond to when their replies come into your in-box.

Before sending out the mailing, schedule your follow-up time on your calendar. Send mailings in small batches, limiting the number of letters to the amount of time you have available.

My rule of thumb is to mail in batches of 20 when my time is tight and in batches of 125 if I am able to schedule a whole day for follow-up calling.

Give Prospects Three Ways to Respond

The challenge with a direct mail letter is that prospects must take the time to do something to respond to you. It is not as simple as e-mail where you can hit "reply" and be done. Rather, it requires picking up the phone, mailing something back, or faxing. Still, there are prospects who like to have something in their hands that they can take with them to the gym to read while on the treadmill or while waiting for a meeting to begin. Direct mail fits that opportunity.

Make it as easy as possible for prospects to reply, providing a minimum of three ways to respond. Some choices include:

- A phone number for contacting you directly or leaving a voice mail message
- An e-mail address for e-mailing you
- A fax number to fax you
- A business reply card if your company has them. If not, a tear sheet at the bottom of the letter that can be mailed back. Appendix A has good examples of tear sheets.
- An address so prospects can visit you in your office if appropriate

In today's selling environment, I recommend providing a phone number that rings directly at your desk and also has professional voice mail, an e-mail address you can check at least three times daily, and a fax number where your responses won't get lost. People rarely use fax numbers for direct mail letter responses anymore unless you are requesting a response to an invitation.

Promise Follow-up

When you give a prospect three ways to respond to you and plan to follow up, let the prospect know you will be following up. You can give a date or range of dates during which you will follow up. In the body of your letter let the prospect know how you will be following up; then keep the commitment and do it.

"Pete, I'll give you a call the week of August 12 to follow up." Or, "Jonathan, I'll give you a call the afternoon of May 29 to follow up." Or, "Janice, I'll e-mail you a quick note next week as that may be an easier way for you to reply to me."

When you keep your follow-up commitment, you demonstrate you are a sales rep the prospect can count on. If the prospect has an interest in your solutions, he or she will take note of your follow-through. The prospect may not respond to your lead generation activity this time but will take note perhaps making him or her more open the next time you attempt a contact.

I can't stress enough: Do your follow-up! This is one of the six keys to success as a sales rep. If you go to all the work to create the direct mailing, follow up. Don't let your leads go to waste.

How to Address Prospects in a Letter

This is a cultural decision. In North America, most of Europe, and Australia, business has become so casual that a letter addressed to Mr. Johnson is automatically screened as direct mail and tossed. The challenge is your database informing you that Mr. Johnson's first name is M. Here you have no choice if you want to use a name. You must write Mr. Johnson or find a way to learn what M stands for.

There is also the challenge of abbreviating names such as William, Robert, and Charles. Don't assume; if you get it wrong, your communication will stand out as an obvious direct mail piece. Here you need to make a decision on how you want to handle the situation. There are three quick choices:

1. Don't mail to this prospect.
2. Use Mr. or Ms. rather than the first name.
3. Do some research to find out the name.

If you choose to do the research, you can call the company's receptionist and ask: "I want to send Mr. Johnson some information and would like to properly address the envelope. Can you tell me if he goes by William or prefers a different name?" This approach quickly gives you the answer.

Receptionists typically help you with such information as their job is to assist people calling the company. Secretaries and assistants are, of course, entrusted with protecting their boss's time so they often screen what you are going to send and may not provide the name you are seeking.

Opening and Closing the Letter

Out of respect for prospects, begin your letter with "Dear."
You have more options for closing. Some examples include:

- Sincerely
- Best regards, Warm regards, or Regards
- Yours truly (although used less today)

Any of these closings is acceptable. It is up to you to decide which one feels most appropriate for the letter you are sending. Using an opening and closing demonstrates respect for the person to whom you are directing the letter.

Letter Length and Other Rules

Try to limit your letter to three-quarters of one business page, one full page maximum. Use an 11 or 12 point font so it looks professional and is easier to read. Use 1 to 1.5 inch margins on both sides. Leave the right margin ragged, not justified. Limit paragraphs to five sentences. Limit sentences to one and one-half lines maximum. Avoid acronyms that may not be easily understood. Avoid uncommon words. *Spell check* and *proof*—every single time.

To stamp or meter? To sign or not? As a sales rep, stamp, yes. Meter, no. There is nothing personal about a metered envelope, and it's the first one to be tossed. Leave metering to marketing, which has a higher budget and more time than you do.

So it goes with signing your direct mail letter. You should sign your letters—legibly. Use a blue pen so it looks more personal. You want prospects to feel you took personal time to contact them, even if they may doubt it in the back of their minds.

Do not use a computer-generated signature on a direct mail letter. That works well for e-mailings, but when you send a preprinted signature, it screams "direct mail." Sign your own letters. I used to sit at my home office desk on Sunday nights, while watching TV, and sign and stuff the direct mail letters I would send the next week. It doesn't take much time yet makes all the difference in your response rate.

Hand address. Hand-addressed envelopes are opened more frequently than computer-generated or label envelopes, so write out the address for your top prospects. For all others, print the envelopes on your laser printer or have marketing print the envelopes for you. If I have time, I choose the top 15 prospects and write their envelopes by hand. For all my mailings I write my first initial and last name as "K. Lee" above the company name in the return address section. This personalizes even printed envelopes and increases the probability of the letter being opened.

Lumpy or flat? Lumpy envelopes with something in an odd shape inside tend to peak a prospect's curiosity and are opened more frequently than flat envelopes, although fat envelopes can be intriguing as well. Think about what you can put in your envelopes that would make them lumpy but still pertain to the message you want to convey.

Print once, mail slowly. I just told you to mail in small numbers, but who has time to print 20 letters once a week, put them in envelopes, stamp the envelop, and then mail them? Using the power of your contact management database, you can set up groups and mail in very small numbers over time.

Because there is never enough time to generate direct mail letters in small batches, I have a trick I use. I print all my direct mail letters at once with dates corresponding to the dates I will be mailing the letters. To do this, I create the small groups I'll be mailing to by using my contact manager and then use my contact manager's word processing merge feature to create letters with different dates.

I print all the envelopes and as I stuff them, I write the date from the letter in the stamp area of the envelope. This is the date I need to mail the letter. When I put the stamp on the envelope, it covers my writing. Until I'm ready to mail, I can quickly sort through which envelopes need to be mailed and which ones should wait. This technique allows me to print six weeks of direct mailings at once, but I can mail them over time.

The best days to mail. Letters received on a Tuesday, Wednesday, or Thursday have much better odds of being read than those received on a Monday or Friday. On Monday there is a greater volume of mail as both Saturday's and Monday's mail is delivered by the company mail room at the same time. On Friday people are in a hurry to get everything done and begin their weekends. They tend to let the mail wait until Monday.

Do some tests by mailing to yourself from your office to see when the letters arrive. This helps you determine what days of the week you should mail to be sure prospects receive the letters on a Tuesday, Wednesday, or Thursday. This test also helps you calculate when you should schedule your follow-up dates.

Proof! Proof! Proof! And proof again. Read it carefully. Verify names, phone numbers, Web addresses, e-mail addresses. If you included product name, verify capitalization and spelling. Find the errors *before* the piece is sent.

Combine lead generation activities. One way to increase your response rate is to combine a direct mailing with another lead generation activity. For example, in the closing of the letter you might tell the person you will contact them by phone on a specific date and time or will send an e-mail to set a time to meet. In Chapter 18 I talk about linking lead generation activities to create campaigns. This is an effective way to increase your response rate because you are touching your contact multiple times in a short period. Multiple contacts keep you top of mind with the prospect.

Watch the message behind gimmicks. Some reps like to use gimmicks to entice prospects to open their direct mail and then grab the prospects' attention immediately. An example might be sending a person a clock and enclosing a note that reads, "I am hoping you can find time to meet with me." Although gimmicks are effective for some reps, they may not properly reflect the image of your company or yourself. There are horror stories, too, of over-the-top or tacky gimmicks that seemed like a good idea at the time but ended up backfiring, alienating the client, or, in the worst-case scenario, getting a rep fired for sending a gimmick her employer felt was in poor taste.

Consider carefully the message behind the gimmick if you choose to use one. It should fit the business issue or need that your direct mailing highlights.

SENDING OUT A QUICK LETTER

There are a few basic steps to getting a simple, highly targeted letter out the door as quickly as possible. This type of letter can be used for any number of purposes and easily personalized using the functionality of your word processor and contact manager. You may choose to send a letter to update a select group of customers or prospects about a new product or service, or to personally invite them to a special event for which they may have already received an invitation, or to update them on some future plans.

Frequently this type of mailing is sent to fewer than 50 contacts, although it can be applied to mailings of up to 100 contacts. For the steps for sending out a quick direct mail letter, see Figure 12.1.

FOLLOWING UP WITH THE NONRESPONDERS

You want a plan in place to determine how you will follow up with the 95 to 98 percent who will not respond to the initial mailing. Your

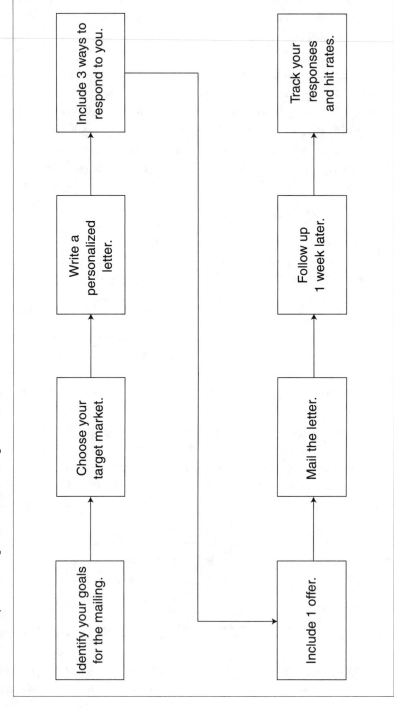

FIGURE 12.1 Steps for Sending a Quick Direct Mailing

plan might include phone calls or another type of lead generation activity as I discussed earlier.

If you are not well known in the target market you are mailing to, you may choose to execute a series of mailings before placing any follow-up phone calls or sending any follow-up e-mails. Your purpose in these mailings is not to get leads, although they would be nice. Although the letter inside must be well written, there is a high probability the envelope will never be opened because the prospect has never heard of you or your company. In this type of mailing, your purpose is to begin creating awareness for your own and your company's name.

An awareness mailing can be an effective way of getting your name in front of new prospects several times over a period of a few months. Then when you call, they have heard of your company and perhaps even heard of you, because they have seen your name cross their desk. This increases your odds of connecting with them even if they never read one of the mail pieces you sent.

VARIATIONS OF DIRECT MAILING YOU CAN USE

There are numerous variations of direct mailing limited only by your imagination. Below are several variations Flo learned about through her conversations with George.

Holiday Greetings

Many businesspeople send holiday greetings in December. Another effective use of holiday cards is to send them during unusual holidays when prospects are not expecting them. Typically, cards are opened and read so you have the opportunity to get your name in front of prospects. You can follow up by phone with a message that fits the card you sent and begin your conversation.

Figure 12.2 includes examples of some successful holidays to use and their key messages. See Appendix A for an example of the Thanksgiving card we like to send to our clients, key prospects, and partners. I find holiday cards are especially successful when sent on a holiday that

FIGURE 12.2 Holiday Messages

Holiday	Key Message
New Year	Wishing you a successful year; looking forward to working with you in the new year.
Valentine's Day	You are special to us.
Memorial Day/Summertime	Wishing you the opportunity to relax and enjoy the warm weather with your family and friends.
Thanksgiving	Thank you for being a client.
December Holidays	Enjoy the holiday season; looking forward to working with you in the new year.

people don't expect a card. I have sent cards for Thanksgiving, Valentine's Day, and the beginning of summer. They always get a strong response even though there is no call to action.

If you are doing business in Asia or Europe, be sure to send holiday cards appropriate to the country you are targeting. Also be careful not to send cards specific to a North American holiday outside North America. They not only lose their meaning but may also hurt your potential relationship with the prospect. For example, sending a summertime card in June to Australia when it is winter won't have the impact you were hoping for; likewise, a Thanksgiving card to the UK!

Recently Published Articles

You may discover your marketing department frequently publishes articles. You can send out these or other articles you have read and believe relate to your target market, enclosing them with a brief note. Articles are an excellent way to get the attention of your prospects because they don't feel as if you are selling.

To increase the chance an article will be read, highlight the particular sections to which you want to draw your prospect's attention, and then write a brief note to the prospect at the top.

If you want to send an article to a larger group and get it out quickly, make copies of the article. Write a brief letter saying you are enclosing the article and why you thought it would be of interest. Do use a proper salutation and closing, signing your name and including your phone number *on the article* and the letter. This way, if the article is shared with others, your name and contact information are shared as well.

Important Company Announcements

Whenever your company has an important announcement, such as a new executive, solution, or acquisition, it may be of interest to your top target markets and prospects. It will definitely be of interest to those on your top ten customer list.

Use this information as an opportunity to send a letter. Develop your content using your company's official announcement.

With both the articles and company announcements, your call to action may be completely unrelated to the article or company announcement.

WHEN NOT TO USE DIRECT MAIL

If your message *must* be heard or is urgent, do not use direct mail. You have no guarantee prospects will open the letter if they don't know who you are and are not expecting it. In this situation, you are better off to use the phone and call.

If you don't have a budget for mail, you won't be able to use direct mail. However, with postage still reasonably priced, direct mail can still be an option even on a limited budget.

If you don't have access to your target market's mailing addresses, it would require work to acquire them before you can send mail. And if you have access to the mailing addresses but would have to handwrite them, it might consume more time than you have. In both these situations, I recommend finding a partner you can share the mailing responsibilities with.

If you have a color printer and find the article on-line, highlight the key sections and print the article in color for mailing. It will look cleaner. If you have e-mail addresses, e-mail the highlighted article rather than mailing it.

SUMMARY

Flo decided her first mailing to her top ten customers was going to be the announcement of her company's office expansion. Although this announcement wouldn't necessarily interest her prospects, Flo wants her customers to know TJ Parker Ideas is a growing organization. Her call to action includes two options: (1) enroll in an event still six weeks away, or (2) get together for coffee to touch base.

In her research, Flo learned that many sales reps tend to e-mail rather than send a letter. Even though marketing departments send direct mailings, they look like direct mailings. If Flo plans her direct mailing pieces appropriately, they will look like letters to her prospects and include valuable business content prospects want to read. For her target markets that may not know who TJ Parker Ideas is, direct mail might be an easy way to begin creating awareness for the name. Flo can see great potential in using direct mail activities as one of her primary methods to generate leads.

13

E-MAIL LEAD GENERATION ACTIVITIES

Flo's new partner, Dave, extols the virtues of e-mail lead generation. Dave is current on all the latest technology and thinks phones are a thing of the past—unless it is a phone line going through his PC. Dave seems to be a successful sales rep and certainly has great ideas. Being one to pick up the phone before all else, Flo is skeptical. Because Dave wants to run their joint lead generation campaigns using e-mail, she decides she better understand this way of selling.

WHAT IS E-MAIL LEAD GENERATION?

E-mail can be a very effective form of generating leads and penetrating accounts with little effort, especially if you have a good database available to you. You can use it as a primary lead generation and relationship-building strategy in your territory. It can be used in place of, or in conjunction with, direct mail lead generation activities. Perhaps the two biggest benefits of e-mail are the ability for a prospect to respond immediately—and it's free! There are no mailing, printing, or paper costs. Of course, you still need a list, and you still have to write and proof your e-mail just as you would a direct mailing.

E-mail includes sending introductory messages, newsletters, cards, brochures, invitations, and more.

WHY USE E-MAIL LEAD GENERATION?

E-mail can be more effective than direct mail because it is so simple to respond to; no phone to pick up or letter to mail. It is also easy to forward on to other people who might be more interested recipients of your message. This gives you the opportunity to reach the right people faster.

Because e-mail is so easy to respond to, you may find yourself holding an entire conversation over e-mail as you respond to prospects' e-mails. This can quickly qualify the opportunity and push ahead a new sale in your funnel.

Depending on the capabilities of your contact manager, you can queue e-mails to be sent on certain dates, allowing you to spread out your lead generation campaign with little effort. You might even be able to set up a string of e-mails in a campaign to be launched over time or based on the type of response you receive. E-mail is a very powerful tool, especially when combined with your contact manager.

HOW TO USE E-MAIL LEAD GENERATION EFFECTIVELY AS A REP

Limit the number you send. As with direct mail, don't send more e-mails than you can respond to. This is especially important with e-mail as people can respond immediately and, in turn, expect a response within ten minutes to one business day. Even more significant, if you send an e-mail and the prospect responds, the prospect expects you to respond right away because you initiated the contact.

I recommend limiting your e-mailings to *no more than* 125 contacts at a time. Some prospects will respond immediately and others may take several days. If you are very busy, limit your e-mailings to between 20 and 25 prospects. If you are looking for a big response quickly, send as many as 125 and be sure you have your follow-up scheduled.

Finding e-mail addresses. If you know the name of the contact with whom you want to connect among your top ten customers and top ten prospects, you may be able to call contacts' receptionists to get e-mail addresses.

You may also try to guess what the e-mail address might be by identifying the company's e-mail naming convention. There are several ways to do this. Bala Swaminathan, Director–Education and Training Department with CompTIA, recommends going to a company's Web site and looking for e-mail addresses that indicate the naming convention. Cheryl Gilinsky of SimPath suggests a great place to start is in a company's "news" section with press releases or its "About the Company" page. Typically, the company provides several contacts' e-mail addresses that may offer clues as to what e-mail address to use for your contact. ("While you are there, do some quick reading to gather valuable business intelligence about your prospect," advises Swaminathan.) You may have to test two or three e-mail addresses to get the right one, but more often than not, you can figure out your contact's address.

For larger target markets, it may make the most sense to get a list, by either purchasing one or obtaining one from marketing based on criteria you define. Many marketing organizations have mailing lists they use that also contain e-mail addresses. Frequently these lists are easily added to your contact manager.

Salutations. It is very unusual to find an e-mail in North America, Europe, or Australia that is addressed to the person's surname or even one that begins with "Dear." An e-mail typically begins with the person's first name or no name at all.

Signatures. Your signature line is another way to provide information to prospects. Although you don't want an eight-line signature, you can include all of the following on its own line beneath your signature:

- Your full name
- Your title
- Your company's name
- Your company's marketing tag line telling what your company does
- A hot link to your company's Web site
- Your phone number, including area code and country code if you do business outside your country

- Your fax number, including area code and country code if you do business outside your country
- Your company's city and state

If you personally do business internationally for your company, be sure to include your country code. Even if you work in the United States and do business in Europe, don't be so arrogant as to assume your prospects should know your country code when you typically have to ask theirs. Including your country code subtly says to prospects, "We are an international business."

Effective subject lines. As with direct mail, the key to gaining access to prospects is to get them to open your e-mail. Your subject line helps prospects decide if they should open your e-mail or delete it immediately. Use subject lines that are not gimmicky but that relate to the body of your e-mail; and keep them business related. Avoid sounding "sales-y."

Figure 13.1 includes some good subject lines I've seen recently and suggests how the reader might interpret them. Two of them refer to prospects' potential business needs in the subject line, allowing the prospects to quickly qualify if this is an e-mail to open immediately.

Avoiding spam *blocking*. Spam blocking is an issue with e-mail lead generation campaigns. You want to avoid its happening to you, especially for your larger prospects where you might be e-mailing multiple people. To avoid it, do not e-mail a large number of people within the same company at the same time with the same subject line. Vary your sub-

FIGURE 13.1 Effective E-mail Subject Lines

Subject Line		Interpretation
Rapid E-learning Development	=	If you need to do E-learning Development, read this e-mail.
Registration discounts for HPI	=	If you are thinking of attending HPI, here are some discounts you can take advantage of.
Complimentary Webinar on Offshore Project Management	=	If you do Offshore Project Management or are thinking about it, this quick class or presentation might be of interest to you.

ject line and the time you send the e-mails so they don't all enter a company's e-mail server at the same time. Be careful to keep your subject business related and not sales oriented.

As much as you may enjoy the graphics capability and the general formatting flexibility of HTML, sometimes graphic-intensive e-mails are flagged as spam as well. Be careful using them because they may carry the wrong message to your prospects, appearing as a marketing e-mail rather than as the personalized e-mail you want to send.

Length. Keep your initial e-mail as brief as possible to ensure it is at least skimmed. Ideally, you want the prospect to read the complete e-mail, which means you need to make it quick and easy to read. Include a strong value proposition that the majority of your target market can relate to at the beginning to quickly grab attention, and then get to your point quickly.

Use line breaks to create paragraphs in your e-mail. As a rule, include no more than four sentences in a paragraph. Try to have only two to three paragraphs in the whole e-mail. Use a one-line sentence as your closing paragraph.

Using links. Include a hot link to your company Web site where prospects can go for additional information. This may be in the body of the e-mail or in your signature line. Don't include so many links that prospects think they're reading a newsletter rather than an e-mail written specifically to them. Limit your links in the body of the e-mail to two.

Give prospects two ways to respond. Even though prospects can easily hit "reply" to respond to you, they may be eager to talk to you right away. Be sure you give prospects the option of calling you directly by including your phone number. I recommend including it in the body of your e-mail as well as in your signature line. Not everybody will scroll down to the bottom of your e-mail to see your signature. But if your phone number is written in the body of your e-mail, your contacts will read it as part of the e-mail.

Don't send too many e-mails too frequently. Over time, as you do more lead generation e-mail campaigns, you want a log of all the people you e-mailed so you can avoid sending too many lead generation e-mails to any one person. This can be tracked on paper if necessary; just monitor how frequently you send e-mails to each target market. If you divide your target market into smaller groups, as I often do, track those subsets as well.

As you begin to link your lead generation campaigns, e-mail will probably become one of the activities in all your campaigns, just as cold calling will be. The more sophisticated you become in subdividing your target market, the greater the chance you will have overlapping lead generation campaigns. This isn't an issue with many lead generation activities, except that your prospects may begin to ignore your attempts to catch their attention. With e-mails you run the risk of annoying your prospects by sending too many unsolicited e-mails, and you want to avoid this. Frustrating your prospects with too many communications has a negative effect on your lead generation efforts.

As a rule of thumb, I recommend launching new e-mail campaigns no more than once every three to five weeks, which doesn't include follow-up on an existing campaign. When you are following up on an existing campaign by e-mail, proactively send an e-mail no more than every two to three days. The concept here is that you want to send a reminder once your e-mail has slipped two screens or more below the main screen in the person's e-mail box and therefore has possibly slipped his or her mind as well. Although prospects who receive 100 e-mails a day see your e-mail slip below two screens quickly, it probably won't slip their mind for a couple of days.

When launching new e-mail campaigns, avoid overlapping a target market where an e-mail campaign is already running. In this instance, your messages from the two campaigns need to be integrated so it appears you are sitting at your computer writing this e-mail to only your prospect—not to 124 other people. Ideally, you want to combine the e-mailings from both campaigns into one e-mail message. When you do this, it *does* appear as if you are writing personal e-mails.

At one point I was running a series of four different e-mail campaigns into the same target market over six months. To avoid sending e-mails with different messages or too frequent e-mails, I wrote them so each e-mail contained the messages from the four separate campaigns. The campaigns involved sophisticated tracking of prospect responses in our contact manager, as well as different messages for different responses, to successfully run for that length of time. It took a great deal of coordination and planning, but the response rate was phenomenal, nearly 72 percent, because it appeared as if I were writing to each person individually.

Give yourself time to follow up. People expect a quick response to e-mail. Schedule time on your calendar to follow up as the responses and returns come in *before* you launch the e-mail campaign. Each prospect requires a personalized response; even a three-line e-mail may take 5 minutes to write, so be sure you have the time to write it. Fifteen responses could take 75 minutes; and if each prospect sends a response to your response, that may entail *another* 5 to 10 minutes of writing time.

Create a set of prepared responses. To reply quickly to prospects' e-mail responses, prepare a set of e-mail replies before launching your campaign. Create them to match the types of responses you expect based on the content of the e-mail you are sending. As you receive answering e-mails, tailor a prepared reply to fit with the e-mail response received from prospects.

Figure 13.2 shows potential responses you might receive from prospects and the initial content you could use in your e-mail reply. It also includes some follow-up steps to take after sending the e-mail.

Queue e-mails. Follow-up is one of the most important skills in lead generation. However, prospects often ask you to call back because they

FIGURE 13.2 Sample Prepared Responses

Potential Prospect Response	Your E-mail Reply
1. We don't need your services.	Thank you for letting me know. I'll touch base back with you in three months to see if anything has changed. Is there anyone else in your organization I should be working with?
	If your e-mail software or contact manager allows it, queue an e-mail to go out on the date you should follow up, forwarding the previous string of e-mails. Copy yourself on the e-mail so you know it was sent and you can follow up if you don't receive a response.
	(continued)

FIGURE 13.2 Sample Prepared Responses, continued

Potential Prospect Response	Your E-mail Reply
2. Please send more information.	Thank you for your interest; additional information is attached.
	You may need to ask a few questions before sending additional information. Respond with no more than two questions that will help you qualify what information to send. If you do not receive a response with the answers within four hours, be prepared to send something. Keep whatever you send brief and easy to read.
3. Check back after a period of time.	Thank you. I've made a note to touch base with you.
	Queue an e-mail to go out on the appropriate follow-up date, forwarding the previous string of e-mails. This way you won't forget and you keep your commitment. Copy yourself on the e-mail so you can follow up if you don't receive a response.
4. Remove me from your mailing list.	You have been removed. Thank you.
	Then remove the e-mail address from your contact manager to avoid any future e-mailings in error.
5. We're already working with another provider.	Thank you for letting me know. We frequently complement many providers. I would appreciate the opportunity to chat with you to see if there might be a fit where we might work together.
	Make a note in your contact manager to touch back with this person in three months as situations change regularly. Begin a process to penetrate this account through other contacts because this company clearly uses the types of solutions you provide.
6. Call me.	Reply that you will call and include a date and time.
	Ideally, call that same day.

aren't prepared to have a conversation with you yet. Often the prospect is not yet ready to address the problem but expects to do so at some future date.

Many reps would log such a request in their contact manager, wait until the time to follow up approached, and then call or e-mail the prospect at that time. With today's technology, you can prepare your follow-up e-mail now for execution in the time frame the prospect requested.

Write the e-mail as if you were going to send it and then use the queue feature in your e-mail or contact manager software to schedule the e-mail to be sent at a future date. This is a time-saving technique. You write the e-mail when the words you want to communicate are fresh in your mind and you know exactly what you want to ask for. You don't need to remember what you wanted to say or what the last conversation was. Rather, you have a scheduled e-mail waiting to be automatically launched on the date you want to follow up.

To help prospects remember your previous conversation, forward the most recent sequence of e-mails as part of the queued e-mail. Then prospects can read down the previous e-mails if they need to refresh their memory as to what they said.

You can queue an e-mail to be sent far in the future. To help remind yourself that the e-mail has gone out and it is time to follow up, blind-copy yourself on the queued e-mail. When the e-mail shows up in your in-box, you know it was sent and that you should follow up if you don't receive a response.

Log your responses. Copy the e-mails you receive and put them in your contact manager so you have a log of your correspondence. Ideally, send your lead generation campaign directly from your contact manager so the original e-mail is already logged in each prospect's contact record. If you are unable to send directly from your contact manager, copy the string of e-mails, including your initial one, into the contact record when you receive a response.

What to do with returned e-mails. Consider logging the returned e-mails you receive as well. This way you know you sent the e-mail and that it was returned.

A returned e-mail does not always mean the e-mail address is bad. The prospect's e-mail server may have been down, or there may be some other transition e-mail. Before you assume the e-mail address is not correct, attempt to resend the e-mail two times. Because a prospect's e-mail server could be down, wait several hours or up to two days between attempts to resend.

If the e-mail still comes back each time, then the address *is* probably incorrect or the contact is no longer with the company. At this point you could call the receptionist of the company (if it is a company) you would really like to break into: "I'm calling to verify Katharine Floyd's e-mail address. I have k.floyd@johnsoninc.com." Pause, and let the receptionist confirm or correct. At the same time, you may choose not to do anything with this contact. Because the e-mail was returned, you may want to remove the e-mail address from your contact manager so you don't mistakenly e-mail to it again in a future campaign. This reduces the number of returns you have in future mailings and reduces your overall e-mail lead generation workload. You can pick this contact up in a different lead generation campaign using direct mail or cold calling.

Following up with e-mail lead generation nonresponders. You may choose to follow up with a phone call, or you could launch another e-mail campaign "to follow up on the e-mail I sent you earlier this month." If you e-mailed a small group, it is easier to follow up by phone than with a large group. Let the size of the group and the importance of the company dictate whether you use a phone call or e-mail to follow up.

VARIATIONS OF E-MAIL LEAD GENERATION YOU CAN USE

Direct mail follow-up. E-mail is also an excellent vehicle for follow-up in a direct mail lead generation campaign. You warmed up your prospects with a direct mail letter and can refer to it in an e-mail to them.

You may even choose to mention in a direct mail letter that you will follow up by e-mail on a certain date. This way a prospect won't be surprised when the e-mail arrives if he or she read your letter.

E-mail may be one of the three response methods you provide in a direct mail letter. Prospects can e-mail *you* to begin discussions. Now you have all the contact information as well as a lead.

Accompany a cold call. You may choose to use an e-mail to accompany a cold call. Leave a cold call message so the prospect can hear your professionalism and your message firsthand. Then mention you will follow up with an e-mail in the event that this is an easier way for him or her to respond. Recap your cold call message in the e-mail and suggest times you might talk.

WHEN NOT TO USE
E-MAIL LEAD GENERATION

If you cannot get a good list of your target market's e-mail addresses, or it is taking you a long time to clean up a list, choose a different lead generation activity. You don't want to slow your lead generation work. Your objective as a sales rep is to quickly generate effective leads. If it is going to take you a long time to get e-mail addresses so you can *begin* a campaign, that will not get you closer to filling your funnel.

If you have a good mailing list, it would be better to plan a direct mail campaign first and then follow it with an e-mail campaign if you think you can get access to the e-mail addresses while the direct mail campaign is in process. If you do not have a good mailing list, plan a cold calling campaign.

Permission restrictions. If you want to e-mail a large list and you are not targeting the message of your e-mails, you need to be aware of permission laws surrounding e-mail campaigns. In many countries it is against the law to send e-mails without the recipient's permission. In such cases, you cannot e-mail unless you can find a way to make the message completely targeted to your audience so it applies directly to it or you have the target audience's permission to e-mail it.

The easiest way to secure permission to e-mail is to get it through another lead generation activity. For example, Flo decided to run a direct mail activity announcing the expansion of their office. Her call to action might be the option to sign up for an electronic newsletter or other type of e-communication. All the people who respond positively have now given Flo permission to e-mail them.

Another lead generation activity that can be used to successfully gather e-mail permissions is speaking engagements. You may perform a speaking engagement for the local chamber of commerce on business issues you know are top of mind to your top target market. At the end of the engagement, you can offer the option to sign up for the company newsletter and other updates on similar issues you might send via e-mail. Everyone who signs up has given you permission to send e-mails.

If you don't use a lead generation activity to get permission, your e-mailing must be specifically targeted to the recipient. It can still have a call to action. However, if it seems like an advertisement, you risk its being screened as spam, deleted immediately, or angrily responded to with a "REMOVE" in the e-mail subject line. If any one of these occurs, you have lost the potential lead and possibly lost all permission to e-mail the contact. To avoid any of these three negative responses, be sure your e-mailings have a message that relates to the person you are e-mailing.

SUMMARY

Dave sold Flo on the advantages of e-mailing! Flo could see there were clear benefits, especially for getting a quick response and following up. Flo plans to add e-mail follow-up to her own direct mailing campaigns and launch an e-mail campaign to her top ten customers. She has their e-mail addresses and believes this may be an excellent way of communicating updates on the projects her company is doing in their accounts while also seeking out new opportunities.

Flo also wants to see if she can get a list from marketing with her top target market's e-mail addresses and try some focused e-mailings: first a summer e-card to create awareness and then one with a strong business issue as the subject. Flo's lead generation plan is taking shape, and she now has many options besides simply dialing for dollars to get the leads she needs.

14

TELEMARKETING AND COLD CALLING ACTIVITIES

If there is one thing Flo knows, it is cold calling! She's been "dialing for dollars" for two years, but it isn't as effective as her manager would like her to believe. Calling on high-level executives of the organization and running through a list over and over haven't been effective for Flo in the past. That's what led her to where she is now: calculating the number of leads she needs, the number of lead generation activities she'll have to execute to get those leads, and investigating different direct marketing activities to use. She's decided to talk with Sally, another rep at TJ Parker Ideas who uses cold calling, too, but she doubts Sally can tell her anything she doesn't already know. Based on Flo's experience over the past two years, cold calling is a technique past its prime.

WHAT ARE TELEMARKETING AND COLD CALLING?

Telemarketing is a quick way to reach a large audience by phone. Cold calling is a form of telemarketing that can be done over the phone or door-to-door. The primary difference between telemarketing and cold calling is that telemarketing is usually a list-driven lead generation activity that involves calling into a large number of companies in your target market over a short period. Cold calling is a highly targeted lead generation activity limited to a well-defined set of companies. You would use telemarketing to call 100 companies in your top target markets and cold calling to call or drop by your top ten prospects.

Typically, you will have done more research prior to a cold call than you will have done before a series of telemarketing calls. You will have a strong value proposition for why your target prospects should talk to you and a specific request to make of the prospects. With telemarketing you have a more general value proposition and a request to meet by phone or face-to-face with the prospects. You use the same basic format and conversation for every call. For this reason, telemarketing calls are often referred to as a "blitz" with a "spiel" rather than as a true value proposition. Cold calling is more than simply picking up the phone and dialing.

WHY USE TELEMARKETING AND COLD CALLING?

I find it interesting that as I talk with different sales reps about their lead generation activities, over 92 percent of them only use cold calling to generate leads. It is by far the most popular form of lead generation among business-to-business sales reps.

Telemarketing can be done by you, the sales rep, a professional telemarketer, an administrative support person, a partner, or almost anybody who has a good phone presence. Cold calling, because it tends to be more specific to a set of companies or contacts, is best done by you.

Both cold calling and telemarketing seem quick. You pick up a list and just start dialing for dollars. Your goal is to find prospects in a list of suspects that fit specific criteria you have set.

However, neither is always the most effective lead generation activity you could use because prospects may know nothing about you or your company. With cold calling you have done nothing to let your prospects know you think you have a good solution that would be of interest to them. Your hit rate may be quite low compared with some other lead generation activities. It can take many calls to gain enough recognition with prospects that they will accept your call or agree to a visit. This can be a slow process when you need a large number of leads coming into your funnel.

If you combine telemarketing or cold calling with direct mail, you can warm up a call by sending information in advance. Prospects may respond with an interest, thus prequalifying themselves. At the least, you have begun to create recognition for yourself and your company in preparation for your next lead generation activity. In combination with other activities, you can actually increase your overall hit rate using telemarketing and cold calling.

HOW TO USE TELEMARKETING AND COLD CALLING EFFECTIVELY AS A REP

With the popularity of cold calling, many books about how to do it effectively are available. Here are a few tips on how to cold call effectively as part of your lead generation activities.

Remember your objective. Your objective in telemarketing and cold calling is to get a conversation started that could result in a lead. As Karena Stocker, branch manager for Excel Personnel, likes to say, "If you don't ask, they cannot say yes, they might need your services."

You usually won't know what a prospect's needs are with a cold call. Given this, you are not trying to "hit" the prospect's exact need with your first call. Rather, you are attempting to get the prospect's attention. You want the prospect to recognize that you might help with needs he or she does have. You want to gain enough interest that the prospect will stay on the phone longer or agree to a meeting where you can spend time understanding his or her needs.

Given that the objective is to simply get the prospect's attention and start a conversation, pick one solution or two related business problems that you can mention to begin the conversation anywhere that will grab the prospect's attention. Even if the prospect replies, "We don't have that problem," the conversation has begun. You can then ask, "What problems *are* you focused on right now?" And you've begun the conversation.

Figure 14.1 provides an example of how we at KLA use two common business problems for nearly all sales organizations for our initial calls to companies. The two problems are (1) increasing sales, and (2) increasing the number of new leads salespeople generate. We call this our cold

FIGURE 14.1 Sample Cold Calling Value Proposition

> Hi Madison, this is Kendra Lee with KLA Group. Many companies we assist are working to increase their sales and the number of new leads their salespeople generate. That's an area we specialize in, and I wanted to call to see if these are challenges you are looking to address in your own company, and if it might make sense for us to discuss how we might work together. Do you have a few minutes to chat now or should we schedule a more convenient time?

calling value proposition. Nearly every sales organization is focused on one of these two business issues.

At KLA, if we are talking with a sales executive, the only change we make is to replace the word *leads* with *opportunities* because it sounds more strategic and less tactical.

If you are going to use cold calling as a primary lead generation activity on its own, figure out what two common business problems you can use for each of your top two target markets and use them with the five-sentence cold call formula.

The Five-Sentence Formula for Cold Calls. Cold calls must be brief and to the point. The Five-Sentence Formula for Cold Calls in Figure 14.2 gets your message out to your prospects quickly and immediately engages them. Provide your phone number and e-mail address so your prospects have it even if they aren't ready to do anything yet.

FIGURE 14.2 The Five-Sentence Formula for Cold Calls

Sentence 1	Give your name and your company's name.
Sentence 2	Tell why you are calling; if you have a referral, use it as part of this sentence; use the business issues you have identified here.
Sentence 3	Tell how you can help with your solutions; if you have a good customer reference, mention it as part of this sentence.
Sentence 4	Give a call to action telling exactly what you would like the prospect to do. Hold a discussion with the prospect.
Sentence 5	Leave your phone number and e-mail address.

Be prepared for voice mail. People are busy today. The majority of the time when you call you *will* reach voice mail. Your objective is to be professional and concise while getting your point across and peaking the prospect's interest. If leaving concise voice mail messages is not your best skill, write out the message you will leave so you are certain not to leave out any information. Then practice the message until it sounds natural. Use the Five-Sentence Formula for Cold Calls from Figure 14.2 to write your voice mail. Your voice mail message should be the same as your cold call message.

After you've left your message, see if you can reach *somebody.* Even a receptionist can give you a new piece of information you may not have. As you listen to your prospect's voice mail, see if the prospect gives you the number of an assistant you can call. If not, leave your voice mail, then call back, and try pressing 0. Most likely 0 will take you to a receptionist or your prospect's assistant. Use the Five-Sentence Formula for Cold Calls and ask if your prospect is the right person for you to talk to. See if you can find out the prospect's schedule, the best time to call, the best way to reach him or her, other people you should be talking to, and other information that will help you break into the company.

What to say to gatekeepers. You can also use the Five-Sentence Formula for Cold Calls with gatekeepers. They can then help guide you to the right person to speak with. While you are speaking with gatekeepers, gather additional information about your prospect. You may even attempt to get an appointment scheduled on the prospect's calendar "to avoid the two of you playing telephone tag," as you can say to the gatekeeper.

Don't ask for the business. Claire Reynolds, regional account executive for Excel Personnel, cautions: "When cold calling door-to-door or on the phone, don't try to get business right then and there. When you cold call, you are gathering information. Your objective is to set an appointment to discuss how you might work together." Don't try to gather all the prospect's needs on the first call or talk too long about your offerings. Get enough information to keep the prospect's interest after you get off the phone, and talk long enough to ensure the prospect will keep your first meeting where you can spend more time together.

Omega Salas, who does cold calling on a daily basis for Wagner Equipment, says the best way to be successful with cold calling is to be up front and honest about your services and capabilities. "Don't overstate what you can do just to get the lead," he says. "Be honest." If during the cold call you learn the prospect is interested in services you can't provide, be up front about it. Let the prospect know what you *can* do after reporting what your company can't do. This way together you can determine where there are opportunities for you to work together.

Engaging a telemarketer. You often don't have the time to make all the calls you might like to. In this situation, engaging a telemarketer can be a great way to keep leads flowing while you are focused elsewhere.

To be successful when using a telemarketer, write the script yourself and schedule time to train the telemarketer on how to use your script as intended. Although you might have a resource or partner write the script, you may want to write it yourself to be sure you are covering all the key points you want to make.

Provide the script in two formats. First, provide a conversational script that you can use to show the telemarketer how the conversation might sound. Second, provide a bulleted script the telemarketer can refer to during the call without sounding as though a script is being used.

The level of complexity of the conversation you plan in the script depends on whom you've selected to make the call. If you are making the call as a sales rep, you can call with a goal and objective and let the conversation flow. If you select an administrative support person or contract telemarketer to call, you want a detailed script of how you'd like the conversation to flow as well as potential objections the telemarketer may need to address.

As you train the person who is making the calls, provide enough background about the target market to make the telemarketer comfortable and somewhat knowledgeable about the people being called. Let the telemarketer know what objections he or she may run into and how to handle them. Give him or her ideas on how to get past gatekeepers to reach the target contact.

Key your telemarketers into the strengths and weaknesses of your company and of the competition so they can better answer questions right away rather than calling back later or asking you. Let them know if you want them to continue calling contacts over a period of days or weeks until they reach the target contact or if they should make only five or six attempts to reach a contact.

Practice the script a few times with the telemarketer. Share your experiences of testing the script. Outline when the telemarketer should call you with an opportunity, question, or prospect's concern.

Make sure the telemarketer is excited about and understands your campaign to ensure he or she makes a much better call, not to mention many more calls per day.

After the campaign. Take time to meet with your telemarketer after the campaign to find out how the telemarketer thinks the campaign went. What could have been done differently to make it even more successful? What does the telemarketer think went exceptionally well that you want to do again? Use these ideas in your next telemarketing campaign. You may choose to involve your telemarketer as one of your resources when you plan your next lead generation campaign. After working with you on several campaigns, he or she will have ideas and recommendations that should help you to improve your response ratio.

How many tries will it take to connect? Over the past two years, KLA has tracked the average number of attempts it now takes to reach a new prospect. Based on our research, we have found the number has increased since the market downturn in 2001. For companies without name recognition it takes approximately nine calls until a prospect takes their call. For companies with name recognition, it takes approximately seven calls.

When you add e-mail follow-up to a cold call, the number of attempts drops. For companies without name recognition, it takes four to five calls and four to five e-mails to get a prospect to reply. For companies with name recognition, it takes only two to three calls and two to three e-mails. Typically, the prospect replies by e-mail. The strategy I recommend is to use the combination of a phone call followed by an e-mail. This way your prospects can respond to you in whatever manner is easiest for them—typically e-mail.

How frequently do you call? Whether you are cold calling or using a telemarketer, this number has changed as well. The rule of thumb used to be to attempt to reach a person as many times as you had time during a day but to leave only one message per day.

With the advent of Caller ID, many prospects now know who tries to call them ten times in a day, which doesn't leave the desired impression. I recommend you not attempt to reach any one contact more than two times a day and leave one message. Because people are so busy in today's work world, call every other day and leave one message rather than calling every day.

At this rate, it could take you four weeks to connect with a new prospect, so you want to be calling new prospects and following up on lead generation activities every day as part of your lead generation plan.

Following up with telemarketing and cold calling nonresponders. When do you give up on calling a prospect? Based on the average number of tries it takes to reach a prospect, you don't want to give up before you have called at least nine times. Phil Harris of Akibia told me one of his top rep's philosophies is that he will continue to call until the prospect does one of three things:

1. Tells the rep, "Don't call."
2. Tells the rep, "I'm the wrong person."
3. Takes the call when he finally has a need.

Regardless of which reason, in this scenario Harris's rep talks with the prospect every time—and never stops calling until he does.

VARIATIONS OF TELEMARKETING AND COLD CALLING YOU CAN USE

If you have the resources to engage a telemarketer long term, do it and use a telemarketer to follow up on your lead generation campaigns rather than doing it yourself. This frees you up to launch other lead generation activities, follow up on new leads, and sell.

PROJECT PLANNING NOTES

1
2
3
4
5
6
7
8
9
10
11
12
13
14
15
16
17
18
19
20
21
22
23
24
25
26
27
28

PROJECT ACTION NOTES

DATE

GOLD FIBRE®

56	55	54	53	52	51	50	49	48	47	46	45	44	43	42	41	40	39	38	37	36	35	34	33	32	31	30

WHEN NOT TO USE TELEMARKETING AND COLD CALLING

Telemarketing and cold calling can move quickly or very slowly, depending on your ability to get prospects on the phone; but combining both methods keeps your name and voice in front of your prospects. Telemarketing and cold calling are always good lead generation methods, even though they may go slowly. You are wise to use both methods in conjunction with other activities to increase your response rate.

Don't use telemarketers to try to gain access to your top ten customers or top ten prospects. These are accounts you have identified as having the greatest revenue potential in your territory. Although you might be tempted to use telemarketers to establish the first contact, make these calls yourself after doing your research. This way you can be certain what message is being communicated and that appropriate follow-up is occurring. You can also seek out new contacts to talk with as you gather new information about the account.

SUMMARY

Sally taught Flo quite a bit that Flo didn't realize she didn't know about how to use telemarketing and cold calling effectively. Flo plans to change her cold calling strategy immediately, using the Five-Sentence Cold Calling Formula to make her calls more effective. She's going to talk with her partners to see if they have access to telemarketers they can use in some of their lead generation campaigns. And she's definitely going to train her telemarketers more effectively than she was trained for cold calling. Flo plans to integrate cold calling into all her lead generation activities. She's beginning to see how direct mail, e-mail, and cold calling could all work together in one integrated lead generation campaign to not only create awareness but also to garner high response rates.

15

EVENTS AND NETWORKING

Successful Events on a Shoestring Budget

A professional event for under $350:

    Purchase a list $75

    Rent a conference room for a morning $125

    Rent projection equipment $100

    Coffee and donuts $20

    E-mail invitations ..... Free

    Engage a speaker .... Free

Attend Seminars, Conferences, Symposiums

    Conference fee .... Free–$1,200

    Travel and expenses .... Free–$1,000

Flo didn't realize holding an event could be affordable for a sales rep with no budget. Thank goodness she'd found this article in her lead generation research.

Their office has conference room space, so it won't even cost her $100 to hold an event. She could reserve the room, request projection equipment from the office manager, have a partner speak, pick up the donuts herself, and use the office coffee. Now all she has to do is get the list—and maybe marketing or the local chamber of commerce can provide that.

WHAT ARE EVENTS?

We frequently think of events as very large trade shows, sporting events, art shows, conferences, or seminars. Events are often planned by the marketing department or your management team. However, events do not have to be large, costly affairs. You can plan events for your target market alone by bringing in partners as guest speakers on topics important to your target market, partners to demonstrate complementary solutions, and local speakers who want to get their own message out. If you want to get fancy, you can even hold social events, such as hosting a golf tournament or attending a local show.

In today's technology environment, events are no longer always face-to-face either. Many events are now Web- or phone-based, including Webcasts and forums on the same topics we traditionally thought of for face-to-face business events: topics related to a business issue, problem, or challenge your target market is facing. These events are definitely very affordable and easily executed if you have access to the technology.

Figure 15.1 shows the four things participants want when they attend an event and the questions they have to be able to answer to get that information. To be successful, any event you choose to host should provide these four things and the answers to these questions.

The level of depth you choose to provide for the event topic determines the type of event to use. For example, at an executive forum or breakfast, participants expect a great deal of information, facts, case studies, and understanding of the business issue, with thought-provoking solutions for them to consider. At a new product announcement, the business issue discussion would be much lighter than in an executive breakfast, as participants know the purpose is a new product announcement. Here the percentage of focus will be on the new solution and how it will help the participant's business. Use Figure 15.1 to discover the four things participants want and put yourself in your participants' position to determine the depth of information to present for a successful event.

Attending Events

You don't need to host an event to meet prospects. Attending events where your target audience will be is an excellent way to network with

FIGURE 15.1 The Four Most Powerful Things a Person Wants from an Event

What Participants Want	What You Need to Provide
1. To **Learn** something new about the topic that drew their participation; a topic they were already familiar with	**What did I learn about this topic that I didn't know before?** Provide additional details on the topic, explaining the root causes that led to the business issue being discussed.
2. To **Discover** something they did not previously know about a different topic	**What did I discover that I had not expected to discover when I chose to attend?** Give a twist on the business issue at hand, another way to think about it, a possible root cause that is typically never considered, or other business issues that may arise from the main topic.
3. To **Know** facts and new information	**What facts and new information did I gain that helped me to understand the topic with more depth?** Here you might provide statistics from a recent analysis, a case study, a reference, and/or a customer speaker providing supporting data on the topic of the event and its importance to participants.
4. To **Understand** how to address what they have just discovered and learned	**What is the solution they might consider to address the business issue they just learned about?** This covers the offerings you have that might help address the root causes and ultimately the business issue.

them while also expanding your knowledge about their business needs. You may attend a trade show, conference, symposium, or Webcast. You should attend the same events your target market attends so you can both learn about their interests and mingle with them.

If your primary reason for attending is to meet prospects and network, I recommend face-to-face events. You'll have an opportunity to speak with them at breaks, sit next to them in sessions, and eat together at conference-planned meals. You'll learn about their business priorities by attending the sessions. As an added benefit, you'll also meet potential partners who are attending for the same reasons as you.

If your primary reason for attending an event is to learn about your target market's industry and business, Webcasts can be a cost-effective way to do this. Webcasts are online seminars and are hosted by publications and associations as well as by large companies. Publications and associations focus on topics related to the industries they serve. The topics can span a wide range—everything from how to sell more effectively to market trends to current business issues. Large companies focus on promoting their solutions by discussing business issues, using a format similar to Figure 15.1. Attending a Webcast hosted by a competitor can be an excellent way to do competitive research—if the competitor accepts your enrollment.

To enroll in a Webcast, you either receive or see an invitation. You might find an invitation in an online publication to which you subscribe or in a print publication giving information about the Web link for enrolling. When you enroll, you are sent a link to the Webcast log-on page, an ID, and a password to attend. Once in the Webcast, you can typically see the names or initials of people who are attending but not their company names, making it an ineffective way to network unless you recognize a participant's name and follow up by phone or e-mail.

WHY USE EVENTS?

Events you host, attend, or speak at provide a great way to get to new prospects while discussing business topics of interest or introducing new solutions. You can easily leverage events your company already has planned. Whether or not the company's target market for the event is your territory, you may still be able to invite your target market and your top ten customer and top ten prospects. Even if you have to prepare and send your own invitations and the event is already running and paid for, that is still less of an investment for you.

Although the lead generation response rate can be considerably higher for small, well-targeted events, they do require perhaps the longest amount of preparation. This is because you need to use a combination of direct mail, e-mail, and telemarketing to drive enrollment to the event itself. This may seem to be a reason not to use events, but, in actuality, it is one of the points in favor of using them. The repeated connecting with your prospects builds awareness for you and your company, making it easier to get their attention. Even if they do not attend the event, they are hearing and learning more about you. This repeated touching makes it easier to connect with them the next time you run a lead generation event.

HOW TO USE EVENTS EFFECTIVELY AS A REP

Leverage the marketing department. If your marketing organization has plans to host several seminars, participate in trade shows, or launch other events that fit within your target market, plan them into your individual lead generation campaigns. Some events to consider include the following:

- **Sporting or arts events.** Use these as a great way to network with new prospects and socialize with current prospects and customers. Follow up with an e-mail and phone campaign to turn new prospects into qualified leads.
- **Radio spots, TV advertising.** Refer to these in your lead generation campaigns. If the marketing messages work in your target markets, repeat them in your written lead generation activities such as direct mail and e-mail. Prospects' familiarity with a marketing message can help you to establish rapport with them more quickly.
- **Seminars, trade shows.** Plan these into your individual lead generation campaigns, including pre-event activities, to let people know you will be present or that the event is happening and they should plan to attend, and follow-up activities to touch anybody you weren't able to meet personally at the event. You can also follow up with all participants just to tell them you are available and why they should care, as well as follow up with people who weren't able to attend the event.

Look for events you can leverage from your marketing organization. As you execute events, use the following recommendations to make the event successful for its target market.

Precall the list. If you have access to a telemarketing department in your organization, plan to precall the list you will be sending invitations to. This is a great opportunity to be sure the list is accurate and to let people know an invitation is on its way. When you precall, you can tell people you will be following up on the invitation as well, so they will be expecting the follow-up call after the invitation is sent. If a partner or you are making the calls, you can treat this as an opportunity to uncover immediate needs. You may find some leads in your precalls even though that is not your objective. Precall your list two and three weeks prior to mailing the invitations.

The invitations. Ten years ago, invitations to events were very formal. Today, invitations can be as simple as an e-mail or as formal as wedding invitations. They might be a PDF attachment, an HTML embedded note, a link to a Web site, a direct mail letter, or a standard card–style invitation. Consider your budget, the type of event you are hosting, those you are inviting, and your objective for the event. Choose the style of invitation to match those considerations.

In all cases, include at least four ways for prospects to reply and accept: phone, fax, e-mail, mail. If you have access to the technology or one is already established, also add a Web link to enroll.

If the event is being run by your marketing organization or is a conference you will be attending, send e-mail invitations telling people you will be at the event and asking to meet with them. See the "Set Up Meetings Before a Live Event" section on page 161.

Include an offer to increase attendance. When you send out the event invitation, either by e-mail or regular mail, include an offer that will really catch invitees' interest and make them want to attend the event. It might be any of the offers I discussed in Chapter 11, such as a white paper, free analysis, case study, or CD. Some companies offer promotional items such as a free T-shirt, a kit to clean your PC keyboard, or a company mug. Your offer doesn't have to be costly; the most effective offers tie to attendance at the event.

The opportunity to meet for coffee, attend sessions together, and then get together as a group following a session could be an excellent offer to accompany an event. In the meeting after the session, you could hold a discussion on what brought participants there, turning it into an opportunity for participants to network with each other. Be creative with your offers, keeping in mind your prospects value something that helps them do their job more effectively or teaches them new information—not a T-shirt or coffee mug.

Some offers to consider for an event include:

- An electronic copy of the presentation—typically provided in a PDF, nonrevisable format
- The opportunity to network with peers
- A discount on services performed by a specific date
- Free software, equipment, training
- A drawing for a free book, product, or service or a discount for one or more attendees
- Breakfast or lunch with you or an executive from your company prior to the event or drinks following the event
- Free services—an analysis based on the topic of the event, a one-hour meeting with one of your consultants
- A trinket with your logo—a clock, pen, or tool (such as a kit to clean a PC keyboard). I've even seen back-scratchers with logos as giveaways. They are fun and people pick them up, but consider if these trinkets help create an opportunity to sell something.

At KLA events we offer what we call electronic tools. Each of our events integrates into the presentation some type of tool people can use to do their job better, such as a strategic thinking plan, checklist, or customer call action plan. We offer these tools free of charge to people who attend our events. Because we do it at every event and have done so for several years, people who have attended previous events expect the tools, which are valuable to them, and come to our events to receive them. Our request form to receive the tools includes the opportunity to sign up for our electronic newsletter, permission to e-mail those who sign, the opportunity to request information regarding specific services, and a request for referral names for us to contact. We have turned our offer into an opportunity for new business beyond just the contacts attending the event.

Plan to follow up on the invitations. To increase visibility for an event, call all the people to whom you sent invitations to personally invite them and reextend your offer. As you call, update your database with changes in contact information and make notes about your conversations. These calls serve not only as a reminder to people but also as another encouragement to attend. Follow up five to seven days after the invitations have been mailed. If you e-mail invitations, follow up three to five days later.

Keep events small. Limit events to between 10 and 40 people. Fewer than 10 participants is threatening to many people, who may feel captive in a one-on-one sales call. With more than 40 people, you can't spend time with each of them.

Live event considerations. Figure 15.2 outlines ten points to consider as you decide to hold an event.

Set up meetings before a live event. Sometimes you have access before you arrive at an event to a list of those who will be attending. Review the list, decide those you want to talk to, and e-mail them to set up a meeting. If you don't have access to a list, e-mail your target market to let it know you will be attending and to see if its members will also be attending. Work to set up coffee or a meal with those who respond that they will be there. You may want to attend a session during the event together and then meet after to discuss its impact on their business and where you can help. Be sure to follow up with these same prospects after the event, thanking them for their time and moving your new opportunities forward.

FIGURE 15.2 Live Event Considerations

1. **How long do you want the event to last?** People like short events because they are easier to fit into their schedule. It used to be you could get a person to attend a three-hour seminar. Not any longer. I recommend 30- to 60-minute Web events, and 60- to 90-minute face-to-face seminar-type events. Clearly, trade shows, new product launches, symposia, and similar events are much longer, ranging from one to three days.

2. **How far do you expect people to travel to attend?** Most people will travel 30 to 45 minutes for a short event, further for a long event.

(continued)

FIGURE 15.2 Live Event Considerations, continued

3. **Do you want to start early in the morning before prospects go to the office, or do you want to try to attract them away from the office?** There are advantages in having an event before prospects have to go to the office as they won't become engrossed and change their minds about coming. However, sometimes events in the midafternoon are effective as prospects treat them as an opportunity to leave early for the day.

4. **Do you want to hold the event at your office, in a building conference room, or in a hotel?** The image and type of event determine the best location. An executive breakfast can be very effective at your office if you have appropriate facilities and can also be very nice in a private room at a local restaurant with good service.

5. **Is parking readily accessible?** This is a must if people are driving.

6. **Is the event more suited to a Web-based delivery?** If so, try Web-based delivery and see what results you get. People may find it easier to attend because they do it from their desk. Some disadvantages to consider: participants are easily distracted by e-mail and open items on their desk and it is more difficult to connect personally with participants. You want to have prescheduled follow-up with each of the participants to get the highest number of leads from a Web-based event.

7. **Do you want to serve some type of food and/or beverage?** People expect a snack at the very least. With Web events you can show a picture of a cup of coffee at the start and tell people to "sit back. Relax. Have a cup of coffee, and join us."

8. **Events are generally well attended if given early in the morning on a Tuesday, Wednesday, or Thursday. Web events are also successful during the lunch hour.** Plan your event for a time that works best for your target audience. Construction workers won't want to lose hourly pay to attend a midday session.

9. **An 8:30 start time virtually ensures your prospect won't go to the office beforehand and become involved in other things.** Absolutely! See number 3 for more.

10. **What will you do if the competition attempts to attend your event and you see them signing in?** Determine if you are going to allow the competition to attend, or politely suggest that it is not appropriate for them to be there. Thank them for coming and ask them to leave. I once had a partner's competitor show up at an event we were hosting jointly. Out of respect for the partner, I couldn't allow the competitor to sit in the room and network with my partner's leads. To avoid confrontation, I asked a manager from our organization to ask the competitor to leave. The manager told the competitor he appreciated his coming, but out of respect for our partner who was hosting, it was not appropriate for the competitor to participate. The competitor didn't want to make a scene in front of his own competitor—my partner—or potential prospects, and he left quietly.

At the start of the event. As you kick off your event or as it progresses, let prospects know what it is you expect from them. Some examples are provided in Figure 15.3. They know you would not hold an event without a reason. They know your job is to sell. They *expect* you to ask for something, so be up front and do it. You improve your chances of success if your prospects know what it is you want them to do. Tell them concisely at the beginning and at the end of the event, but avoid making it sound like a sales pitch unless you really want it to be one.

FIGURE 15.3 Tell Your Prospects What You Expect from Them

Your Goal	What You Might Say
Generate interest	Thank you for coming today. We believe you will find this session/topic of interest to your business because _____. Following this session, we would like to know _____.
Establish awareness	Thank you for coming today. Although you may know quite a bit about our company, we wanted you to know about _____ because we believe it can help your business _____. Following this session, we would like to know how you believe it might help your business.
Set an appointment for a personal follow-up visit	Thank you for coming today. Based on what we know about each of your companies, we believe that a _____ will be of value to your company because _____. However, we believe that before we can confidently recommend this solution to you, we must understand more about your business. After you have heard our presentation today, we would like to set up a personal follow-up visit to meet with you to better understand your individual objectives and needs, and how you see _____ assisting you in achieving them.
Order on the spot	Thank you for coming today. You have heard a lot about _____ today/over the past few weeks or months. You know how ____ fits your business requirements. You may have a few questions remaining, and our goal today is to answer those questions so you can order _____ before you leave today.

At the event. Make the most of your networking opportunity! Make yourself get out there and *meet people you do not yet know.* Create an agenda ahead of time to start conversations. If you have a choice where you sit, choose to sit with people you have never met. Attend all the sessions, even if you are a speaker or host. Change your seating, and talk with the people around you before and after the session. During sessions, ask questions. Give your name and your company name so people know who you are and can approach you later.

After the event. Send a thank-you note or an e-mail within 48 hours. Personalize it to a conversation you may have had together or to a comment a prospect made during the event. If you send an e-mail, you can suggest next steps. If you send a written thank-you note, promise a follow-up call—then call.

When I attend multiday events, I use late evening or early morning hotel room time to queue e-mails to people I have met. I write a quick e-mail while our conversation is still fresh in my mind and then queue it to send out the morning of the day following the conference. I copy myself on the e-mail as a reminder and for easy forwarding. My thank-you e-mails are out of the way when I get on the plane.

For those who are not attending. Reply to people who say they are not attending an event you will be attending and ask if there is anything in particular they are interested in that you could listen, watch, or look for on their behalf. Set appointments to meet with these people after returning from the event to debrief—and see where you might be able to work together. This is also effective for trade show, conference, and symposium events.

After the event, use a follow-up e-mail and phone campaign to turn new prospects into qualified leads. Contact them with a few interesting observations or findings to share from the event, and again offer to get together and discuss what you learned that might be of interest to them.

Using customer speakers at events. Customer speakers can be very effective spokespeople for your solutions. If you are able to secure customers to speak at one of your events, treat them like royalty. Make sure they know exactly what the schedule is. Escort and introduce them around. Many people are uncomfortable in groups where they don't know people. In addition, many people don't like speaking in front of large groups. Your goal is to make your customer speakers comfortable and as relaxed as possible, considering how much you value their assistance and your relationship.

TIPS FOR SUCCESSFUL NETWORKING AT EVENTS

Events provide one of the biggest opportunities for networking, whether you are hosting or attending, and no matter if they are business or social. You want to take advantage of the opportunities these events provide to network. Through networking you can meet potential customers, partners, and resources.

Networking should be integrated into your lead generation activities—especially events, PR activities, and referrals. These are activities where you will meet a number of people and have the opportunity to stop and get to know them. As much as I prefer to sit by myself or hide behind a potted plant, I've learned that the connections I make through networking can be invaluable both professionally and personally. Following are some tips to make your networking a success.

Set your agenda. Before you walk into an event, know what you want to talk with people about. Plan your first three questions to use with anyone you meet. That way you're prepared to have a valuable conversation rather than talking about the weather or traffic. Know with whom you want to connect and what you want to talk about. Plan your conversation in your mind before it happens.

If you have the chance to see the participant list before the event, identify those people you want to meet. If the list is not distributed, know the types of people you want to connect with. I tell people I am the first person to hide behind the potted plants in the lobby, but this is your opportunity to connect with people. If I can avoid talking with people, I will. I am truly shy, even though I am a public speaker and salesperson. I use an agenda to help me identify with whom I want to talk and what I want to talk about. It makes me more comfortable approaching people because I have a plan. Without an agenda, you reduce your odds of networking success.

What will you give? Your agenda is the first piece of your networking plan. The second piece is knowing what you will give peple who speak with you. What will they take away from a conversation with you? You want to make their time spent with you just as valuable as you would like your time spent with them to be. Think about the type of event you are attending. If it is a business conference, what good ideas and information do you have to share that would make it interesting for people to talk with you?

What do you want to get? The third piece of your networking plan is identifying what you want to get out of your networking conversations. What are the questions you want to ask? What is it you don't know that you need to know to help you sell more effectively? You might be looking for some new partners, information about your target market, and prospects. Knowing what you want to get out of conversations with people helps guide your conversation with the people you talk with.

Joining a group. One of the most difficult moments in an event is when you walk into a room full of groups, where people are chatting comfortably with each other, and it looks as though there is nowhere for you to go—except behind the potted plant! You can look around for someone who is not part of a group and head over there to start a conversation. You can also join a group.

To join in a group, walk over and gently touch a person on the arm. The group will automatically open up and allow you to join in. Listen carefully to the conversation. Use active listening, such as nodding and smiling, to show you are participating in the conversation. Take a moment to listen to the conversation. Once you have an idea what is being discussed, listen for an opportunity to add to the conversation, and then join in verbally. Be careful not to interrupt.

Introducing yourself. Make it easy for people to begin a conversation with you. When you introduce yourself, add a tag line they can latch on to and ask a question. A tag line is a brief sentence you say after you introduce yourself. The tag line I use most frequently in business situations is, "Hi, I'm Kendra Lee with KLA Group. I help companies improve their sales results."

A tag line gives just enough information for the other person to ask a question to begin the conversation. Two common questions following my tag line: "So you work mostly with salespeople?" or "How do you help improve their sales?"

Depending on my agenda, I tweak my tag line to match my agenda. Or I follow my agenda with a question related to my agenda. "Hi, I'm Kendra Lee with KLA Group. I help companies improve their sales results. I'm writing a book on lead generation, and I was wondering what the best way is for a salesperson to gain access to you?" I've made it comfortable for the person I'm speaking with by giving him or her something specific to talk about, and the conversation begins quite naturally. Think about the tag line you want to use *before you arrive* at the event.

Remembering names. One of the best ways to connect with a person is to remember the person's name and use it judiciously in the conversation. The method I have found most successful for remembering a person's name is to use it right away. I look into the person's eyes, studying her face at the same time, and then say, "It's nice to meet you, Elizabeth."

Part way through the conversation I use the person's name again to cement it in my memory. If I have forgotten it already, I ask right away. Because I've just met the person, I'm comfortable asking again. "I'm sorry. Your name again is . . . ?" After Elizabeth repeats her name to me, I'll say, "Thank you, Elizabeth. I'm Kendra." Repeating my name avoids Elizabeth's being embarrassed if she's forgotten my name—which she typically has!

At the end of the conversation thank the person by name once again: "It was so nice to talk with you, Elizabeth. Thank you!"

Starting conversations. Listen for other people's tag lines to begin a conversation. A person may have an unusual name, may mention his or her job, or may work for a company you aren't familiar with or are very familiar with.

I often hear, "I've only known one other Kendra," allowing me to respond, "And where did you know her from?"

You can also use your agenda to ask initial questions to begin the conversation.

Expanding on cliché conversation starters. Yes, there are people who talk about the weather and the traffic, but you can still turn conversations that begin with a cliché into valuable conversations.

Be prepared with a few questions to ask if you are given cliché questions. Give forethought to how you can twist those questions toward your agenda.

"The traffic was terrible, wasn't it?"

"It sure was! What other events have you recently attended that had such terrible traffic, Elizabeth?"

Fact-finding through conversations. Networking provides an excellent opportunity to learn more about your target audience, its business issues and needs, its industry, and your competition. Use your questioning to interview people during your conversations. Remember the "5 W's and How" from English? Use them here to gather more information—who (the person you are speaking with), what, where, when, why, and how—related to your topic:

- What did you find most interesting about that last session?
- Had you heard that before? Where? When?
- Why do you think that is such an issue today?
- How is your company addressing it?

Be careful not to interrogate the person with questions as if you were a television reporter uncovering the story of the century. Rather, use the questions to guide the conversation and create an interesting discussion.

Ending conversations. It's easy to find yourself joining a group for the duration of an event or a section of the event. In doing this, you limit your networking possibilities. You want to meet a variety of people, and to do so you need to mingle among groups.

- **Listen for a natural close in a topic and excuse yourself.** "It's been so nice speaking with you and I look forward to talking with you again throughout the event. I'm going to circulate and meet some other new people."
- **If there is a person clinging to you, bring her along or introduce her to another person.** "Let's go speak with that group, Elizabeth,"

and head over to a new group together. Or "Elizabeth, I'd like you to meet Jeffrey. We work together to assist companies such as your own."

Effective networking. Before you arrive at any event, you can take five planning steps to make it a successful networking opportunity for yourself—and the people who speak with you:

1. Your agenda
2. What you will give
3. What you want to get
4. Your introduction tag line
5. Cliché question responses

Following up with event nonresponders. For those prospects who do not respond to an event invitation, send an e-mail following the event that covers some of the highlights of the event and offer to debrief further with them in a phone meeting. If you learned something especially relevant to your target market or picked up an interesting handout, you may be able to create an offer for them. Ask that they e-mail you if they would like a copy. When they do, you can set a time to talk with them.

VARIATIONS OF EVENTS YOU CAN USE

Webcasts. A Webcast covering topics of interest to your target market is a way to provide value to your prospects without their having to leaving their offices. The topic can be anything of interest to your customers or prospects. Whatever the topic, be sure the Web seminar demonstrates your expertise; you want to show your level of professionalism and value.

To deliver a Webcast, prepare PowerPoint slides and deliver them using an online tool such as Microsoft Live Meeting. People log on to the online tool, watch the slides, and listen to you deliver them. If you work for a larger company, your marketing department may use its own tool that you can reserve for a specific time.

One-hour Webcasts covering relevant business issues draw a large number of people. Typically, you take a few minutes at the beginning and end to talk about your solutions that are relevant to the topic. Or you weave your solutions into the business issues being discussed.

Executive breakfasts. Choose a topic relevant to executives, and invite one of your own executives or a partner executive to speak at a breakfast.

Forums, conference calls. If you don't have access to online tools to host a Webcast, you can host a forum or phone seminar. Reserve a conference phone line and discuss topics you feel are of highest priority to your target market.

You can set these up as a one-time event or an ongoing event, depending on the time you want to invest in it. For example, I host a monthly Sales Executive Forum open to sales executives in the IT industry. Each month we discuss an issue, challenge, or initiative that is uppermost in their minds. I facilitate the conversation by posing questions and sharing my thoughts, but it is their discussions that make the time together so valuable and keeps them coming back. These sales executives are all prospects for our consulting services and hear about our expertise through the conversations we have.

Association events. Join associations in which you are likely to find your target audience and get involved. Attend their events. Join a committee. Speak. Write articles for their newsletters. Associations can be a very inexpensive way to network with your target market in a soft-selling environment.

"To maximize the value of association events, bring a partner with you," suggests Holly Simon of KLA Group. "Look at joint solutions you can bring to this common market. Showcase your partner's solutions within the association."

Leverage partner events. Another potential for events is through partners. Do joint events focusing on your complementary products and services. Join in on events your partners' companies have planned. Split the work in promoting and hosting them and reap the rewards together.

WHEN NOT TO USE EVENTS

If you need a response quickly from your target market, events may not be the best lead generation activity. The exception to this is an event already planned that you expect to take advantage of within the next two weeks. Otherwise, most events typically require a 30- to 60-day lead time before you actually connect with prospects.

Events you are hosting usually take a minimum of 30 days to plan. Most events hosted by sales reps take six to eight weeks to plan and execute effectively because of the number of activities leading up to the event. This is the case whether you are doing a face-to-face or Webcast event. You want to be sure you give people enough advance notice so they can plan to attend. That means you want invitations in their hands at least three weeks prior to the event. Before sending the invitations, you must choose the topic, secure the location and speaker, and write a compelling invitation. Typically, those activities take at least two weeks, although they can be completed in a matter of days, especially if this isn't the first time you have hosted an event.

For events you attend, you still want to send out an e-mail saying you will be there; and try to schedule coffee or a meeting with people you think will also be there. These e-mails should be sent at least two weeks in advance, and ideally three weeks in advance to be sure you can schedule time on their busy calendars.

SUMMARY

With events so cost effective, Flo decides to use one to begin her lead generation efforts with her newest partner, Jeffrey. Flo's marketing organization is hosting a new product launch in a month. Marketing's target market for the event is outside her territory, but she believes the topics will still be relevant to her contacts. Flo speaks with Jackie, who is running the event. Jackie doesn't see any conflict in having Flo's target market attend the event and gives Flo permission to invite the 150 contacts she and Jeffrey have identified.

Jackie has some extra invitations to give Flo but does not have funding to prepare and mail the invitations. Flo and Jeffrey address and mail the invitations themselves and enclose a personal note to each contact. Other than following up on the invitations and setting individual meetings with people who will be attending, Jeffrey and Flo don't have much preparation for this event, leaving them free to follow up on leads and work other opportunities already in their funnel.

In planning her networking conversations for the new product launch, Flo realized she had a great deal to offer her prospects: she knew a lot about some key business issues in their marketplace, and she understood what other companies in their market were doing and how they could use her and Jeffrey's solutions to solve those business issues. During the conversations Flo wants to gather information in return: which of her target market participants are interested in the new product being announced; how her participants think they might use the product; what business issues they think the new product might address; and who, in their organization, they would need to begin talking with about the new product.

Flo plans to integrate this new information into a follow-up direct mailing to people who don't come to the event. She is also going to hold a Webcast targeting several of the top business issues her participants believe the new product solves. The event will launch several additional lead generation activities in this target market for Jeffrey and Flo! This is an excellent use of her time, with the possibility of a high return through multiple lead generation campaigns.

16

PR ACTIVITIES
FOR SALES REPS

Jane was the only sales rep Flo knew who was actively trying to get articles published. Jane hadn't been successful yet, but Flo thought she could learn from what Jane was doing.

Jane was happy to talk with Flo, even though her attempts to get articles published in the local business journal had failed. Jane had called the editor (albeit late in the day when he was on deadline) and coerced him into spending a few minutes on the phone with her. Her idea would be to contribute an article that celebrated the fact that one of her customers had a great new health care product coming out. In Jane's mind it was information everyone would be interested in and in turn cause her phone to ring off the hook! Instead of agreeing with her portrayal of things, the editor gruffly hung up the phone with barely a goodbye.

So Jane tried him again the next day and the day after that, thinking that somehow she hadn't emphasized her point strongly enough. She never was able to get through to the editor again. But lo and behold, her competition had an article in the journal the following month, and Jane noticed some differences she shared with Flo. Primarily, the article shared tips and pointers about how to use a new technology sweeping the medical industry. It never mentioned manufacturers by name, but the point did come across, and Jane's competition looked like a true expert—so much so that the competition was seen fairly often in the journal.

This sounded pretty risky to Flo. It seemed as if she needed to figure out how to do PR activities the right way before she contacted anybody.

WHAT ARE PR ACTIVITIES?

PR stands for public relations. These activities include such things as writing and publishing articles and press releases, and speaking at meetings and conferences. PR activities are a great way to build awareness and create credibility for yourself and your company with your target market. Over time these activities help to increase your response rates from your other lead generation activities as your target market recognizes your name.

By publishing articles in key target publications, you are able to reach a much broader audience. Likewise, your prospects stop and pay attention to what you have written about a particular topic if they have a need or an interest. And this could lead to instantaneous success for you.

WHY USE PUBLIC RELATIONS ACTIVITIES?

Salespeople frequently struggle with credibility within their target market. Until your prospects get to know you, they assume you only want to make a quota. They don't recognize that you want to help them. PR activities can help you change this perception. Articles give you the opportunity to express your opinion on issues and how you would address those issues with your company's solutions. Because they are published, articles appear more credible than a direct mail piece or marketing slick with the same type of information.

HOW TO USE PUBLIC RELATIONS ACTIVITIES EFFECTIVELY AS A REP

Leverage the marketing organization. PR is typically done within your marketing organization, but not all companies use PR. You can leverage PR work already completed by your marketing organization, sending articles, press releases, and newsletters to your target market and top ten customers and top ten prospects. If your company doesn't use PR, you can do some on your own by writing articles and newsletters in your target market.

Write articles. Write articles for local business publications, industry magazines, and online publications your customers read. As a sales rep, you can target one article every four to six months and fit that within your busy schedule. You want to build a relationship with editors at a publication so you know what they are looking for in articles. Editors will look forward to your articles as you build relationships with them and they see that your articles are timely and relevant to their readers. To get articles accepted, keep them focused on an issue of interest to the publication and its readers. For example, local business journals like articles about local business issues and referencing local companies. Get their attention by using local companies as examples in your articles.

Because articles are public relations activities rather than selling activities, keep any selling references subtle. The best way to sell through articles is to tell a story, such as a brief case study, or discuss a business issue and how to solve it, and then include your tag line at the end of the article.

Include a tag line. Every article includes a few short sentences at the end about the author. This is your opportunity to say what you do and to provide your contact information. I have found this is especially effective in online publications where readers can respond right away to an e-mail address you provide.

Figure 16.1 shows a tag line I use. Notice it includes information about my company and our services, our target customers, and three ways to contact me directly: phone, e-mail, and Web site.

FIGURE 16.1 Sample Article Tag Line

Kendra Lee is president of KLA Group, a highly skilled training and consulting company that provides training, assessments, market planning, and research for all customer-facing organizations including sales, marketing, professional services, and customer service. The KLA Group provides services for a variety of companies throughout the United States, Canada, Asia, Latin America, Europe, and Australia. For more information, Kendra Lee can be reached at (303) 741-6636, klee@klagroup.com, or at http://www.klagroup.com.

Be careful not to make your tag line too long or publications will abbreviate it, perhaps removing key information you wanted the reader to know.

Sell to editors. Working with editors of publications is similar to selling. You need to pitch your ideas to them and get them accepted. Treat them just as you would a customer and respond quickly when you receive their go-ahead for an article. Be careful not to take advantage of your relationships with editors or a specific publication. Sending them too many ideas, especially if they're not good ideas, will turn an editor against you. Think about the news value of your information and present it in a way that you're confident will be useful to your editorial contacts.

According to Paul Suter, president of Suter Media Relations, a well-respected PR firm that works with editors throughout the country, there are five key things every businessperson should know about editors and how they work. These keys can be found in Figure 16.2.

Choose the right publications. Target publications that your target market and top customers will read. In your region, you may choose to write for the local business journal to grab the attention of your top customers. Choose an industry publication to gain target market visibility. To identify the publications you should write for, ask current customers in your target market what publications they read and what they like about them. Use this information to determine what types of articles you should write and what your customers would read.

While you interview your current customers about the publications they like, read those publications to learn what topics they like to cover

FIGURE 16.2 The Five Keys to Working with Editors

1. You need them more than they need you.	Editors are contacted by dozens of people every day with story ideas. It's for this reason that you need to make your pitch stand out in the crowd and display relevance to the editors and their publication.
2. It's not news because you did it.	Even though you may have achieved something tremendous in "your world," it doesn't mean it will be viewed with the same amazement by an

FIGURE 16.2 The Five Keys to Working with Editors, continued

	editor. Make sure the idea you are presenting is something that will be useful—and of interest—to people outside of your circle. It must be of interest to the publication's readers.
3. Be accessible.	If you've established a relationship with an editor, make sure you treat the relationship with respect. If the editor (or an assistant) calls you with a question, do everything you can to get back to him or her within an hour. It's likely that the editor is on deadline and needs the information right away. If you're not available to help, the editor may turn to your competition with the same question—just so the job can be finished.
	While this can be very difficult for you as a busy sales rep with a heavy schedule, it is an important point. Editors expect you will be able to respond to them quickly. If you respond, they will continue to call you. If you cannot respond, they will find other people to call.
4. Journalists aren't cut from the same cloth.	A newsroom doesn't operate in the same manner as a boardroom. Journalists seek to share important information and expose truths, whereas a corporation is focused on the bottom line. This truth impacts the way a journalist views a business and the way a journalist views what you're "pitching."
5. It's not an ad.	If an editor agrees to interview you for a story, don't expect to be able to review the story before it runs. Journalists who interview you want to share your expertise in their story. But remember, the story belongs to their publication, and they won't ask you to review the article and provide comments before it runs. For this reason a published article is viewed with much more credibility than an advertisement and is also the reason why a positive article about you or your company can do far more for your marketing efforts than an ad campaign could ever accomplish.
	To avoid any negative information in an article, be conscious of the journalist's objective to publish a good story as you are being interviewed. Be aware that anything you say in the interview could end up in print. Speak deliberately and thoughtfully to avoid quotes you didn't intend to be published.

and the styles of articles they publish. As you read the publication, you get a sense for the length of article they prefer and how they position topics you might submit. For example, there may be a special section each Thursday in the local business journal in which articles about the section topic are highlighted. If there is a section on your topic scheduled for publication, you may have a better opportunity to get an article accepted for the special section than for the general journal sections. Editors publish their special section topics annually or semiannually. Once you know what publications you are targeting, you can request a list of any special sections or issues those publications have planned.

Get copies of the publications to see who the editors are and what types of articles they publish. Use this information and the information gained from talking with your current customers when you approach the editors about writing for them.

Send articles. You don't need to write all the articles you want to use in your lead generation activities. As you speak with your marketing department about the press releases, ask if any key people in your organization have published articles. Consider how you can integrate these articles into your lead generation plan. Send articles that have been written by others in your organization to your target market. I talked about the value of this in Chapter 12, "Direct Mail Activities," as well.

Be available for interviews. Journalists are always on the lookout for good resources. If you've been able to impress the media with your expertise, always make yourself available for interviews. Figure 16.3 provides some tips for conducting a great interview.

Use the Internet. Chat sessions, online groups, and networks give you the opportunity to get in front of people as well. Be careful, though, as these can eat into your time very quickly. Before you know it, you can spend half a day chatting or responding to e-mail chains and have no leads to show for it.

Speak professionally. Scary as it may sound, public speaking is an excellent way to reach your target market. You have a captive audience in a room for 45 to 90 minutes and the opportunity to demonstrate your credibility through your presentation. People come up to you afterward

FIGURE 16.3 Tips for a Great Interview

- **Have an agenda.** Think about and memorize the four or five key points you want to make with a journalist and make sure you share them. Don't wait for the journalist to ask the "right" questions either; go ahead and make your points over the course of the interview.
- **Don't "talk down" to a reporter.** Reporters aren't asking stupid questions; they're just trying to share information in a way that makes sense to their readers. Keep this in mind as you are explaining a topic or service that may not be as easy for other people to understand.
- **Tell your story.** Reporters leave it to you to share the information that's relevant. Feel free to get into details and control the interaction. This helps to ensure your key messages come across in a story.
- **Bring materials.** Numbers, research, and graphics are all things a reporter loves. The more information and documentation you can share, the better.

to talk with you, and you can mingle with the audience before and after the event.

Speaking is similar to writing articles. People don't want a sales presentation. They want to listen to a presentation on a topic of interest to them. Stories, case studies, and current business issues make excellent speaking topics for both large and small audiences. As you speak, discuss the topic thoughtfully, offering your recommendations and providing examples. This keeps the audience engaged and builds your credibility. Figure 16.4 lists numerous speaking opportunities you might find.

To find speaking events, approach your local chamber of commerce, associations your target market belongs to, and user groups. As you attend presentations, pay attention to the speaker's style and note what you

FIGURE 16.4 Speaking Opportunities

- Customers' or prospects' own internal meetings, executive events, companywide meetings, kickoffs
- User groups for your solutions
- Industry events, shows, and conferences
- Associations related to your target market's industries
- Local radio talk shows about the things you are doing for your customers, upcoming events, and key industry topics
- Local charities' meetings or training sessions where loaned executives from your target market may be serving
- Seminars, Webcasts, and other events for your own company

like that could be used in your own presentations. If the audience is a good target market, introduce yourself to the speaker to find out who engaged him or her and ask for an introduction. The contact may be right there in the room providing you the opportunity to immediately discuss an idea for a presentation. You may quickly find yourself scheduled to speak at an upcoming meeting. You may even mention your availability for speaking engagements to your customers and prospects. If they know you are available to speak, they may refer you to groups they participate in for speaking opportunities.

If speaking is not your top skill, you may want to find a local speakers organization associated with the National Speakers Association. Here you can take classes to improve your speaking and learn how to find speaking engagements.

FOLLOWING UP WITH PUBLIC RELATIONS ACTIVITIES' NONRESPONDERS

PR is something you aim toward a large audience and then wait for them to respond to what they have read or heard about you. It is an awareness-raising technique. It is not an activity you can proactively follow up on as with other lead generation activities. Rather, you can use the fruits of your PR, the PowerPoint presentation from your speaking engagement, the article, press release, or newsletter as part of another lead generation campaign you would proactively follow up on.

VARIATIONS OF PUBLIC RELATIONS ACTIVITIES YOU CAN USE

Send letters to magazines. If you are concerned that you don't have time to write articles, another option is to send letters to the editors of the magazines your customers read. Make them thought-provoking responses to articles you have read in the publication. Do this every three to four months to stay in front of your target market.

Newsletters. Newsletters are a form of PR that can be a very effective way of creating awareness for your target market. Consider writing a simple newsletter to send out quarterly to your top ten customers and prospects. The typical weekly or monthly newsletter would be difficult to manage as a rep, but a quarterly newsletter may be more achievable. This can be a great way to build awareness for yourself and your company in top accounts. E-mail the newsletter so it's easy to respond to, and include a call to action at the end of each issue inviting people to contact you.

Involve clients. If your customers are doing something that's newsworthy, ask them if you can present their story to one of your media contacts. Doing so will show clients that you are active with, and respected by, the press; and it will provide your media contacts with another good story angle. It will be a win for your clients, the press, and yourself.

WHEN NOT TO USE PUBLIC RELATIONS ACTIVITIES

PR activities are a soft way of building awareness and creating credibility for yourself and your company with your target market. These activities work best over time. They won't necessarily have immediate results. If you are looking for short-term lead generation results, PR activities may not be your best option. They are a good choice if you are trying to build your creditability as well as awareness for yourself and your company.

SUMMARY

Flo can see a great deal of potential for PR activities. Because it builds awareness and credibility over time and she needs to build her funnel right now, Flo decides she is going to wait until next year to build PR into her lead generation strategy for her top target markets. She will do other activities to quickly build her funnel this year and then integrate PR into her plan next year.

Flo sees one area where she would like to use PR activities this year, and that is for her top ten customers and top ten prospects. Because she is going to target those companies specifically with their own lead generation activities, Flo thinks it will take less time to get the attention of her target contacts through PR. She feels PR can help her build her credibility quickly while at the same time helping her gain access to key executives faster than other lead generation activities might.

17

REFERRALS

Bill is a star at getting referrals from customers and turning them into new customers. Because he has referrals coming in, Bill spends fewer hours on the phone answering voice mail messages and returning calls. He runs fewer lead generation campaigns and finds referrals take his calls faster than do new prospects who have responded to lead generation activities. Referrals seem more willing to speak with him and, as such, actually return e-mails and phone calls to him and willingly set appointments with him.

Flo's manager had suggested she speak with Bill to find what she could learn from him. Her manager told her referrals were diamonds in the rough waiting to be polished. He said if she could collect some referrals, it would speed her sales process and reduce the number of leads she needed to get on her own. Flo had never received many referrals in the past, but her customers liked her, so maybe this was an opportunity she had overlooked.

WHAT ARE REFERRALS?

Referrals are recommendations from another person to contact someone that person thinks could be a potential customer for you. Referrals can come from anyone: a current customer or prospect, partner, friend, or business associate. They can come when you are anywhere: visiting a customer or prospect, attending a conference, speaking at a business meeting, out for dinner, or at a party.

Some of the best referrals come from current customers. Many reps don't ask for referrals from their customers because they're uncomfortable asking customers to do something for them. However, customers are often delighted to provide referrals for a sales rep who has served them well.

WHY USE REFERRALS FOR LEAD GENERATION?

Referrals help you reduce the length of your sales cycle significantly and gain qualified prospects quickly. Aaron Linkow, president of Classic Doorways, says he built his business on referrals and ranks them as his favorite technique for generating leads for just that reason.

Most referrals come from three sources: customers, prospects, and partners. By using referrals, you're getting your clients to do your prospecting for you. You can actually assign them a piece of your quota, just as you assigned a quota to your partners (see Chapter 9, "Quota'ing Your Partners"). The only difference is that you won't expect your customers to remember to give you referrals as you *would* expect from a partner. Thus, you add *asking* for referrals from your customers on a quarterly basis to your lead generation plan.

With partners, you should plan to ask about referrals each time you touch base with them—and you should offer to provide referrals to them in return. Partner relationships are built on the recognized need to help each other succeed. As you partner with people who you can trust and you speak with them frequently, offer referrals and advice to help them succeed. Then let them return the favor with a steady stream of quality referrals to help you succeed.

Perhaps the seemingly most risky type of referral to request is one from a current prospect. You may have a prospect that you believe will become an ideal customer but has not yet bought anything because of a long sales cycle. If you have a strong relationship with this prospect, have fully demonstrated the value of working with you, and have indicated the solutions your company has to offer, you may be able to ask the prospect for referrals even though you have not yet completed the sale.

When you have a strong foundation in place with a prospect, you absolutely can ask for a referral: "Frank, we've been working together on this proposal for several months now. I think I have a good feel for your needs, and we've agreed you are pleased with the way we are progressing together. What other people do you know who might have needs similar to your own that I should be working with?"

Your prospect may give you names because you two have worked so closely together and you have helped figure out what the prospect should be doing to address his or her needs. The prospect appreciates the hard work you have done and wants to assist you.

You have nothing to lose in asking, as the worst a prospect can do is say no. Wait until you have built a good relationship with a prospect and demonstrated the value of working with you before asking for referrals. Once you have done both, do ask, as prospects are another good source of referrals for you.

HOW TO USE REFERRALS EFFECTIVELY FOR LEAD GENERATION AS A REP

The best time to ask for referrals. The best time to ask for a referral or a reference is when customers have just told you how delighted they are with your solution. Another ideal time to ask is when you make follow-up calls. Ask for referrals every two to three times you meet with customers. Customers meet new people all the time, just as you do. You don't know if any of them are prospects unless you keep asking for referrals. You may not receive a referral every time you ask, but you do communicate that referrals are an important part of your business, and your customers remember that. After asking several times, your customers begin to recognize how important referrals are to you and begin to look for referrals on your behalf. They expect you to ask for referrals and want to be ready with some qualified names.

What to ask for. When asking for referrals don't settle for a name and phone number only. Make sure you can use your source's name. Ask for extra information, such as why your source believes this person would want to speak with you and how your solutions would help this person's company. The more information you can secure from your source, the better prepared you will be when you place the first call, and the faster you will move your sales process along.

How to ask for a referral. Asking for a referral can be intimidating to many salespeople. They don't want to bother their customers with unnecessary requests. The steps in Figure 17.1 can make it easier for you to ask for referrals.

Pause. Give the person 15 seconds to think after you ask for a referral. Do not say *anything* while the person is thinking. Use your listening skills and wait patiently.

Use your questioning skills. Use open-ended questions when asking for a referral. Don't ask such closed questions as "Can I tell Joe you suggested I give him a call?" Ask instead: "Is there any reason why I can't use your name with Joe?"

Make a suggestion. Help your contact think of a referral by giving him suggestions of possible referrals. "Anyone in the new department?

FIGURE 17.1 Seven Steps to Easily Asking for a Referral

1. Ask if any other departments might need your service. Or if the customer (or contact) knows of any business associates who might find similar value in your solutions.
2. Ask for the names, titles, direct telephone numbers, and e-mail addresses of the people the customer (or contact) gives you. If the customer shows you a business card, note the fax number and the address too.
3. Ask for additional information through open-ended questions, such as "Why do you think Joe would find value in our solutions?" Try to get to business reasons Joe would need your solutions.
4. Ask when would be the best time to call the prospect.
5. Ask your contact to provide a personal introduction. "Would you give Joe a call or drop him an e-mail and let him know that I will be contacting him and why you thought he would be interested in speaking with me?"
6. Send a handwritten note or e-mail to thank your contact within 24 hours of receiving the referral.
7. Follow up with your contact on how your conversation went with the referral. Periodically follow up with how the relationship is progressing. These follow-ups are especially effective as brief voice mail messages. In each message, be sure to again thank your contact for the referral.

Anyone in the professional association you chair? Someone in your bowling league?"

Use a referral letter or e-mail. Send an introductory e-mail to your referrals and copy your contacts. Then send a separate e-mail to the contact who made the referral. Ask your contact to forward this e-mail to the referral with his or her endorsement. The e-mail from your contact motivates the referral to reply more quickly.

If e-mail is not heavily used in your industry, tell your contact that you would like to send his referral a letter about how you might be able to work together to help his or her business and how you have helped improve your contact's business. Then ask the contact if you can send the letter to him or her complete with an addressed and stamped envelope, and ask the contact to write a quick note to the referral at the top of the letter.

Use a positive approach to the referral. Don't tell your referral you know all his or her problems because your contact told you. Rather, tell the referral that your contact recommended you call because of what you specialize in. Mention the business reason your contact thought it made sense that the two of you talk. Make your call as positive as possible regardless of what your contact told you:

> "Joe, Frank Ratcliffe from The Drafting Experts suggested I give you a call because we specialize in helping companies increase the number of leads their sales reps generate in new and existing accounts. He mentioned that a top priority for you this year is new business generation and thought it might make sense for us to talk."

Mention the referral contact. Refer to your referral contact throughout the conversation with your new prospect. This strengthens your connection to the prospect through the referral source. One way to do this is by discussing how you handled specific projects for your referral contact, people you might have worked with across the contact's organization, how you approached their issues, or your excellent service record with the contact's company. Don't simply drop your contact's name in the conversation or discuss your solutions; this sounds too arrogant or sales-y. Rather, make the conversation relevant to this prospect based on the knowledge you have from working with your customer's company and from the value your customer thought you could provide to the prospect.

FOLLOWING UP WITH NONRESPONDING REFERRALS

The challenge with referrals who don't take your call is that you have a responsibility to the person who gave you the referrals to follow up on his or her recommendation. You can use this responsibility to your advantage. Call and e-mail nonresponding referrals and let them know you would like to connect with them so you can update your contact on how the conversation went:

> "Joe (the prospect), I'd very much like to touch base with you so I can let Frank (the referring contact) know that we talked."

You aren't asking Joe to make a decision to work with you, only to talk with you. Once you get together on the phone, you have the opportunity to discuss how you might be able to help Joe's company based on what Frank, your contact, told you.

After nine tries (the number of calls I said it takes to connect with a new prospect in Chapter 14, "Telemarketing and Cold Calling Activities"), let your contact know that you are having difficulty connecting with the referral. Because the referral may have been out of the office, ask, "Has Joe been out of the office or busier than usual, do you know? Your referral is very important to me, Frank, and I want to be sure I connect with Joe." See what Frank tells you. Joe may have been out of the country on business, recently changed positions, or experienced a family emergency. Frank can advise you what to do, even if that advice is to stop calling.

Should your contact suggest you stop calling because the referral must not be interested, reduce your number of calls but add the referral to your lead generation list in the correct target market. If appropriate, add the referral to your list of top ten prospects. This way you haven't lost the referral, who will be contacted as part of your normal lead generation activities.

VARIATIONS OF REFERRALS YOU CAN USE

Ask your prospects for referrals. As I discussed earlier, you can also ask your prospects for referrals. If you have built a relationship with some of your prospects, ask them for the names of people they know who could benefit from your solutions. Even if your prospects haven't purchased, you want to have established rapport and trust before asking for a referral. Asking prospects for referrals is especially relevant if your sales cycle is long. Sales reps with 18- to 24-month and longer sales cycles build strong relationships with their prospects. If your sales cycle is a long one, you will get to know your prospects' businesses and many contacts within them quite well. With this knowledge and a long sales cycle, you should ask for referrals. If you wait for a sale before asking for a referral, it could take another 18 to 24 months or longer before you close that sale. By asking for a referral 6 to 8 months into the sales process rather than waiting until the sale closes in 18 to 24 months, you may speed your time to sale with that referral by as many as 6 to 8 months. (See Figure 17.2.)

Look for referrals *for* your customers. Seek out referrals to *give* your customers in addition to asking for referrals. The more referrals you offer, the more you will receive. And referrals you give can be in the form of a hard worker looking for a new job, an executive from another company to network with, or a sales lead. *Help* your customers as you want them to *help* you. They won't expect this, and it will differentiate you from your competitors as well as from other sales reps overall.

FIGURE 17.2 Reducing Your Sales Cycle Using Prospect Referrals

	Ask for a referral after closing	Ask for a referral during the sales process
Length of your sales cycle	18–24 months	18–24 months
Ask for a referral	18–24 months	6–8 months
Begin second sales cycle	At 18–24 months	At 12–16 months
Close second sale	36–48 months later	30–40 months later
Saved time when asking for referral during the sales process		6–8 months

Get referrals from noncustomers. Gwyneth Short, owner of Complete Performance, suggests "building relationships in the industry you are targeting. Meet individuals of 'influence' who will refer you to companies that might be interested in your services." Here you can use PR activities to join associations in the industry you are targeting, attend meetings and conferences your prospects attend, and speak at events they attend. As you mingle and network, you naturally discuss what you do and find yourself on the receiving end of referrals from people you have just met. See Chapter 16, "PR Activities for Sales Reps," and Chapter 15, "Events and Networking," for additional ways to network and be seen in places where you would meet noncustomers.

WHEN NOT TO USE REFERRALS FOR LEAD GENERATION

Don't request referrals if the implementation of your solution is not going well, if there is a customer satisfaction issue, or if your relationship with the contact is not strong. Resolve these issues first and then ask for a referral.

One interesting observation from the customer service industry is that customers who have a problem that a company resolves are likely to be happier than are customers who have never had a problem. So if you do have a customer satisfaction issue to resolve, don't let it keep you from asking for a referral once the issue is handled. Customers now are able to talk, not only about your solutions, but how well you handle customer issues.

SUMMARY

Flo realizes she has let many referral opportunities pass her by because she never thought to ask for a referral. As she thinks about the number of leads she needs to generate, Flo realizes referrals are probably the fastest way for her to get new leads—both in current customers and in new prospect accounts. She plans to ask for referrals to other contacts within her list of top ten customers as well as referrals to other companies immediately. She is sure there are opportunities she is not aware of, and who better to guide her than her key contacts who already like her?

Flo also plans to try asking three prospects for referrals and see where it leads. If it goes well, she'll try it with other prospects.

18

CREATING YOUR OWN CAMPAIGN

W*atching the political campaigns gave Flo an idea. She would create a campaign of her own—a "sales campaign." She had learned a great deal about lead generation in her conversations with different salespeople. What if she pulled it all together into her own sales campaign? Flo wouldn't be making posters or running ads, but she would implement a planning and execution process similar to a political campaign.*

Flo chose an e-mail campaign for her top target market, inviting potential participators to a Webcast she and her partner Michael would be cohosting. Rather than just e-mailing, Flo and Michael wanted to make sure they had a way to follow up on the e-mails in case the people they e-mailed didn't respond quickly to their offer. As part of the campaign, Flo and Michael planned to include the e-mail itself, plus several follow-up methods, to touch those people who had not yet responded.

WHO DO I FOCUS ON?

To be successful at lead generation, it is better to work on getting continual exposure with a smaller target group than it is to try to focus on many target groups with only a few exposures. By focusing on two small target groups with continual lead generation activities, you increase your results as your prospects begin to hear and see your name more frequently.

You want people in your target markets to receive e-mail and direct mail from you, read articles you have sent them, attend events you are hosting, see you at business events, look up your company on the Web, and hear about you from their business associates at other companies through referrals, references, and testimonials. You want to be everywhere your target contacts are—just as in a political campaign. These are the types of lead generation activities you want to incorporate into your territory plan to give your target market continual exposure to you and every opportunity to buy from you. I'll talk more about creating an overall lead generation plan for your territory in Chapter 23.

WHAT IS A LEAD GENERATION CAMPAIGN?

Effective lead generation that provides this level of exposure requires a careful planning process. Just as a well-laid-out political campaign is backed by a detailed project plan, so should your lead generation activities have a well-thought-out strategy, with each critical step documented. This planning and execution process is called a *lead generation campaign.*

A lead generation campaign may include only one activity, such as an e-mail campaign, or it may be a series of lead generation activities strung together to provide continual contact with your target markets or top customers and prospects.

As part of a campaign linking activities, you may choose to call all nonresponders. Or you may elect to send a follow-up email as a reminder and then call all nonresponders to this emailing. Of course, you would not want to e-mail or call those people who responded to the previous e-mailings. Use your contact manager to track all the people who responded to be sure they are eliminated from the follow-up communications. Campaigns give you more opportunities to connect with your target market and your top ten customers and top ten prospects, identified in Chapters 6 and 7, on a regular basis with a consistent message.

As you put together your territory plan for the year, you plan groups of activities in the form of campaigns to be executed across each of your target markets and your top ten customers and top ten prospects. As you will see in Chapter 23, you execute the campaigns at different points throughout the year as defined in your territory plan. This allows you to connect frequently with your top target markets. These campaigns make you more effective in filling your funnel quickly with new qualified leads.

WHAT ARE THE STEPS TO A GREAT LEAD GENERATION CAMPAIGN?

You can design an effective lead generation campaign quite easily. The process is basically the same for all your lead generation activities. If you commit to the process, it becomes second nature to you as you design new campaigns in the future. You can adapt the process to include lead generation activities cosponsored with your partners or used on your own.

Figure 18.1 outlines the process for the three lead generation activities most frequently executed by sales reps: telemarketing, e-mail, and an event. This outline demonstrates how a campaign for each activity would flow and the number of business days you would need to allow in your planning process to successfully execute the activity.

FIGURE 18.1 A Typical Campaign Process for One Lead Generation Activity

	Time Frame in Business Days		
Campaign Steps	**Telemarketing**	**E-mail**	**An Event**
Decide to do a campaign	14 days prior	30 days prior	46–54 days prior
Hold a planning session to outline key steps; assign roles and responsibilities	9–12 days prior	22–25 days prior	39–47 days prior
Choose a location	—	—	32–45 days prior
Choose a target market and pull the data lists	7–9 days prior	19 days prior	Pull data 32–40 days prior
Design an e-mailing, direct mailing, or invitation	—	17 days prior	31–39 days prior

FIGURE 18.1 A Typical Campaign Process for One Lead Generation Activity, continued

Campaign Steps	Time Frame in Business Days		
	Telemarketing	E-mail	An Event
Get e-mailing, direct mailing, or invitation input from key resources	—	12 days prior	29–37 days prior
Write a simple phone script	3–6 days prior	—	—
Precall target market mailing list and update database	—	15 days prior	24–32 days prior
Test script and make appropriate changes	2–5 days prior	—	—
Review and practice script with callers	Day of call or day before	—	—
Telemarket/Cold call	Call	—	—
Proof the e-mailing, direct mailing, or invitation	—	9 days prior	26–34 days prior
Print the direct mailing or invitation	—	—	24–32 days prior
Choose refreshments; provide setup information to location coordinator	—	—	21–28 days prior
Set up the e-mailing in your contact manager or e-mailing software	—	7 days prior	—
Mail the direct mailing or invitation	—	—	17–25 days prior
Call to confirm receipt of the mailing	—	—	12–20 days prior
Send a follow-up e-mail to nonresponders	—	5–7 days following first e-mailing	—
Call to get people enrolled	—	—	7–15 days prior
Confirm location, room, and equipment setup and refreshments	—	—	5–7 days prior
If an event, place an event reminder call to enrollees	—	—	1–2 days prior
Hold the event	—	—	Event
Make follow-up calls or send follow-up e-mails	—	—	1–5 days following

Until you gain experience planning campaigns, allow enough time to complete each major step in your campaign. You don't necessarily want to spend time completing each step to perfection, but you do want to ensure the right actions are taken at each stage. You would be horrified if an e-mailing were sent with a typo in it or an event didn't have sufficient refreshments available. To avoid potentially embarrassing and unprofessional mistakes, be conservative in the number of business days you allow yourself to complete each activity. The activity time frames will be considerably shorter if your resources or partners are able to respond more quickly to your support requests. And as you become accomplished in your lead generation campaigns, your time frames tighten up.

THE CAMPAIGN PLANNING SESSION

Each campaign should start with a planning session, no matter how informal the campaign. Depending on the size of the campaign, you may or may not choose to hold a formal planning session. If the campaign is large, it will involve a significant dollar and time investment and will focus on a large target market. A formal planning session including all the key resources you will involve is a good idea. On the other hand, if the campaign is focused on a small target market with a minimal dollar investment, you may choose to skip the formal planning session step and do the planning on your own with input from a few key people.

The formal planning session. If you choose to hold a formal planning session, invite key people who understand your territory and your target market for this campaign and will have a role in your campaign. These people will assist you in targeting the right audience, identifying the target audience's business needs, and outlining your company's strengths and weaknesses in relation to your competitors' in the target market. They will also assist you in completing the different steps in your campaign, from securing and preparing the list to editing content or reserving the projector. You want these people to fully understand your campaign objective and plan. You want their input in refining your target market as well as in defining the appropriate steps to execution.

The informal planning session. If your campaign is small and you don't need a formal planning session, approach a few key people with your campaign idea and ensure that you are on track with your target market and audience. Determine who will handle each step and begin execution.

During the campaign planning session. Whether you are holding a formal planning session meeting with the key resources involved or outlining your campaign on your own, you want to answer the questions in Figure 18.2 during your planning session to ensure you stay focused on your goal.

See some examples. Appendix B, Sample Lead Generation Campaigns, includes a flowchart of a complete lead generation campaign and the text for a sample e-mail campaign. Use this as a model for your own campaign planning.

THE CAMPAIGN PLAN

During the campaign planning session, clearly define the major tasks in your campaign, including the start and end dates and owners for each task. If you have multiple lead generation activities planned, include

FIGURE 18.2 Campaign Planning Questions to Answer

---

1. **What is your campaign goal?** Do you want to create awareness with a PR campaign, but you aren't expecting any leads from this campaign? Do you want 12 or 32 leads? What will you consider a measurement of success for this campaign, and what do you want the final measurement to be?
2. **Who is your target market?** Specifically, who will you include?
3. **Who is your target audience?** What titles within the companies will you contact?
4. **Why have you chosen this target audience?** Reviewing this information gives your resources the opportunity to suggest aspects you may not have considered. They may expand your target audience or suggest adjustments. They will help you refine your target audience to get the best return on your investment.

(continued)

FIGURE 18.2 Campaign Planning Questions to Answer, continued

5. **How will you get contact names, titles, e-mail and/or mailing addresses, and phone numbers?** Where will you go to secure the list? Will it cost money? Is it easily available in a format you can use?

6. **What lead generation activities do you want to include in your campaign?** Will you be sending a direct mailing for an event? Will you be doing a telemarketing precall, a reminder call, or a follow-up letter or call? What are all the different lead generation activities you want to include to ensure the highest overall response rate possible?

7. **Why did you choose these activities?** This is another place your planning session participants can assist. They may suggest activities you had not considered or provide recommendations on how to execute the activities differently to increase your response rate.

8. **What offer are you making?** What will you offer your target audience as part of each lead generation activity in the campaign?

9. **What is the target audience's problem or the opportunity you will address?** What business problem or need will you choose to target with your lead generation activity? What will you say that will grab the audience's attention and persuade it to respond?

10. **What will your solution do for the target audience?** Although you don't want to assume what solution you will sell before you've spoken with your target audience, you do need a solution for a business problem or a need to have in mind as you write the content for your activity. This helps you position your content, making it relevant to the target audience.

11. **How can your solution help the target audience solve this problem or help its business with this opportunity?** Given the business problem and solution you have identified, what makes your solution unique for the target audience?

12. **What are your company's competitive strengths in relation to this problem or opportunity?** In your content you want to focus on your competitive strengths. Use the people in your planning session to help you identify them if you don't know them yourself. If you do know them, tell the planning session participants so they can help support you more effectively.

13. **What action do you want your target audience to take after each activity in the campaign?** Based on your campaign goal, determine for each lead generation activity in the campaign what you want people in the target audience to do. Do you want them to enroll in an event from an e-mail campaign, request a white paper during the event, and/or accept a phone call following an event?

14. **Who will assist you in executing the campaign?** What roles will each person play? What are each person's responsibilities? Will you be coordinating the campaign or will someone else? Will you have regular meetings to discuss the details?

15. **Optional: What is your campaign budget?** This topic may or may not be appropriate for inclusion in the campaign planning session depending on who you have participating. At some point you want to determine your campaign budget.

them. Use a project plan format such as Figure 18.3 to outline the major tasks, owners, and start and end dates. You may also want to create a flow-chart of the campaign as an easy-to-follow format, such as the example in Appendix B.

This document, whether in a project plan or flowchart format, becomes your campaign plan. It is your working document as you execute your lead generation campaigns and should never be far from your reach.

FIGURE 18.3 Campaign Plan

Campaign Plan

Target Market: Health Care
Lead Generation Activity: Event

Key Tasks	Start Date	End Date	Assigned To	Results
Campaign planning session	3/1	3/1	You	Done
Get a list of all the contacts in our target market	3/5	3/10		Done
Prepare invitation	3/5	3/20	You/partner	In process
Plan event	3/5	3/30	You/partner	In process
Include in quarterly newsletter	3/14	3/23	Marketing	In process
Put on Web site	3/14	3/23	Marketing	
Send invitation	3/20	3/24	You/partner	
Follow-up invitation with telemarketing	3/27	4/1	Telemarketer	
Call top 25 and personally invite to event	3/27	4/1	You/partner	
Place reminder calls to everybody enrolled	4/11	4/13	Telemarketer	
New product launch event	4/15	4/15	Corporate	
Follow up on event w/ attendees for opportunities	4/16	4/18	You/partner	
Follow up on event with nonattendees to see if we can assist in any way	4/16	4/30	Telemarketer	
Prepare event overview to send in direct mail campaign	4/16	4/30	Telemarketer	
Launch direct mail campaign	5/1	6/30	You	

WHAT TO MEASURE

Throughout your campaigns, track your results so you know what is working and what is not. During the planning session you defined your goal for the campaign. Now you want to know how you performed against the goal.

Tracking measurements tells you what you need to change and what you should do more of. As you track your results, some measures you want to take include:

- Costs. Lists, paper, postage, time, labels, food, space, professional assistance, telemarketing, equipment rentals, and any other costs you have incurred
- Amount of time to develop the activity. Did it take two weeks, a month, three months to develop? You want to know so you can be better prepared the next time you choose to engage in a similar activity.
- Number of pieces sent or number of calls made
- When mailing or e-mailing, the number of responses by method—phone, fax, mail, e-mail, Web site
- When calling, the number of contacts made and number of positive responses to offer
- With an event, the number of enrollees and number of attendees

Once you have this information, you know what lead generation activities work well for you within that target market and possibly within other target markets in your territory as well. You can also continue tracking your leads through different types of closure: the prospects purchased, put the decision off, or chose a competitor. By tracking your leads through closure, you can demonstrate the number of leads closed for each investment the company made in your territory. This information can be helpful in justifying future expenditures, especially if you want to execute a costly lead generation activity.

Using your measurements for the lead generation campaign, you can make some simple decisions in relation to the territory plan you will create in Chapter 23 and future lead generation campaigns you have planned. Figure 18.4 gives you a list of questions to ask yourself and,

FIGURE 18.4 Adjusting Your Territory Plan Based on Measurements

Questions to Ask Yourself	What to Adjust
1. Do you want to use this lead generation activity again?	Was the activity easy to execute? Is this an activity you would like to repeat? If not, consider why and what you could do to improve the process to execute the activity, or the activity itself. Consider removing it from future campaigns if appropriate.
2. Did the activity cost too much to execute?	If the activity cost too much in relation to the projected sales results or the number of responses you received, change or eliminate the activity.
3. Were the results lower than you expected?	If the sales results of an activity are low, determine if the activity, the target market, or the product is the root cause. If it was a result of the activity, eliminate the activity. If the target market is wrong, change it and try the activity again. If the solution cannot be promoted effectively via this activity, change activities.
4. Did prospects actually call you to complain about the activity?	If prospects don't like an activity, check the applicability to your target market first and then eliminate the activity if the target market was correct. (Dissatisfaction can often occur with incorrectly targeted e-mails, direct mail, or telemarketing.) If you choose to continue using the activity, review the planning and execution process and make necessary adjustments.

based on how you answer, guides you in identifying what to adjust in both your territory plan and your future campaigns.

SUMMARY

Flo has pulled all her lead generation ideas together into a series of campaigns. She knows exactly how many leads she wants to get from each activity within each campaign. She has identified the resources and partners she wants to involve in her planning and execution process and has scheduled three planning sessions to be sure everybody is in sync with her strategy.

Flo is almost ready to execute. She thinks her ideas are good but now wonders how she can leverage her hard work to execute the same campaigns with multiple contacts in one company. Is this possible?

19

TARGETING MULTIPLE CONTACTS

F*lo has a number of fairly large compa-nies in her territory. Her largest customer has nearly 1,000 employees, but Flo works with only one main contact. After talking with all the sales reps in her lead generation activity research, Flo recognizes one of the keys to success is having multiple contacts in an account. That way, if one contact isn't ready to do any-thing, there may be another contact who is.*

As Flo begins creating her lead generation plan, it strikes her that there must be a way to touch many contacts in an account at once, just as she touches many companies at one time with her activities. This could help her gain access to a new account faster and, ultimately, close a sale faster. It could also help her build her name within each new company faster.

THE TYPICAL STRATEGY

Many reps think only of approaching lead generation synchronously: one contact per company until that contact says no, then perhaps ap-proaching another contact. This isn't the best strategy, as it limits your ability to get in the door and your overall response rate per lead genera-tion activity. One specific contact from one company must see the lead generation message you have sent. If one person throws away or deletes the message, your opportunity to get in the door with *that* company from *that* lead generation activity is gone—poof! As a result, targeting only one contact at a time increases the amount of work you have to do to get the leads you need to generate to meet your goals. This strategy is particularly ineffective when trying to penetrate large accounts where there could potentially be 10, 20, 50, or hundreds of contacts.

COMPARING STRATEGIES

A lead generation campaign is made up of a series of activities you execute within one of your top target markets or for your top ten customers and/or your top ten prospects from Chapters 6 and 7. Figure 19.1 shows the typical strategy a rep uses when trying to break into new accounts. Out of six contacts at six different companies, one contact has responded to the rep's lead generation campaign. If the rep needs a large number of leads, this is a very slow way to get them. At this pace, the rep will need to run lead generation activities continuously.

You can see how long it could take you to break into one new company if you are targeting only a single contact at a time. Although you might be thrilled to get the new lead, this is a great deal of work to do for just one lead.

One lead won't be enough to achieve any rep's goals. Rather than begin a new campaign, you may decide to continue the campaign with several additional activities. You might choose to target a different contact with the second activity and a third contact with the third activity. The average set of activities takes a minimum of six weeks from planning through follow-up. Before you know it, you have invested 18 weeks in this lead generation campaign and received three leads, as illustrated in Figure 19.2. Even though you have secured new opportunities, you still have not been as effective as you could be.

A more effective strategy for you is to target multiple contacts within a company as part of the overall lead generation campaign and launch those activities *simultaneously*. This greatly reduces the time to achieve a new lead. In addition, if you are targeting multiple people in the organization, you may generate conversation among those different people, further driving up your success rate and increasing the number of new

FIGURE 19.1 Targeting One Contact at a Time

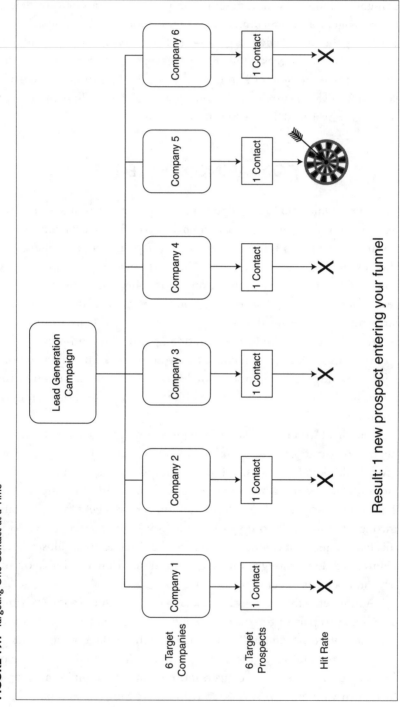

opportunities, possibly in multiple organizations within a single company. You no longer need to worry if one contact throws away or deletes the information you send; there are other possible contacts who may read it or pass it along.

Using this approach, you touch multiple contacts within the company using similar lead generation activities at the same time. You can even choose to use the same lead generation activity with several different contacts. Figure 19.2 shows how to launch numerous campaign activities within the same target company.

Let's say you decide to send an e-mail about a business problem you know companies in your top target market are experiencing. You have a number of customers who have addressed a similar business issue using your company's solutions, and they have been very pleased. You gather information about the results they have experienced and why they chose your company over other vendors. During interviews, your customers will tell you how this business issue impacts organizations within a company, such as human resources, operations, logistics, and finance. Once you have this information, you know which organizations you should target with your e-mail and what key business messages to use in it. For each contact, tweak the e-mail slightly to fit the role of that contact, even if the message is similar. But don't send the *exact* same e-mail to everybody in the event they forward the e-mails. If this happens they will realize they have been "hit" as part of a lead generation campaign, and this could hurt your credibility in their company.

In Figure 19.3, within the same six-week investment as shown in Figure 19.1, you are now attempting to connect with three contacts per company. You follow up with each contact just as if you were targeting only one contact at a time. During your conversations you may mention that you plan to speak with the other two contacts unless you feel this may jeopardize your selling abilities. Often, mentioning you are speaking with other contacts helps you get access to new contacts more easily. Use your sales "sixth sense" and skills to guide you in how much to disclose, but don't hide the fact that you are going to talk with other people. Having these contacts can strengthen your position overall as you learn more about the organization and where you might be able to assist it. Calling each of the contacts to follow up demonstrates your attention to detail, allows you to gather additional information about the company, and helps you identify potential incremental leads.

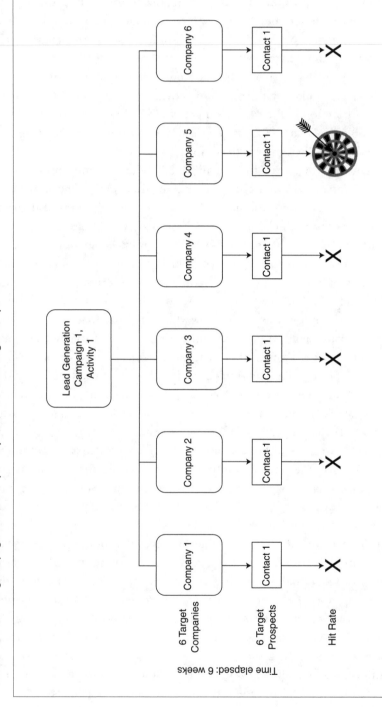

FIGURE 19.2 Launching Campaign Activities Sequentially within the Same Target Companies

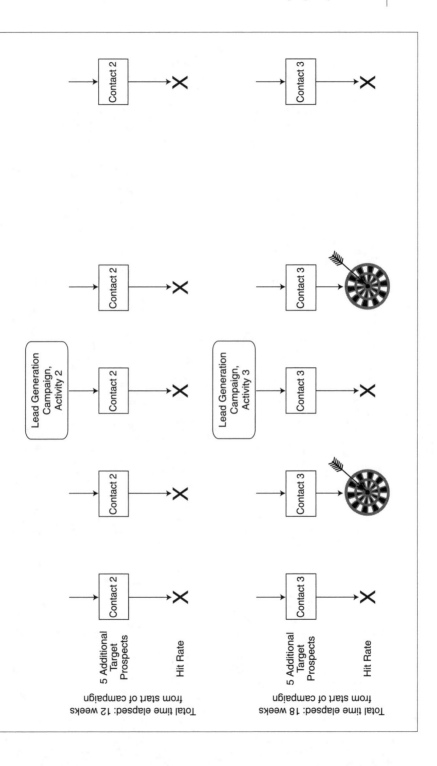

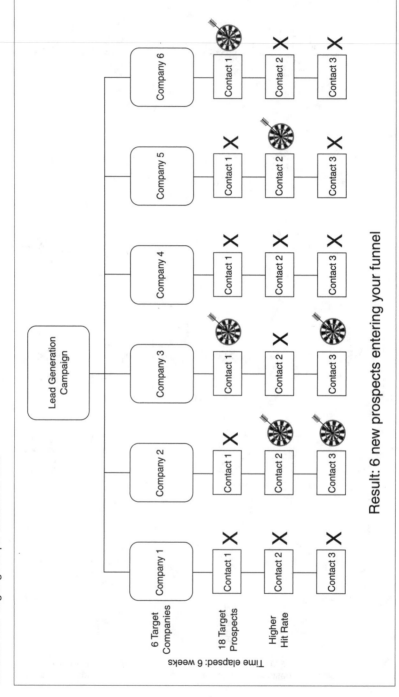

FIGURE 19.3 Targeting Multiple Contacts at Once

TARGETING MULTIPLE LEVELS IN THE ORGANIZATION

Another strategy you can consider is targeting various levels within the same organization or multiple organizations in each company. The same theory applies here. You never know who might be thinking about solving a problem your solutions can help with. You also cannot be sure at what level that person might be within the organization. Problem solvers, influencers, recommenders, and decision makers exist at all levels within organizations. Ideally, you want your lead generation efforts to connect with people who have the desire to take action in areas where you can assist, but you won't know who those people are before you speak with them. You increase your probability of connecting with the right people in a shorter time frame by targeting additional contacts at multiple levels. You will be top of mind when the people who have the desire to take action are thinking about doing so.

If you are going to include targeting multiple contacts and levels in your lead generation plan, you want to know this as you begin to think about the content to include in your activities. Your content will vary slightly based on the roles and responsibilities of the contacts you are targeting. People will feel you have done your homework and you will grab their attention. I'll talk more about this in Chapter 20, "Where to Find Good Content."

SUMMARY

Flo knows she needs to generate a lot of leads. She wants to get her name in front of as many people as possible, as easily as possible. After doing the math, Flo realizes it makes more sense to target multiple contacts simultaneously within a company while she is running one lead generation campaign. She also recognizes the value of having multiple contacts in a company during her sales process—especially in her large, top ten customers and top ten prospects. Not only does Flo choose to target multiple contacts simultaneously within a company, but she also decides she is going to target multiple organizations.

Feeling energized, Flo sets three goals for herself:

1. *Every lead generation activity she runs in medium-sized companies is going to touch at least three contacts.*
2. *Every lead generation activity she runs in large companies is going to touch at least six contacts.*
3. *Flo wants to be the top lead generator in her office with the results to prove it.*

FINDING ACTIVITY CONTENT AND LISTS

Content and lists play a primary role in the success of your lead generation activities. Use Part Four to identify places to find good content and lists. You'll also learn to write your own content and position yourself against your competitors.

20

WHERE TO FIND GOOD CONTENT

Flo is ready to launch her first big lead generation campaign with her partner Michael. Chapter 18 explained that they chose an e-mail campaign, inviting Flo's top target market to a Webcast she and Michael are cohosting and following it with a direct mail letter. The campaign will include an e-mail invitation plus several follow-up methods to touch those people who do not respond. Michael and Flo held the campaign planning session, and now it's time to write the content—a task Flo accepted.

Flo understands the concept of infiltrating a prospect's mind with key business messages that lead to her solutions. The problem was learning the most effective way to write those messages to grab prospects' attention and make them take action. Customers had often told Flo they were thrilled with the solutions she had sold them and what a great job she did in helping them determine the right solution, but Flo didn't know how to take advantage of those comments. How did marketing come up with all those great words?

MARKETING

There are excellent places for you to locate content for your lead generation activities. You don't need to create much on your own; you just need to know where to look.

As mentioned in Chapter 11, your company may have a marketing organization that focuses on direct marketing activities for the company. It creates content that can be the basis for the content of your own lead generation activities. You can use your marketing organization's brochures, case studies, Web content, and articles. Because its messages are targeted to customers, you may be able to easily condense the content and reposition it to your target market's specific business needs. You might even find your target market's business needs documented in some of the materials.

You may also find content in product training materials. These often include good sales positioning phrases and value propositions that, with slight rewording, will fit a customer communication. Product training materials typically tell you which customer contact titles to target with your messages, allowing you to further refine your content with confidence.

Look for phrases, value propositions, business terminology, business issues, and solution descriptions you can use as you write e-mails, direct mailings, event invitations, articles, and other lead generation activity content. You might even find customer quotes to include, or use quotes from your own customers.

Look for content that is 80 percent of what you need, and then make the subtle changes necessary to tweak it to your target market and the message you want to communicate. As you become experienced in your target markets and learn all the ways they implement your offerings, you'll be able to enhance product marketing's messages to be an even closer fit to multiple contacts.

CUSTOMER REFERENCES

References are testimonials from customers about the value of your solutions to them and their organizations. If your customers are thrilled with the solutions you have sold them and with how you have helped them determine the right solutions, consider interviewing them to gather quotes about:

- How your customers use your company's solutions
- Why your customers chose your company's solutions
- What your customers like about working with you and your company
- The business issues your company's solutions will—and won't—solve

Once you have gathered this information, combine it with the marketing information you have collected to create content tailored to your target market. Using customer reference information makes your message more compelling, and it appeals more directly to your target audience, resulting in an increased response rate to your lead generation activities.

While interviewing your customers, also ask who within the organization you should approach about your offerings. This helps identify potential prospects in areas within the company where you have not yet begun to penetrate.

You can secure references in a number of ways. One way is through a phone or in-person interview where you ask the questions above. A phone interview is not difficult because you already have an established relationship with the customer. You are very comfortable working together, and the customer will be just as comfortable providing a reference over the phone. If you don't know the contact too well, you may prefer to meet in person for the interview. This would be the case if you were interviewing a customer executive for a reference, but your key contact for the project was a person who works for the executive.

During the interview, request a testimonial or reference letter that you can quote in lead generation activities, articles, speaking engagements, customer meetings, events, proposals, and the like. Ask the customer if you can quote him or her; customers frequently agree to do this without hesitation. You may also choose to have your customer act as a reference in a phone conversation with a prospect.

Always send a thank-you note or gift to show your appreciation after your customer gives you a reference. If you quote your customer in an article, send a copy of the article as a thank-you. If you want to use your customer in a case study, it is common practice to share the case study in advance of final publication to allow the customer to approve it. Companies often look on case studies as documents their marketing organizations need to approve. Keep this in mind and learn what your customer's company's policy is regarding case studies and follow it.

Getting a reference letter. You want to be indispensable to your customers. Your goal is to build their trust so they *want* to refer you to their colleagues, peers, and friends. As you build their trust and begin gathering references consistently, you can "quota" your customers with new leads outside their companies just as you quota your partners. Rather than assign specific customers with a number of leads in your plan, you can quota them as a group; for example, five leads from customers. If you have customers you can count on to provide leads, you may choose to quota them by name.

To earn references from your customers, follow through on your promises to them. If you promise customer service will call, confirm that customer service placed the call. If you promise a customer a second product manual, provide it. Respond quickly to their requests. At the same time, provide thought leadership, bringing them new ideas and recommendations you gather from working with their people or other customers. Offer to brainstorm with them, attending their team meetings and positioning yourself as a valuable member of the team.

Once you have done these things, your customers will be happy to give you a reference when you ask for it. However, many customers don't know how to write a reference letter and aren't sure what you want said in it. To make it easier for your customers, offer to write the reference letter for them:

"Sam, I know how busy you are and I appreciate your agreeing to write a reference letter for me. Because you are so busy, I would be happy to write up a sample one for you. You can use it as an example when you write your letter, or feel free to have your assistant copy this one. Whatever is easiest for you. Thank you!"

In this example, you give Sam a sample reference letter on a page with no letterhead. Sam's assistant can copy it to Sam's letterhead using a copier if that is easiest or can retype it for Sam's signature.

Make an audiotape. Consider making an eight-minute audiotape or CD of customers recording how pleased they are with your company's offerings. Interview customers on tape about why they chose your company over others, other companies they considered before they made their decision, and what kinds of benefits they have experienced from your solution. Use the tape during presentations, events, key meetings, and prospecting activities. For your prospects, the tape provides another customer's perspective in the customer's own voice.

Capture the satisfaction. Take advantage of the latest technologies. Take digital pictures of smiling, satisfied customers standing around your solutions or your consulting team in their office. Use the pictures in newsletters and on your Web site. They also make an interesting slide show at an event as people are arriving, especially for Webcast events. Include captions under the pictures telling why these people chose your company.

If you are sponsoring a joint event with a partner, try to get pictures of some shared customers. During the event, elaborate on how you helped the customers solve their business problems.

As you take their pictures, ask if you can use them as referrals. If your customers agree to be referrals as well, include their contact information in the picture caption.

Get customer authorization. Be sure to get your customers' signed authorization to use their pictures or quotes to avoid any legal concerns. Typically, this is not difficult when the customer is satisfied, but some organizations are very careful about their publicity. You may find your customers have to get permission from their marketing or legal departments, or they have strict guidelines on how their name can be used. Don't be discouraged if some customers refuse to have their picture taken or to provide a quote. Often it isn't your service but their publicity policies guiding their decision.

As you enter the sales process with new prospects, use the referral consent to suggest qualified prospects call your customers: to understand how you helped them address their business challenges, as references when customers are validating your capabilities, and as part of your value proposition early in the sales process to get in the door.

PARTNERS

Partners often have marketing organizations and marketing materials just as you do. Combine materials to create a fresh, different way to approach your combined target market. For example, use each other's art work and pictures as well as their content.

"Use your partners to provide another perspective on your content, to identify benefits to highlight, and to uncover business needs that you might not recognize in your target market," recommends KLA Group's Holly Simon. Partners can bring a fresh perspective to your content, even if their content is not included.

LINK TO WEB SITES

The Web has tremendous amounts of information. Rather than try to repeat all you think your prospects need to know, include hot links in e-mail communications and electronic newsletters. Give a synopsis of why you are providing the link to generate a prospect's interest. This is especially effective in e-mails and electronic newsletters, as the links can be executed immediately with a click.

If you are writing an article for an online publication, provide a link to your company's Web site at the end of the article and also include your e-mail address, thus allowing prospects to easily get more information or begin a discussion with you. Where you reference information that may be available in other places on your Web site—for example, in a newsletter, current events section, solution description, or an article—provide links. Use these techniques to make it as easy as possible for your prospects to learn about your company and its solutions.

INDUSTRY PERIODICALS AND SURVEYS

Industry periodicals and surveys offer content focused on the business issues your target market may be experiencing. When you quote their findings, their data lend credibility to your content.

Periodicals have excellent content about the most current issues relevant to their readers. In an event format, you can use this information to discuss an issue and demonstrate how your company helps address it. In a direct mail letter, e-mail, or cold call, use the information to create a compelling value proposition for talking with you. Starting from the business perspective demonstrates you know something about a customer's industry and perhaps even the customer's own business.

Industry surveys provide data you can quote to support the business issues discussion. People like to hear numbers, as they lend credibility to the topic at hand. If you are good at analysis, provide some insights and recommendations to your prospects in a cold call, e-mail, or article based on conclusions or suppositions you have drawn from the data. These conclusions or suppositions can begin some valuable conversations for prospects and differentiate you from your competition through demonstrated thought leadership.

CONFERENCES AND TRADE SHOWS

Conferences and trade shows are another ideal place to find business issue content. Here you have the opportunity to speak with experts in their field and network with vendors selling in your top target markets. Attend sessions to hear what people are talking about—both vendors and customers—and listen for topics you can use in your lead generation campaigns. You may find an opportunity to jointly author articles with experts you meet, thus sharing the burden of writing the article and increasing the circulation to contacts in both your target markets.

Conferences and trade shows are events, so prepare for them as you would any event. See Chapter 15, "Events and Networking," for strategies to maximize your lead generation opportunities at conferences and trade shows.

LISTS OF TOPICS FOR ACTIVITIES

Appendix D, "Lists of Topics for Lead Generation Activities," is organized by type of lead generation activity to give you ideas of topics that you might choose to use for each type of activity. Turn to it for more content ideas.

WRITING FOR SUCCESS

To write successful lead generation letters and e-mails—letters that are actually read—there are a few basic steps you want to take. Don't worry about finding the perfect word or formatting it correctly in your first draft. Rather, get your thoughts down on paper and then go back and polish the words, flow, and formatting.

Effective writing is a three-step process:

1. Define your purpose for writing. Get your thoughts out in simple bullets using the Writing Action Plan found in Appendix C. (Spend 10 minutes.)
2. Write your e-mail or letter based on your Writing Action Plan. (15–30 minutes)
3. Revise your e-mail or letter. Edit, polish, spell check. (10 minutes)

Writing a first draft often comes to you quickly if you are familiar with your target market and have done research. If you are struggling with the final draft, ask another person or two to read it and make recommendations. They often have ideas you haven't thought of that will help you quickly finalize your piece.

Know exactly what you want the readers to do. As you begin writing, have a clear understanding of exactly what you want your readers to do as a result of reading your letter. Once you have determined the action you want them to take, tell them in your writing. Clearly state exactly what you want readers to do or what you plan to do. Let the readers know exactly what to expect from you, and then include follow-through on your commitment in your lead generation campaign. Even if prospects aren't available to take your call, you still display trust and reliability by keeping your commitments. A prospect is more likely to e-mail you than to e-mail another salesperson who has not taken the time to display these same qualities.

Edit, edit, edit! Proof, proof, proof! Several years ago I met with an executive prospect who agreed to a meeting with me based on a personalized direct mail letter I had sent him. He said he met with me because my letter was well written and his name was spelled correctly. He explained that he had once received a letter from a sales rep with mis-spellings throughout—including his name. The prospect allowed the rep to meet with him only so he could humiliate the rep. The prospect told the rep that he would never do business with him or his company and told him exactly why.

Don't let this happen to you. Reread what you wrote, make changes, and read it a second time. Make your letter or e-mail brief, to the point, and easy to read. Be sure the prospect's name and the company name and address are spelled correctly.

A guide to help. Appendix C, Writing Action Plan, has a handy guide for organizing your thoughts before you write. Use the Writing Action Plan to think through exactly what you want to accomplish and what you will write to accomplish it.

TIPS FOR HIGH-IMPACT WRITING

As you write, your objective is to create high-impact communications that increase your odds of securing an introductory meeting. Use the following tips for writing commanding content for all your lead genera-tion activities.

Do your research. Focus on the prospect, not on your company. Research your target market, gathering information about its terminol-ogy, top priorities, concerns, and strategic direction. Gather statistics and examples you can refer to in your content. Research the top com-panies in your target market and consider writing content specific to them. Use that information to tailor the content you are creating for the target market to those top companies.

Immediately refer to your prospects' successes. In your opening, im-mediately refer to a prospect company's past accomplishments or results:

"We recognize and respect the strides CD Telecom has made
in the telecommunications industry by being named to the Inc.
list of the 500 Fastest Growing Companies within only four years
of founding the business."

Use the prospect's terminology. Use industry terminology or the terminology of your target market. This may not necessarily be your own. Don't use acronyms that may not be recognized. Use active verbs and descriptive nouns your prospects use in their industry.

Use "you" twice as often as "I" or "we." Focus on your prospects by phrasing your letter from their point of view. Spend less time talking about yourself or your company and more time discussing their issues.

Remember your goal. Your goal is to find a new lead and secure a meeting, not to sell solutions. It's too early in the sales process to talk solutions in your lead generation activities. If you want to allude to your solutions, do it through customer references or condensed case studies a prospect will find interesting and relevant. Mention your products only if you are trying to find leads for a specific, time-sensitive offer, such as a discount. If this is your goal, recognize you are engaging in a product-focused sale rather than a consultative sale.

Suggest other potential contacts. In your communication, suggest recipients share it with other people in their organization who might benefit from the message. This helps you broaden your contact base and identify potential new opportunities with people you have not yet met.

Call for a specific action in the last paragraph. "I will contact you (or your office) on May 13 in the hope of setting up a meeting for the week of June 1 or June 7." Always include your phone number in a visible, easily distinguishable location in the event your prospect has an immediate need and wants to call you.

Don't use your title unless you are a president. Titles tend to work against you unless you are a president or on an obvious executive level. Sometimes they can detract from your message rather than enhance it. If you have an impressive title, use it. If you don't, simply sign your name.

Be positive. Avoid negative statements within your writing as they turn people off. Resist telling your readers what you don't want them to do; instead, focus on positive statements. Many people read very quickly and, most likely, your readers may misinterpret your negative statement for a positive one. You may write, "Our technical team cannot meet with your project team on October 28." However, in reading quickly, a contact may read instead: "Our technical team can meet with your project team on October 28." Reframe your statement to be positive, focusing on the solution and what you *can* do rather than on the negative and what you cannot do. "Our technical team can meet with your project team on October 25 or October 26."

Write so your words will be understood. Write so there is no chance of being misunderstood. When you write that you will call as soon as possible, to you that may mean you'll call in four or five days. To a prospect it may mean that you'll call the next day. Write exactly what you mean. "I'll give you a call on Friday afternoon between 2:00 and 4:00, Jack."

After you write it, schedule it on your calendar to be sure you don't forget.

Use plain, simple language when you write. Don't change your communication style to long, complicated words that people don't readily understand. Say exactly what you mean in a form similar to how you would say it if you were speaking in person. Use conversational language to hold the contact's interest.

Make it easy to read. I try to keep my paragraphs relatively short but varied. To accomplish this, I may have one paragraph that is three sentences long and another that contains five sentences. None of my paragraphs is over five sentences unless the sentences are very short. I like my content to appear both easy and quick to read, leaving the impression it won't take a long time investment to read it. Varying the paragraphs is one way to accomplish this objective.

Another technique is to make your e-mail or letter spacious and airy whenever possible. Use 11–12 points for text fonts and 14–16 points for heading fonts in letters. Use 10 points for e-mails.

Net out your content, condensing your message, especially in an e-mail, so it is very quick to read and respond to. I continually edit my content, working to condense it to the point it is concise yet easy to read. People have so little time today. I am conscious of this and strive to make content relevant and easily actionable.

Focus on your benefits. In written communication, use your strongest business benefit first to get your reader's attention. If you have three benefits, position your weaker benefit second and a second strong benefit at the end. This leaves the reader with a strong benefit top of mind. If you have two benefits and one is obviously weaker than the other, use only the strong benefit and leave out the second.

Use grabber words for high-impact writing. Certain words grab people's attention and lead them to read more than they might normally. Hang the grabber word list in Figure 20.1 on your wall to refer to when writing lead generation content.

If you hang this list on your wall, you may find yourself using these words in telephone conversations as well. They imply strength and instill

FIGURE 20.1 Grabber Words for High-Impact Writing

• You	• Successful	• Money
• Now	• Eliminate	• Safe
• Today	• Stronger	• Protect
• Immediately	• Trend	• Learn
• Free (better than	• Accomplished	• Know
complimentary)	• Reduce	• Understand
• Save	• Productive	• Quality
• Specialize	• Breakthrough	• Trust (not "count
• Increase	• Connections	on")
• Selection	• Innovative	• Proven (can also
• Recent	• Quickly	use "tested")
• Expertise	• Improve	• Discover
• Growing	• Enhance	• Leading-edge (as an
• Choice	• Loyal	adjective)
• New	• Savings	• Reasonable
• Well-known (adjective	• Replace	• Easy
before noun)	• Superior	• Effective
• More	• Niche	• Special
• Flexible	• Results	• Value
• Proven	• Growth	• Effortless
• Personable	• Satisfaction	• Efficient
• Less	• Creative	• Best
• Control	• Affordable	• Speed
• Latest	• Powerful	• Faster
• Caring	• Reliable	• Accurate
• Fewer	• Unique	• Better
• Opportunity	• Help	• Streamlined
• Industry standard	• Profit	• Dealing with
• Fair		

confidence in your prospects. Pick out a few you like and integrate them into your everyday sales conversations to increase your credibility with prospects, customers, partners, and resources.

SUMMARY

Flo is relieved to know there are places where she can go to find good contacts for her lead generation activities. She isn't a marketer by trade, and although she isn't a bad writer, she certainly isn't a superior one either. Now she realizes she doesn't have to create communications from a blank page. She has access to many types of content and plans to tap into all of them. Flo is confident she cannot only write a compelling e-mail that will draw people to their Webcast, but that a follow-up direct mail letter will secure additional prospect meetings as well. She was concerned she would let Michael down, but now she sees she has all the tools she needs to write the content for their joint campaign.

21

IDENTIFYING YOUR COMPETITORS AND COMPETITIVE DIFFERENTIATORS

*"***A***nd in this corner, please wel-
come the next great middleweight boxing contender! He weighs in at a very hefty
220 pounds, especially considering his short stature! He has a weak left jab and
is susceptible to being knocked out because of a 'glass jaw.' And if the match lasts
longer than five rounds, he'll probably be too exhausted to continue fighting. . . .
Ladies and gentleman, I'm happy to introduce the 'Italian Stallion'!"*

*As Flo sat watching the boxing match on TV with her husband, she wondered
who her 220-pound competitors were. How could she position herself more favorably against them as she wrote the content for the Webcast lead generation campaign? Flo knew her competitors' solutions were not a strong fit in the finance
department of her target market. Using this knowledge, she made a decision to
execute her lead generation campaigns targeted to the same departments as her
competitors, plus the finance department. She would tweak her lead generation
content to mention her company's strengths in the finance department. Now all her
department contacts would be aware, not just the finance department contacts.*

HIGHLIGHTING YOUR STRENGTHS

Like a boxer, you need to be able to identify your own strengths and what will help you land the knockout blow to your competition. You need to know who your competitors are and how to position yourself favorably for a win from the very first communication.

There are times you choose to write your own content for your lead generation activities. When creating your own content or adding to existing content, you want to know what you should highlight as key points and what to avoid bringing up. Your content should focus on your company's differentiators that help you penetrate your target markets more effectively. Your differentiators help you increase your response rate, and they ultimately impact your close ratio.

To focus on your company's differentiators, you need to know your company's strengths and weaknesses as they relate to your competitors' in your target market.

YOUR COMPANY'S STRENGTHS AND WEAKNESSES

Your strengths are what make it easier for you to get in the door with a prospect. Your weaknesses are the objections the prospect may bring up in the first few meetings. Your objective is to neutralize your weaknesses and highlight your strengths in your lead generation communications.

As you consider what the strengths and weaknesses are, think about them from your company's perspective, not your prospect's perspective. Consider not just your company's strengths and weaknesses but also your company's solutions, operations, and people.

In many instances you have strengths and weaknesses that are not recognized by your target market. If your target market does not recognize a strength, you want to find a way to emphasize it in your lead generation campaigns so that it can become a differentiator for you. With foresight, you can use your company's strengths to your advantage or to play down and neutralize any weaknesses. During lead generation, you want to use your strengths to penetrate your target market more effectively than does your competition.

Use a format like Figure 21.1 to identify your company's strengths and weaknesses. Consider doing the exercise with your top partners to get a fresh and different perspective. Other strengths and weaknesses to look at include yourself, your partners, and your resources. You could be considered a strength if you have extensive experience in your target market. This is especially true if you have developed exceptional knowledge through research, interviewing customers, reading industry studies and articles, and talking to your marketing department about their target marketing. Other strengths might be your team's selling advantage or technical expertise.

Use the confirmed column to note if your target market recognizes each strength or weakness.

YOUR COMPETITORS' STRENGTHS AND WEAKNESSES

You can be certain your competitors know your weaknesses. They mention them to your prospects right away. You need to be prepared to

FIGURE 21.1 Our Company's Strengths and Weaknesses Analysis Worksheet

	Confirmed?	
Strengths	**Yes**	**No**
Weaknesses		

address those objections, and, if possible, use your lead generation activities to neutralize them before the first conversation. Examine your competitors' strengths and weaknesses, using a worksheet similar to Figure 21.1, and then build a strategy in anticipation of your competitors' lead generation actions.

As you analyze your competitors' strengths and weaknesses, consider their people and operational processes as well as their solutions. Market perception should also be a consideration. Does the market view a competitor as stronger than your company? Are your competitors' processes recognized as exceptional? If the answers to these questions is yes, examine how you can better position your company and highlight your strengths.

As with your own company, in many instances your competitors will have strengths and weaknesses not recognized by your target market. However, be aware. Even if the target market does not recognize your competitors' strengths in certain areas today, your competitors could be developing a strategy to emphasize those strengths.

USE YOUR ANALYSIS DATA FOR CAMPAIGNS

As you plan your lead generation campaigns, focus on using activities that highlight your competitive differentiators. One way you might do this is by targeting a specific department within a company where your differentiators are acknowledged and valued.

Another technique is to execute a campaign in a target market your competitors have not yet reached. You may be able to have greater impact in that target market by being first to communicate with it. Your response rates may be quite high because the audience is not bored or overstimulated with your message.

You can have a similar impact in a target market in which your competition is already focusing lead generation campaigns. To create impact, choose a series of lead generation activities your competitors are *not* currently using combined with a message different from your competitors. If my competition is cold calling and sending direct mail, I send e-mails wrapped around a Web event and two published articles. This makes my lead generation campaign appear fresh and unique.

ANOTHER USE FOR YOUR COMPETITIVE DIFFERENTIATOR INFORMATION

Not only can you use your strengths and weaknesses analyses for determining your competitive lead generation strategy, but you can also use it to determine your target markets. You have defined your target markets, so now you have the opportunity to do a preliminary test to see if you have chosen wisely. Use the analysis in Figure 21.1 to decide if you have a strong enough overall offering for your top target market. You can look at your company, your solutions, and your successes with other companies in this or a similar market. If the weaknesses outweigh the strengths, you want to choose a different target market.

For each target market you test, repeat the exercise in Figure 21.1. Your strengths and weaknesses may vary considerably between target markets as will your competitors'.

If your strengths indicate you should pursue this target market, next look at your competitors' strengths and weaknesses in the market. Can you overcome them? If you can overcome them, you have chosen a good target market, one you can successfully position yourself to sell into.

SUMMARY

Flo is pleased she had not yet begun to write her content for the Webcast lead generation campaign. She now has some additional information she wants to take into consideration as she prepares it. Knowing her strengthens and her competitors' weaknesses has helped her determine which business benefits she wants to highlight in her e-mail and direct mail letter. It has also given her ideas for content recommendations she and Michael should make to the Webcast speaker to reinforce several of their differentiating strengths.

22

WHERE TO FIND GOOD LISTS FOR CAMPAIGNS

F*lo has her campaign lead generation activities outlined in a plan. She knows the content she wants to include. She has her target market identified. Now she needs to find lists of contact names with phone numbers and mailing and e-mail addresses to execute them. The Yellow Pages aren't detailed enough. Her manager isn't interested in purchasing a list. Her contact manager software has some contacts in it, but she called them all during her dialing-for-dollars days. She'd like some new names. Where will she get a list?*

USE MARKETING'S LISTS

Your contact list determines 40 percent of your success, with success being defined as people responding to you. Without a good list, the best content will never be read by the people targeted when you wrote it.

Very often your company has prospect lists that marketing has purchased for its marketing campaigns. Make marketing your first stop in search of a good list. Prospect lists are frequently available through your sales database or contact manager, and you just need to understand how to have reports created for the target markets you have identified. If marketing controls or manages the sales database, it can help you create reports for your target markets.

Once in a while, marketing has its own database. If this is your case, understand the process for accessing marketing's database. Marketing may be able to load your target market contact information from its database into your contact manager, allowing you to create your own groups of people to target.

It is not uncommon for marketing to have companies identified in its databases by the NAICS codes discussed in Chapter 6, "Segmenting Your Territory into Target Markets That Work for You." If your company's database has NAICS codes, you will be able to create refined lists of contacts by industry groupings quite easily. Meet with your marketing organization to determine how you can get access to its lists or create lists from your own sales database.

MAILING LIST SUGGESTIONS

If your marketing department doesn't have lists and your sales database is tired, consider purchasing lists. You may be able to justify the expenditure if you can demonstrate a well-thought-out lead generation plan with high potential. Alternatively, you may be able to convince a partner to buy the list. If a partner's company purchases the list, your partner probably won't give it to you but might print a list for you to use for follow-up calls. You can then add people you make contact with to your database and perhaps ask a resource to add the other contacts to the database.

You can also secure accurate mailing lists from many organizations, some for free and others for fee. If you attend an event, you can ask for the list of participants. If your company has a booth at a trade show, it should receive an electronic registration list as part of the booth fee. Marketing typically receives the list and may make it available to you.

If you attend a convention, you can call for the mailing list. Many conventions often sell their lists. If you attend a conference, often a list of attendees is published. Although the list is published on paper, you can hire a low-cost resource to input the information into your database.

If you speak at a conference or an event, you should receive a copy of the registration list as well as feedback evaluations from participants. These contain contact information, although typically they are on paper.

Other places you may choose to secure lists include:

- List brokers, such as Dun & Bradstreet, Hoover's, and Lead 411
- Google, America Online, Microsoft Internet Explorer, and other Web-based search engines
- Chambers of commerce
- Association directories, business directories, and additional organizations that maintain member directories
- Trade show, convention, conference, and event organizers for the group you are targeting
- Trade journals
- Industry magazines
- Local libraries
- Local universities
- Yellow Pages
- Partners

Patrick O'Liddy, sales and accounts manager with Creator Mundi, has had great success with using Google to identify different organizations and companies he should approach. He uses key words to find company names and then goes to their Web sites to gather information. Once he has prequalified they are a fit for his target market, he adds them to his lead generation campaign lists. This approach works well if you are targeting a select set of companies. If you want a larger list quickly, this would not be the best approach.

If your territory is not in your city, you can call the libraries or chambers of commerce in the key cities in your territory to purchase lists from them. You can even go online to pull Yellow Pages listings in those cities.

How Much Will I Pay?

The type of information you want from your list determines where you should go to purchase a list as well as how much you can expect to pay for that list. The format you would like also factors into the cost. Electronic formats are more expensive than paper, but if you can load the electronic list into your database easily and save the cost of someone's inputting it by hand, it may be worth the additional fee. Lists from nonprofit associations may be less expensive than lists from periodicals. Lists from associations to which you are a member may be quite afford-able with member discounts.

DATA TO GET WITH YOUR LIST PURCHASE

As you consider purchasing a list, you may have many options as to information you can secure about prospects. Before you purchase, think about the information you require to target well for your lead genera-tion campaigns. The more accurate your targeting and list, the higher your response rates from your lead generation efforts.

Some information might include:

- Company name
- NAICS industry classification code
- Executive names and titles
- Revenue
- Number of employees
- Number of salespeople
- Number of locations
- Headquarters address
- Web site address
- Executive contact information, including e-mail addresses
- Installed computer equipment
- Number of buildings owned
- The company's financial rating

ANALYZE THE LISTS

Before executing any lead generation campaign, review and clean the list you are using, asking yourself the following questions:

- Does every company have a contact name?
- Are the contact names really names or only initials?
- Who is on the list you know will never buy from your company?
- Which contacts do you know are no longer at the companies listed?

- Is the address complete?
- Which companies have old addresses?
- Which companies are no longer in business or have merged with other companies?
- Do you have multiple contacts in most companies so you can run simultaneous lead generation campaigns to contacts in different departments, such as operations, manufacturing, and distribution?
- Do the contacts have titles listed to easily sort against?
- How large is your target market? Is it too large to run lead generation campaigns that you can follow up on in a timely manner?
- Can you slice your list into minute minitarget markets and create very specific messages to those smaller markets?

Your objective, as you review your list, is to determine how accurate the data are before you put effort into a lead generation campaign. If the data are not current, the first step in your campaign should be to use a low-cost telemarketer to clean up the data or run a simple lead generation activity that will help you clean up the data for minimal time and money.

ALTERNATIVES TO PURCHASING A LIST

"I never buy lists because I can't afford it," quips SimPath's Cheryl Gilinsky. "I use the Internet to get the names of the contacts I want to approach based on the vertical markets I am targeting."

Gilinsky culls online magazines to see which companies and contacts are mentioned in articles and which ones are advertising. She looks at magazines in her target industries to identify the movers and the shakers and builds a list from what she learns. This is an excellent strategy for your top ten customers and top ten prospects as you glean new information about the companies. Using search words, you can even use this strategy to define the top ten customers and top ten prospects in your target markets.

As you attend events, look to see who is attending. Pick up business cards. When provided, input the attendee list into your database.

Competitors' Web sites are an excellent source of potential leads. Look for lists of competitors' customers—these are qualified purchasers of solutions similar to your own and make excellent additions to your list. Sometimes they even include success stories detailing what customers purchased. You can determine if the company has purchased any solutions similar to your own.

Check to see if your company invests in online business databases. You may have access to Web-based companies, such as Hoover's Online or Dun & Bradstreet, to look up one customer and then do a search to see who their competitors are. All of these companies and contacts can be added to your list.

Sometimes competitors make mistakes and e-mail you or your company as part of their own lead generation efforts. Not only does this give you insight into how they are positioning themselves in their lead generation content, but it may also give you access to *their* list. Joan Geardino, director of technical training with Advanced Network Technologies, confided, "Some of our competitors who are doing very targeted e-mailings will mistakenly send their lead generation e-mails to us—with all the e-mail addresses clearly displayed. We use the "reply all" feature of e-mail to capture the e-mail data and add those people to our own lists!"

MAINTAINING YOUR LIST

To garner the highest response rates, maintain your list. As you receive returned e-mails and mailings, encounter disconnected phone numbers, and learn that people have left a company, update your database. Telemarketing and e-mailing activities can be quickly implemented if a fairly current database is in place. But if your information is old, inaccurate, or incomplete, your lead generation will be significantly slower while you clean your list.

Often reps call from lists and aren't sure if the contact names are accurate. This can be true whether the list is purchased, is acquired, or is internal to your company. If this is your case, make sure you take that into consideration when you plan the campaign. You may want to have a telemarketer make calls to verify the contact information before you begin your lead generation campaign.

As you receive returns and new information throughout your lead generation campaign, your telemarketer, an administrative assistant, or a partner resource might be able to update your database for you. Consider where you can get resources to help you maintain your lists.

SUMMARY

Flo hadn't realized there were so many places to get a list. She spoke with her marketing department and found it does have a list she can use for the Webcast. Michael's marketing department has a list from a recent speaking engagement. Flo and Michael plan to compare their lists and remove duplicates. Flo has a telemarketing resource they are going to use to call both lists and update contact information before sending the Webcast e-mail invitation. The telemarketer will be able to gather missing e-mail addresses as well. The telemarketing is scheduled to occur two weeks prior to the e-mailing, thus keeping the contact information accurate. The direct mail letter will go out two days following the event. Flo and Michael anticipate a high return rate as a result of their thorough list strategy. They are hopeful this will improve their response rate and are excited about how their campaign is coming together!

CREATING A TERRITORY LEAD GENERATION PLAN

Part Five helps you pull together all of your lead generation campaigns into one integrated territory plan. In it you learn what to include in your plan, how to ask for additional resources, when to make adjustments to the plan, and how to execute it to achieve the goals you have set for yourself.

23

CREATING YOUR ANNUAL TERRITORY PLAN

Flo had never talked to her manager *about an annual territory plan, but she thought it would be a great strategy to create one anyway. She knew it would help keep her on track to achieve her goal of $1.2 million in sales. Flo views this as a journey that will take a year to arrive at her destination. As with any long trip, she wants a map outlining exactly how she will get there. Flo doesn't feel she can afford any wrong turns. She wants all her partners and resources in step with her strategy. And she wants a plan to guide her when she becomes distracted.*

WHAT IS AN ANNUAL TERRITORY PLAN?

As a territory sales rep, the Strategic Territory Action Plan, a sample of which is found in Appendix E, is your road map to success in your territory. In it, you deliberately plan what lead generation actions you will take to successfully penetrate and sell to your territory. Your plan pulls together all the work you have done to determine how many leads you need and where you will get those leads. It includes your top two target markets, top ten customers and top ten prospects, your partner and resource information, and your lead generation campaigns. You may also

> A territory plan is your business plan guiding the actions you will take, resources you will engage, and investments you will make based on a defined revenue objective.

choose to include some of your analysis work, such as the partner quota calculations, key business messages by target market, and competitive strengths and weaknesses.

The longer you stay in the same territory, the easier your success planning becomes. Your first year is a building year as you define your quota based on your goals rather than on your manager's goals. During this time you change your lead generation strategy from dialing for dollars to a series of integrated lead generation campaign plans; you put all the resources in place: analyze your territory; identify your target markets and top ten customers and top ten prospects; create partner relationships; gather together your resources; learn the capabilities and capacity of your marketing department; research the competition; collect content; interview customers; and develop lead generation campaigns. You *will* achieve success in your first year with this plan. In your second year, you achieve success far beyond the first as all your plans come together, the leads begin flowing freely, and you follow up on new opportunities. Even if your territory changes in the second year, you still achieve superior success because you have your support structure in place and an existing plan to adjust.

If you are able to maintain the same territory for two or more years in a row, you have your results from previous years to review as part of your territory plan. Analyzing your historical performance gives you insight into where you need to make changes versus where you want to maintain your current strategy. You see clearly where you have been overwhelmingly successful and where you have been less than satisfied, allowing you to fine-tune your lead generation strategies.

WHY CREATE AN ANNUAL TERRITORY PLAN?

To many sales reps, creating an annual territory plan feels like busywork. Many reps like to be spontaneous, doing what feels right based on how customers are responding. But spontaneity has a price in the amount of stress a rep may endure attempting to make his or her quota. Even if your manager doesn't require an annual territory plan, putting one in place helps you achieve your goals. As you grapple with setting aside good selling time to pull together a plan, remember why creating a territory plan is a good idea.

First, a solid territory plan gains your manager's buy-in that you know how you will succeed in your territory. A well-thought-out and presented plan keeps your manager focused on other people's territory and leaves you to run your own.

Second, you want your manager's support in your lead generation activities. You need additional resources to execute the lead generation campaigns you have in mind, and you want your manager to agree to provide and fund those resources. A territory plan serves as a business plan, justifying the careful consideration put into how you will spend additional funding and the results you expect to achieve. It is easier to secure the approvals required with a strong territory plan. You will receive a larger portion of your manager's overall budget for even risky lead generation ideas if you are able to demonstrate how and why you will use it.

As I joined a new company, I put together a territory plan outlining how I was going to approach the territory, target markets I would approach, lead generation campaigns I planned to run, partners I would use, and resources I felt I needed. As part of my resource request, I asked for telemarketing support, outlining the campaigns I wanted telemarketing to participate in and its role in those campaigns. I received the resources I requested, but my team was angry with me. The team members didn't understand why my manager had given me telemarketing support when they didn't have it, and my peers saw it as favoritism. But I had presented a well-thought-out plan with sensible business justification that my manager could understand. Planning makes a difference.

Your territory plan is your road map to success. It outlines exactly how you will achieve the goals you have set. It is your *business plan* and should never be far from reach.

ELEMENTS OF A STRATEGIC TERRITORY ACTION PLAN

There are 12 key elements that make your strategic territory action plan an invaluable tool. They are listed below in the order you would present them:

1. **Territory Quota Goals** from Chapter 2, "Lead Generation Begins with Your Goals," help you determine if you have an action plan to achieve or overachieve your territory goals, leveraging as many resources as possible to do the work for you. This element includes both your goals from Chapter 2 and the number of leads you need in your funnel at all times from Chapter 4, "How Many Leads Are Enough?"

2. **Territory Profile** in Appendix E, "Sample Strategic Territory Plan." This exercise allows you to slice your territory multiple ways and look for obvious target markets. You'll be able to see more clearly where you can generate new leads across your territory.

3. **Historical Performance** from Chapter 6, "Segmenting Your Territory into Target Markets That Work for You." Here you examine which target markets performed and which did not over the past two years, indicating a possible need for change in lead generation focus.

4. **Top Five Territory Target Markets** from Chapter 6, "Segmenting Your Territory into Target Markets That Work for You." This element defines where you will focus your lead generation activities and campaigns to get the biggest return on your investment of time, energy, and money.

5. **Top Ten Strategic Customers** from Chapter 7, "Generating Leads in Named Accounts." Here you identify those customer accounts in which you already know large opportunities exist. Remember, you identify what "large" means to your territory and choose your top accounts based on those criteria. In some territories, large may be $1 million because an average sale is $250,000. In other territories, large may be $75,000 because an average sale is $3,500. You define where your largest opportunities exist.

6. **Top Ten Strategic Prospects** from Chapter 7, "Generating Leads in Named Accounts." You identify those prospects where you believe large, or potentially large, opportunities could exist. Highlight these prospects because they may fall outside your top five target markets, but you want to be sure to focus lead generation activities on them too.

7. **Strengths and Weaknesses Analyses** from Chapter 21, "Identifying Your Competitors and Competitive Differentiators." As part of a territory plan, you want to consider the territory strengths

and weaknesses of your company and your key competitors to better understand your position within the territory and your target markets. These analyses help you define your positioning in your top target markets and the key positioning and messages to use in the content and planning of your lead generation activities.

8. **Territory Partners and Resources** from Chapter 8, "Identifying Partners Who Can Help You." List the partners and resources you can leverage in generating and closing leads within your territory. Include the lead generation quota you believe they can contribute to your territory from Chapter 9, "Quota'ing Your Partners."

9. **Marketing Strategy by Top Target Markets,** from Appendix E, "Sample Strategic Territory Plan." This element identifies the strategy you plan to use to generate and win new opportunities in a defined target market, including which partners you will engage to assist you, what your company's strengths and weaknesses are in the target market, and a list of the lead generation campaigns you would like to execute. Your lead generation activities action plan is not included in the territory plan. Rather, it is your daily working document as you execute your lead generation campaigns.

10. **Lead Generation Campaign Overview** from Chapter 18, "Creating Your Own Campaign." This element is the overview of all your lead generation campaigns by target market. It includes one campaign overview per target market you are covering this year.

11. An example of one of your **Campaign Plans.** These plans are the detailed plans behind your campaign overview for each target market. Include one activities action plan example in your territory plan to demonstrate to your manager that you know what you are doing and how you will use the resources you are requesting. Be sure not to take on all responsibilities for activities yourself; you can't do it all alone.

12. **Territory Resource Requirements** in Appendix E, "Sample Strategic Territory Plan." This indicates where you ask for the resources you require to be successful in executing your lead generation campaigns within your target markets and territory. Be sure to ask for the resources you believe you need.

THE PROCESS TO DEVELOP YOUR TERRITORY PLAN

Figure 23.1 shows the process to use to develop the components of your territory plan. Notice your activities are not included in your territory plan. Rather, the plan includes the weekly to-do items you will use to execute your plan.

Appendix E, "Sample Strategic Territory Plan," demonstrates how all the elements of the plan come together. It puts all the forms in one handy place for you to create your own plan. As you review it, you will note the territory plan in Appendix E is organized in the format you would use to deliver your plan rather than in the format you would use to develop it.

ASK, ASK, ASK . . . FOR THE RESOURCES YOU NEED!

You have a vision you are passionate about for your territory. You have identified your target markets, your top ten customers and top ten prospects, and the partners you need to work with to achieve your personal quota. You have developed a marketing strategy you believe will help achieve your goals. Now you may need resources to get the job done and execute your campaign plans.

You *must* ask for those resources. They are necessary to execute your lead generation plans. When you ask, the worst your manager can say is no. If you don't ask, you will never get the resources you require.

How do I ask? Ask for slightly more than you need as a negotiating tactic. You have a goal to meet. If you get more than you require, use the additional resources to execute your lead generation plans on a bigger scale.

When asking, know exactly what you are asking for. Use the format in Figure 23.2 to prepare yourself for a resource conversation with your manager. List the resources you require, who you think can approve or supply the requirement, and the date you need each one. Be prepared to request substitute resources in the event you receive a negative answer.

FIGURE 23.1 Territory Plan Development Process

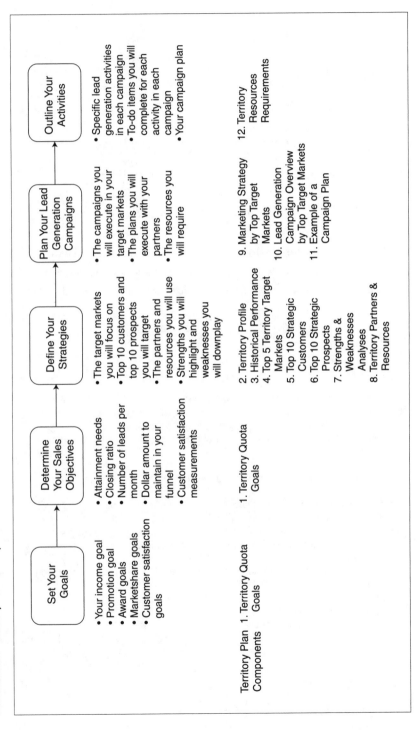

FIGURE 23.2 Territory Resource Requirements

Requirement	Assigned To	Due Date

What do I ask for? Ask for any resources you need and cannot provide on your own to execute your lead generation strategy. Figure 23.3 includes some of the resources to consider as you create your territory plan.

FIGURE 23.3 Resource Requirements

- Funds to execute a lead generation activity
- Executive focus for events, such as a speaker, or other areas
- Additional equipment, for example, a laptop projector
- Additional software, such as special presentation or contact management software
- Lists
- Training to learn more about the target market's industry or to gain speaking skills
- Additional people on your team, such as administrative, telemarketing, or inside sales assistance
- Additional business partners working with your company, where you think it might be beneficial to have a more formal arrangement between the companies
- Changes to existing customer contracts where the contracts may impede selling
- Trials
- Special promotional offerings for a lead generation activity
- Special offerings to gain a foothold in a top ten customer or top ten prospect account or a target market, such as packaging a set of products and services into a special offer specific to an industry or a large company need

CONSIDER INVESTING IN YOURSELF

If, for whatever reason, your company does not give you the critical resources you need to be successful, consider making the investment in those resources yourself. Hire a telemarketer from a temporary employment agency. Or hire a public relations agent to write and submit articles for you, saving time getting in the door and working with editors. Another good investment might be in the equipment necessary to do effective lead generation: a good printer, a camera cell phone, contact management software, and more. You can purchase lists and pay for postage. If necessary, you could even negotiate with a printer to publish event invitations if marketing can't print them. Remember, your territory is *your* business to invest in.

If you need to make the investment to blow away your quota, do it! The additional income and awards you earn will offset your expenses. And if you are successful, your company may reimburse your out-of-pocket costs at the end of the year.

HOLD A TERRITORY PLANNING REVIEW MEETING

After completing the annual territory plan, hold a territory planning review meeting. At the review meeting, present your territory plan in a formal presentation, giving each participant a copy. As with an annual meeting, this is your opportunity to communicate your plan to achieve your territory goals, solicit additional ideas, get people's support, and request the resources you need.

Invite those people whose support you need to successfully execute your lead generation plans. Invite your manager and one other sales manager, a peer sales rep or two you respect, your administrative support person, your sales support person, a marketing person, and one or two service support people who work with your customers. Hold a separate meeting with each of your partners individually to review your plan with them.

SUMMARY

The review meeting was a tremendous success for Flo. So much so that Flo decided she will hold a territory planning review meeting every six months to discuss her progress, share adjustments she plans to make, gather new ideas, and review where she needs additional assistance in the coming six months.

What Flo didn't realize is the additional good things that would happen because she took the time to create and share a plan. Not only did she now have a complete strategy she and her partners could follow, but she knew her path to achieving her goals. She didn't have to guess the direction to take—it was in the plan with logical reasoning supporting it.

Even better, once Flo's plan was complete and she shared it with her manager, she had full company support. Her manager was so impressed by Flo's initiative and ability to think through some of the goals and challenges of an entire year that he was more willing to give her the resources she requested. Nothing could stop her success this year if she executed her plan!

24

USING YOUR TERRITORY LEAD GENERATION PLAN EFFECTIVELY

F*lo's goal was to achieve her quota by September 30 so she wouldn't have to work so hard the last month of the year— and she far exceeded it. Not only did Flo learn about generating leads to meet goals, she also learned how to manage consistent, targeted lead generation in her territory. Flo was awarded Salesperson of the Year at TJ Parker Ideas. Her planning really paid off!*

HOW DO I USE MY TERRITORY PLAN TO IMPROVE MY ODDS OF SUCCESS?

You have done a lot of work to reach the point where you can outline your lead generation campaign strategies and create a territory plan to achieve the goals you have set for yourself. Don't let your plan sit in a file and gather dust. Filing your plan won't help you improve your odds of achieving your quota and income goals. Use your plan as your lead generation strategy for the year.

To get started, create a to-do list based on your lead generation campaign plans that is compiled in the Campaign Overview section of your territory plan. After presenting your territory plan in the territory review meeting, pull your campaign plans apart to use each week. They determine your weekly to-do lists. In selling, a rep's calendar is dynamic—at the whim of customers. As such, even though you might think you can complete an activity by a specific future date, you may not be able to do so when that date arrives. To position yourself for success, allow a week to complete a set of activities. Assign yourself specific activities you can complete within a week or a week and a half. This gives you a period to complete activities and avoids the stress of late nights at work writing lead generation content or putting stamps on envelopes.

Look at your territory plan each month to determine if you are on track with your original plans. Review your lead generation campaign plans every week to stay focused on the activities outlined in your plan. I strongly recommend maintaining your territory plan, campaign overview, and campaign plans electronically for easy sharing and updating. My primary tool is a spreadsheet that allows easy copying, sorting, expanding, contracting, and reporting of my campaign plans. I can quickly make changes to the spreadsheet, track it using version numbers, and e-mail it to my support team. Once you have outlined your plan in the spreadsheet, keep a paper copy close at hand for easy reference and planning.

As discussed in Chapter 23, "Creating Your Annual Territory Plan," share your territory plan with your manager, partners, and resources. You have a team of people supporting you. They know what their responsibilities are in your plan and how you will support them. Check in with them periodically to see what assistance they need from you and how well they are doing with those responsibilities.

In sales, thinking about numbers leads to success. You know your statistics and your goals. Another number to consider is the 13-month year. If you create your plan in November and present it in December, you give yourself a 13-month year. Your lead generation plans begin in December for launch to prospects immediately following the holidays. As the year draws to a close, your partners will be quota'ed and on board with your strategy, and lead generation campaigns will be designed and queued for launch. You will jump into the year immediately on January 1 while your competitors are just beginning to plan their new year!

DETERMINING THE RIGHT ACTIVITIES
TO FOCUS ON

Your territory plan and lead generation campaigns contain many, many action items, and at times you may feel overwhelmed by them all. To avoid this feeling, first work with partners and resources to divide the work. If you are still feeling overwhelmed, focus on only those activities in your top target market, top two to three prospects, and top five customers.

Look for ways to consolidate your campaign plans. You can often consolidate several similar activities into one campaign plan, allowing yourself to complete similar to-do items at once even though they may pertain to different target markets. For example, if you are holding three events on similar topics but for different target markets, you can plan the invitations, book the locations, and write the event invitations at the same time. You can also reuse campaign plans with new dates when you are running the same set of activities across multiple target markets. Using an electronic spreadsheet for the campaign plan makes this especially easy and you don't "reinvent the wheel" for each campaign.

Once your lead generation campaigns are running smoothly in your top two target markets, you are ready to begin activities in your next target market. The next target market is the third one you identified in the top five territory target markets in your territory plan from Chapter 6 "Segmenting Your Territory into Target Markets That Work for You." To bring on a new target market, determine the lead generation campaigns to execute and create a Marketing Strategy by Top Target Markets from Appendix E, "Sample Strategic Territory Plan."

Don't concern yourself if you cannot get beyond your top two target markets, top two to three prospects, and top five customers in one year. It may take you a full 12 months to get your lead generation engine running smoothly. That's okay. Once the engine is running smoothly and you are pleased with the results, then you can push it and add the next top two to three prospects, top five customers, and additional target markets.

Give yourself time to be successful before trying to take on too many lead generation activities. If you push to do more too quickly, you may find your efforts ineffective or, worse, resulting in a negative image within your target markets. Just as you took the time to plan, take the time to execute your plan deliberately and effectively.

MONITORING AND ADJUSTING YOUR TERRITORY PLAN

Not every activity in your lead generation plan will have the results you are seeking. Therefore, monitor and measure your results as discussed in Chapter 18, "Creating Your Own Campaign." When you discover a specific lead generation activity is not performing successfully enough, adjust it, or even stop it. Don't stick with an activity that isn't working just because it's part of your plan. Adjust your territory plan and move on.

In the same vein, if there is a lead generation activity that is working particularly well for you, consider how you might change your lead generation campaign plans to take advantage of the high market response. You may choose to repeat the activity in other parts of your territory or again in a few months in the same target market. Be careful not to reuse the same activity too frequently as the market may become immune to it and response rates will drop.

Use your territory plan to guide your daily, monthly, and quarterly activities. It is a living document that you want to adjust as you see the results of your efforts.

SUCCESS BEGINS WITH YOUR TERRITORY PLAN

There are six keys to success. If you follow these six keys, you will far exceed your goals, achieving unexpected rewards and accolades as well:

1. A vision
2. A plan
3. Die-hard execution
4. Constant and consistent lead generation
5. Follow up! Follow up! Follow up!
6. Understanding of and caring for your customers and prospects

Even if you don't have the seemingly innate talent of some of your peers, you *can* be an extremely successful sales rep—through your territory plan. It is your key to success. It is the business strategy and plan that encompasses the six keys of success in your territory. It outlines your goals and all your plans to achieve those goals. If you execute your plans, you *will* be a success.

Looking back on the previous chapters in this book, there are ideas, strategies, and examples of the things you can do as a sales rep to achieve success. All of the information is based on years of experience, knowledge, and input from people who have—and are currently experiencing—the same challenges and victories that you have. The key to success can lie in these pages, but the true measure of success is in you. Use what you've learned in this book as a guide, but look upon yourself as the person who can make it all happen.

Good luck and great selling!

A

SAMPLE LEAD GENERATION ACTIVITIES

HOLIDAY LETTERS

Thanksgiving Thank-you Letter to a Customer

This text can be sent as a letter, card, or e-mail.

Happy Thanksgiving!

November 18, 2xxx

Jerry Jacobs
Beehive Manufacturing
2835 Broadway
Devon, WI 34967

Dear Jerry,

During this holiday season of Thanksgiving, please accept my thanks for being my ABC Co. client this past year. I look forward to continuing to work together in the New Year. I value your support, and ABC Co. values you as a client.

Jerry, please let me be the first to wish you a happy Thanksgiving, a happy holiday season, and a prosperous New Year!

Best regards,

Randy Young

Thanksgiving Thank-you Letter to a Prospect

This text can be sent as a letter, card, or e-mail. It can be sent to a subset of your target market or prospects you have been talking with who will all recognize your name.

Happy Thanksgiving!

November 20, 2xxx

Jerry Jacobs
Beehive Manufacturing
2835 Broadway
Devon, WI 34967

Dear Jerry,

During this holiday season of Thanksgiving, please accept my thanks for working with me this past year. I very much enjoyed our conversations. Even though we did not get the opportunity to work more closely together through my services in 2xxx, Jerry, I would very much look forward to doing so in 2xxx.

Please let me be the first to wish you a happy Thanksgiving, a happy holiday season, and a prosperous New Year!

Best regards,

Kendra Lee

Client Happy New Year's Letter

February 9, 2xxx

Jerry Jacobs
Beehive Manufacturing
2835 Broadway
Devon, WI 34967

Dear Jerry,

Happy New Year in February! By now you are well on your way to setting your 2xxx business goals, if not already putting your action plans in place. You are busy determining who can help you achieve those goals, and we would like to help.

As your local XYZ Company team, our goal is to keep you informed as new technologies are introduced and old technologies are enhanced. Think of XYZ as the architecture for rapid business change. As business cycles shrink and you strive to become more competitive, to be more cost effective, and to introduce more products faster, you need an information architecture that can adapt quickly. We can do that.

We want to work with you to help you achieve your 2xxx business goals and to architect your business to respond quickly to the changes in your industry. Watch for XYZ updates, like the enclosed one, that outline topics and products important to maintaining your competitive edge.

2xxx will be an exciting year. Many new XYZ products are slated for release this year—a new release of the base server, a parallel server, an exciting indexing technology for lightning speed ad hoc queries, and more. This year will also see a significant focus on data warehousing, a process you implement to fit your organization's requirements rather than a product that you squeeze your organization to fit. Upcoming events, seminars, and mailings will continue to bring the flexibility and power of Client Server computing to your organization.

As your local team, we want you to feel you can be an enthusiastic reference on our behalf. In addition, we want you to excitedly refer us to your colleagues as a team that provides exceptional service for your company. That means we need to be working with you as a partner to meet your business requirements. Please help us. Tell us what we are doing well and where we can improve. Call us when you need us if we haven't called you. Let us help you achieve your key business goals.

We look forward to working with you this year to assist you in achieving your 2xxx goals. Call on us at 303-555-8943 with any questions you may have. Thank you for being an XYZ client! We'd like to help you achieve your ideal information architecture—one that consistently adapts to your changing business needs.

Warmest regards,

Daniel Osnow,
Scott Simon, & Mark Jones
Your local XYZ sales team

Prospect or Target Market Happy New Year's E-mail

Subject: Can we talk by phone next week?

Happy New Year, Jerry!

It's hard to believe it's the New Year already! Even though we have not yet had the opportunity to work together, I would very much look forward to doing so this year. Can we set a time to talk by phone next week to discuss your strategic priorities for 2xxx and how we might be able to work together? I want to be sure I focus my efforts in line with your objectives for the year.

Best regards,

Daniel Osnow
Tag line
Phone number
Web address

Thank-you Letter or E-mail

From: Cheryl Gilinsky [mailto:cheryl.gilinsky@simpath.com]
Sent: Tuesday, December 14, 2004 11:21 AM
To: 'jjack@bigcar.com'
Subject: Information on SimPath Learning for Big Car

Dear Judith,

Thank you for taking the time with me on the phone today; it was a pleasure speaking to you. As promised, some documentation for your reading pleasure.

SimPath Learning offers customized, self-paced eLearning and simulation learning solutions to customers and partners worldwide. Attached please find information on SimPath Learning, plus Features and Benefits and some frequently asked questions (FAQ) on simulation-based learning.

"I Hear and I Forget, I See and I Remember, I Do and I Understand"—Confucius

Simulation is more than just eLearning; it is "learning by doing." By using an advanced simulation platform, we capture business processes, system screens, and contextual settings, then model them into effective learning scenarios. What businesses have been experiencing is that system application implementations (e.g., ERP) often fail to achieve the desired business benefit. The reason often cited is lack of appropriate training as users apply old behaviors to new environments.

The staff at SimPath Learning brings many years of experience and understanding in developing a broad range of simulation-based eLearning solutions for business-critical applications. This type of learning targets a positive change in the learner's behavior when faced with new (or changing) business processes and systems.

I have highlighted a few points explaining what SimPath Learning can offer you:

- **Develop customized training solutions that address your specific needs.**
- **Blend soft skills training with systems training for a complete solution.**
- **Create simulation training of integrated systems and/or processes.**
- **Consult with you to obtain the best Learning Management System for your needs.**
- **Adapt courseware for multiple learning audiences (e.g., role-based).**
- **Effectively blend our simulation learning solutions with your existing training strategy.**
- **Provide self-paced foundation training that will allow you to focus on learners who need extra help (i.e., additional mentoring).**

Please feel free to visit our Web site at www.simpathlearning.com for further information and examples of our work.

I look forward to the opportunity to discuss your specific needs in more detail. If you need additional information please let me know.

Regards and thanks,

Cheryl Gilinsky
Alliances & Business Development

SimPath Learning
323.654.1102 (o)
323.650.5300 (f)
323.314.0000 (c)

www.simpath.com

October 16, 2xxx

Jerry Jacobs
Beehive Manufacturing
2835 Broadway
Devon, WI 34967

Dear Jerry,

Thank you for taking time out of your busy day to speak with me today. In today's business world, time is precious. You can rest assured that I will always be respectful of the time you invest as we discuss the possibility of a mutually beneficial business opportunity.

I appreciate the opportunity to speak with you and would look forward to working with you to help achieve Beehive's goals and objectives. Thank you again, Jerry! It would be a pleasure to work together!

Best regards,

Sally Smyth

INTRODUCTORY INTEREST GATHERING
E-MAILS AND LETTERS

From: Cheryl Gilinsky [mailto:cheryl.gilinsky@simpath.com]
Sent: Thursday, January 06, 2005 10:16 AM
To: Bill Thomas
Subject: Can you direct me regarding eLearning?

Hi Bill,

Good day to you!

My name is Cheryl Gilinsky, and I am with a company called SimPath Learning. We provide Customized Simulation Training. I was hoping that you would be kind enough to assist me regarding your eLearning initiative. If you are not the correct person, could you please be kind enough to forward my details?

Do you know what direction your company will be taking regarding eLearning for 2005, and would it consider using a contractor?

My e-mail address is cheryl.gilinsky@simpath.com
Our Web site address is www.simpath.com
My contact number is 323.654.1102.

I thank you in advance and wish you and your family Happy Holidays!

Best wishes,

Cheryl Gilinsky
Alliances & Business Development
SimPath Learning
323.654.1102 (o)
323.650.5300 (f)
323.314.0000 (c)

www.simpath.com

Sample E-mail—2

This is a short introductory e-mail leveraging a best practices guide the marketing organization has placed on the company Web site. Marketing also did a postcard mailing to some companies. This e-mail could be used even if you aren't sure the postcard went to your target market.

Karen,

I'd like to take this opportunity to introduce you to Akibia, the largest independent provider of **UNIX** and **Linux support services.** For over 17 years, Akibia has been delivering flexible **Multivendor Systems Maintenance** services to Fortune 1000 companies, such as **Bear Stearns, Nomura Securities,** and **Allmerica,** enabling them to reduce their IT support costs by **25 to 40%.**

Serving as a single point of contact, Akibia provides hardware maintenance and operating system support for complex, multi-platform environments, including Sun Microsystems, Hewlett-Packard, Compaq, and Dell, systems running on UNIX and Linux platforms.

I would like to set up a meeting to discuss your support requirements and identify how Akibia can reduce your IT support costs by up to 40% while increasing your system's availability and quality of service. I will call you at 10 AM on Tuesday for a brief discussion about your service requirements. If you are not available, please reply and suggest a more convenient time.

I am also e-mailing you to follow up on a postcard we recently sent you offering a **complimentary Best Practices Guide** on how to **Maximize the Value of Your IT Support Investment.** To view the Best Practices Guide, please visit **http://www.Akibia.com/Savings** or call me directly at 111-555-1234.

Best Regards,

Ron
Akibia
111-555-1234
<u>e-mail</u> address
Company tag line

P.S.: To learn more about Akibia's Data Center Support services, please view **IDC's** objective profile of Akibia at http://**www.Akibia.com/Knowledge,** or visit our Web site at http://**www.Akibia.com/Support.**

Introductory Letter to Set Up a Phone Appointment or Meeting Based on a Referral

This letter could also be modified for use when you don't have a referral and for e-mail.

December 3, 2xxx

Jerry Jacobs
Beehive Manufacturing
2835 Broadway
Devon, WI 34967

Dear Jerry,

Jeff Reynolds of ABC Company suggested I touch base with you about how we might be able to work together to more effectively service your members and ultimately increase your profits.

I would be very interested in setting a phone appointment to discuss your business initiatives for 2xxx and how I might be able to assist you in addressing those. Inevitably during this time of growth at Beehive, many outside firms are vying for your attention, so I want to thank you in advance for taking the time to speak with me.

The Widget Sales Co. has developed _____ specifically aimed at _____ then closing them for large financial institutions. Our products and services focus on _____, _____, and _____. Our goal is to _____.

Jeff felt our insights and strategies could be of great value to your organization and asked that I contact you. Is there a time the week of December 15 that we can speak to discuss how we might work together?

I will call you on December 8 to see if we can set a phone appointment. In the meantime, you can reach me at 303-123-4567. I look forward to speaking with you, Jerry!

Sincerely,

Mark Littlejohn
Sales Representative

FIGURE A.1 Typical Event Lead Generation Campaign

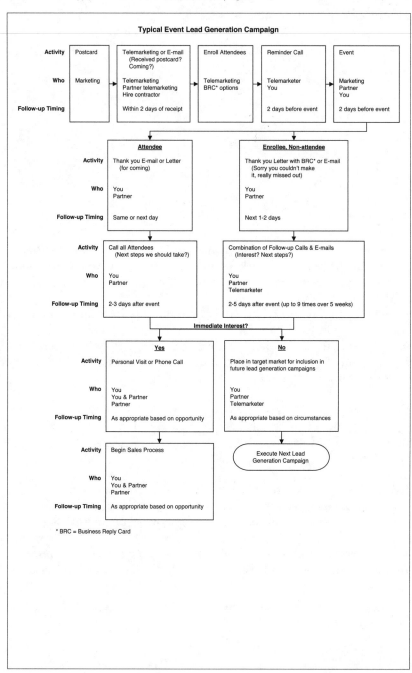

Sample 1 Voice Mail (specific reference to the postcard the prospect or customer might have received)

Hello, this is Ron Davis from Akibia. I'm following up on a postcard we recently sent you offering a complimentary Gartner white paper on how to assess your company's level of IT process maturity. Many Akibia clients, such as Bear Stearns, Nomura Securities, and Allmerica, have found this to be a valuable tool that helped them move to a more proactive systems maintenance model. To obtain the Gartner white paper, please visit Akibia.com/Gartner or call 111-555-1234.

Sample 2 Voice Mail

Hello, this is Ron Davis from Akibia. I'm following up on a postcard we recently sent you offering a complimentary Gartner report on how to assess your company's level of IT process maturity. Many Akibia clients, such as Bear Stearns, Nomura Securities, and Allmerica, have found this to be a valuable tool that helped them increase efficiencies in their IT infrastructure. To obtain the Gartner report, please visit Akibia.com/Gartner or call 111-555-1234. Thank you!

Sample E-mail

Short introductory e-mail leveraging the Gartner white paper referenced in the postcard as the hook.

Jim,

I'd like to take this opportunity to tell you about Akibia, the largest independent provider of **UNIX** and **Linux support services.** For over 17 years, Akibia has been delivering flexible **Multivendor Systems Maintenance** services to Fortune 1000 companies, enabling them to reduce their IT support costs by **25 to 40%.**

Serving as a single point of contact, Akibia supports the critical data centers of many leading companies, such as Bear Stearns, Nomura Securities, and Allmerica, helping them increase the reliability and availability of their critical systems. For more information about Akibia and our Data Center Support services, please visit http://www.Akibia.com/Support.

I am also following up on a postcard we recently sent you offering a complimentary Gartner white paper on how to assess your company's level of IT process maturity. Many of Akibia's clients have found this to be a valuable tool that has helped them move to a more proactive server maintenance model. To obtain this white paper, please visit http://www.Akibia.com/Gartner, or call me directly at 111-555-1234. Thank you!

Best Regards,

Ron
Akibia
111-555-1234
E-mail address
Company tag line

In-Your-Area Intro Letter

These e-mails and letters are very effective for remote geographies that typically don't get the attention larger metropolitan areas receive from salespeople. This letter can be modified for an e-mail.

June 9, 2xxx

Mr. Dave Pierce
Medium Size Insurance Agency
2889 S. Broadway
Leadville, CO 80905

Dear Dave,

I will be in the Leadville area Tuesday, July 17, and would enjoy the opportunity to meet with you. As the XYZ Company sales representative assigned to insurance firms for Colorado, I assist many agencies such as yours in making computer hardware and software decisions.

Today's marketplace offers many choices, from personal computers to large systems. I work closely with a variety of companies to provide the solutions required to effectively operate firms such as your own.

On your behalf, XYZ Company has trained me to understand the insurance environment and to be a consultant to you. This spring I held an Insurance Agency Institute in Denver aimed at keeping people like yourself current on your industry. My knowledge expands beyond computers and software alone to how to keep your agency successful in your own changing marketplace.

I would enjoy the opportunity to discuss your business priorities and how I can assist you in meeting them. If you are available to meet, simply return the tear off sheet below, e-mail me at ssmith@xyzcompany.com, or call me directly at 303-555-1234. I'll give you a call to set up a mutually convenient time to meet.

I look forward to working with you and your firm.

Sincerely,

Sarah Smith

___ Please contact me to set up a time we can meet on July 17.
I prefer: ☐ morning ☐ afternoon *(Check one)*
___ Another date would be more convenient. Please call me to arrange another time.

Mr. Dave Pierce
Other contact _____
Medium Size Insurance Agency
2889 S. Broadway
Leadville, CO 80905
Phone _____

Please return to:
Sarah Smith
XYZ Company
1234 Houston St.
San Diego, CA 80244
Phone: 303-555-1234
Fax: 303-555-1288
Email: ssmith@xyzcompany.com

E-mail Follow-up to a Missed Cold Call Visit

Subject: Sorry I missed meeting you

Leonard,

I am sorry that my schedule did not permit me to visit with you as I had planned Tuesday or Wednesday, February 27 and 28. As you will recall, on February 15 I sent you an e-mail regarding Foothills Telemarketing. We are a telemarketing service provider for those companies that require telemarketing but do not wish to bear the expense of bringing it in-house.

Utilizing Foothills Telemarketing will provide you:
- Experienced, highly productive telemarketers
- Increased customer and prospect satisfaction
- An influx of qualified sales leads
- Decreased costs compared with an in-house telemarketing group
- Proven, streamlined telemarketing and follow-up processes

On Friday, April 11, and Tuesday, April 17, I will be in your area again and would like to introduce myself and the Foothills Telemarketing Organization to you. We have assisted numerous companies in your area to increase their sales and their customer satisfaction. We would appreciate the opportunity to work with your company to provide you these same benefits if these are objectives you are currently focused on.

Is there a time that might work best for you on either April 11 or April 17 for us to meet?

Best regards,

Kristen Singer
Account Manager
816-123-456
kristens@foothillstel.com
Company tag line

EVENT INVITATIONS AND AGENDAS

Event Invitation

The following is an excellent example of a simple, low-cost event you can put together with your partners. Because it combines so many different seminars and Webcasts, it appears bigger than it really is. Notice the offer of a free consultation. This is actually an initial sales call where you consultatively guide people based on the topics they would like to discuss with you.

Even though the technologies mentioned in this event invitation are old, the concept is extremely effective today. It can also be combined with offers of one or two free articles, a white paper, or a newsletter to create an effective, long-term lead generation campaign.

May 5, 2xxx

XYZ Company 2xxx Legal Institute

Did you know that some law firms are billing their clients for a "technology" charge? Does your firm analyze its business development? Are you able to analyze who are the profitable clients and the not-so-profitable clients you do business with today? Did you know that 98% of most businesses store their valuable information on paper so that if a disaster destroys their offices, they could be out of business within a matter of weeks? Do you know how to choose the right technology options for your staff? Do you know. . . .

For the past two years, XYZ Company has brought you the XYZ Legal Institute. We've kept you current on trends in the legal industry and how your firm can remain competitive in today's volatile marketplace.

This year we're expanding the XYZ Legal Institute to include a month of seminars and Web events. Specialists on trends in the legal industry, PCs, Unix, Linux document management, business development, and more bring you these events devoted solely to law firms. We'll give you answers to all of the above questions, and more.

Attached is a list of the events we'll be presenting during the June 2xxx Legal Institute. From accounting to employee benefits and payroll. From document management to image technology. From individual computer system consultations to XYZ Service for law firms.

We're covering the topics that are important to you *TODAY*.

Read through the seminars and pick out one, or many, to attend. There is no charge. To enroll, simply fill in the form below and return it to the XYZ Denver office, or log on to our Web site at http://www.xyzcompany/legalinstitute. You can enroll yourself, your colleagues, and your legal administrator.

For questions, contact me, Sarah Smith at 555-1234 or my assistant, Carolyn Jones, at 555-1235. We look forward to seeing you there!

Sarah Smith
XYZ Company
303-555-1234
ssmith@xyzcompany.com

XYZ Company 2xxx Legal Institute

___ Please enroll me for the events checked below and e-mail me a confirmation.

___ I cannot attend. Please send me information regarding the event(s) I've indicated below.

Name _____	Return to:
E-mail _____	Sarah Smith
Name _____	XYZ Company
E-mail _____	1234 Houston St,
Name _____	Denver, CO 80244
E-mail _____	303- 555-1234
Firm _____	303-555-1288
Address _____	
_____	
Phone _____	

___ 6/6 8:30 AM *Appleby Law Basics*

___ 6/6 1:30 PM *Info Explorer*

___ 6/13 8:30 AM *CGS Legal Technology*

___ 6/13 1:30 PM *Desktop Publishing*

___ 6/14 2:00 PM *XYZ User Legal Panel*

___ 6/18 8:30 AM *CLS Financials*

___ 6/18 1:30 PM *Perfect Write Unix*

___ 6/19 8:30 AM *CLS Professional*

___ 6/19 1:30 PM *XYZ Services for Law Firms*

___ 6/24 8:30 AM *PC Networking & Integration*

___ 6/28   *Computer System Consultation*
   ___ 8:15   ___ 9:25   ___ 10:35   ___ 11:45

XYZ Company 2xxx Legal Institute

June 6
1:30–4:30

Appleby Computer Systems—Law Basics is a case management system that organizes and provides instant access to important legal information. Complete calendaring and an integrated docket control make deadlines a priority. Appleby is a local firm with a wide range of installations nationwide. Platforms: Windows and Unix

June 6
1:30–4:30

Info Explorer—InfoGuide includes pseudoimagining, scanning, and document management to give you a unique way to organize your cases, documents, and incoming documentation. Platforms: Windows, Unix, and Linux

June 13
8:30–11:30

CGS Legal Technology—With the competitive instinct hitting law firms, see how you can utilize this financial, accounting, cost recovery, and business development package to help your firm grow. Platforms: Midrange, Windows, Unix, and Linux

June 13
1:30–4:30

Desktop Publishing for Law Firms—See how easy desktop publishing can be for developing your own newsletters and updates locally using Quick Publish. If you're an innovative firm considering marketing yourself, this is an excellent tool. Platforms: Windows and Unix

June 14
2:00–5:00

IBM User Legal Panel—A panel composed of four XYZ-installed Legal Administrators discusses the trials, tribulations, and results of their automation decisions and the decision-making processes they employed. Platforms: Windows and midrange systems

June 18
CLS
Financial
Applications

See some of the latest technology in tracking time and integrated accounting on one of the fastest-growing multiuser platforms. This package includes all aspects of financial application: time, billing, accounting, and cost recovery. Platforms: Windows and Unix

June 18   **Perfect Write Unix**—Multiuser Perfect Write Version 7.0
1:30–4:30   can save a law firm hardware dollars by utilizing
                   inexpensive terminals rather than PCs. Integrate Unix
                   Perfect Write with DOS Perfect Write for the best of both
                   worlds and add time and accounting applications that can
                   grow easily with your firm. Platforms: Unix and Linux

June 19   **CLS Professional Applications**—Announcing a brand-new
8:30–11:30   Case Management application addressing the issues that
                   Financial Systems users have raised. Platforms: Unix and
                   Linux

June 19   **XYZ Service Offerings for Law Firms**—Disaster recovery
1:30–4:30   planning, end-user services, relocation, cabling, consulting
                   services, and maintenance for the thriving law firm. XYZ
                   offers firms many services to alleviate hassles. Platforms:
                   All hardware platforms

June 24   **PC Networking & Integration**—In order to assist you in
8:30–11:30   successfully establishing communication links in your
                   computer system, PC Dealer 1 has developed the
                   Network Center of Perfection. This network can connect
                   PCs successfully to each other and to midrange systems.
                   Platforms: All hardware platforms

June 27   **Choosing a PC Platform**—How to chose the right personal
8:30–11:30   computer platform for your firm, including the difference
                   between numerous personal computer manufacturers.
                   Learn how to choose which options you really need
                   and what the total cost of computing will be. Various
                   equipment on the market will be discussed as well as
                   service and software considerations. Demonstrations
                   of personal computers and laser printers will follow.
                   Platforms: All personal computers

June 28   **Individual Computer Consultation**—Two XYZ Systems
By Appt   Consultants will be on hand to discuss your firm's particular
                   computer system needs. This will be an individual one-
                   hour consultation by appointment with an XYZ PC
                   Specialist and an XYZ Midrange Specialist. Topics
                   include, but are not limited to, networking your PCs,
                   adding additional equipment, remote communications,
                   office application, accounting, cost recovery, and more.
                   Appointment times are 8:15, 9:25, 10:35, and 11:45, or by

special arrangement. Platforms: All PCs and midrange systems

Please join us for these complimentary events.

To enroll, please call 303-555-8765

fax us at 303-555-9876,

or visit http://www.xyzcompany/legalinstitute.

For Inquiries, contact Sarah Smith at 303-555-1234.

All seminars above will be held at:

1234 Houston St.
Training Room 3
Denver, CO 80244

Webcasts will be delivered live to your office.

Log-on information will be sent with your enrollment confirmation.

Event Invitation

June 23, 2xxx

John Sheppard
Small Insurance Agency
300 America Ave.
Milwaukee, WI 70256

Dear John,

Many insurance agencies today utilize a computer system in their business. And yet, are you using your computers as profitably as possible in your agency?

You receive software from many different carriers. You correspond with your clients, and track potential clients. You have the option of communicating with a number of different carrier locations. And the choices go on. How do you know what's right for your own agency?

To understand the many options open to you, XYZ offers free consulting services for insurance agencies. In conjunction with our authorized dealers, we are able to assist you in finding the right solutions for your firm using both XYZ and non-XYZ services and solutions.

If your agency would like a centralized approach to access and share information among the office, we can teach you how. If your agency is upgrading its current system or purchasing one for the first time, we can also help—with PCs and larger systems. And if you want to figure out how to communicate from home or with another insurance company, we may have the answer.

On Wednesday, October 8, we are devoting a morning to one-hour individual consultations to discuss your own agency's needs. An XYZ PC Specialist will be on hand. Specialty areas include PC networking, portable computing, remote communication, and more.

Individual consultation times are: 8:15, 9:25, 10:35, and 11:45, or by special appointment. To sign up, simply return the tear sheet below to us or e-mail me at ssmith@xyzcompany.com. If you are unable to attend, but would like assistance, e-mail or fax me your questions, a diagram, or a cry for help! Appointments will be held in the XYZ Conference Room 2 at 1234 Houston Street.

Please schedule me for an insurance agency PC consultation, Wednesday, July 8, at the time checked below and contact me with a confirmation.

___ 8:15   ___ 9:25   ___ 10:35   ___ 11:45   ___ Other

Name	_____	Return to:
E-mail	_____	Sarah Smith
Firm	_____	XYZ Company
Address	_____	1234 Houston St,
	_____	Denver, CO 80244
Phone	_____	303-555-1234
		303-555-1288

___ I cannot attend. Please contact _____ at the above address and phone number with further information.

B

SAMPLE LEAD GENERATION CAMPAIGNS

Figure B.1 is an example of a lead generation campaign using multiple activities over a period of time in the same target market. Variations of this example could include:

- Send an e-mail instead of a letter and follow up by both e-mail and telemarketing.
- Precede the letter with a newsletter that preannounces the event.
- Make the event a Webcast rather than a live event.
- Send an e-mail after the event offering a free synopsis of the event and have people who are interested reply to you to receive it.
- Follow up with an e-mail and a call to all interested people.
- Follow up with all people who did not attend or enroll in the event but were interested, and offer a free synopsis of the event.

Figure B.2 is an example of an e-mail lead generation campaign spanning nearly 12 weeks. This campaign could easily begin with an offer to attend an event, a new product announcement, or a holiday greeting. Here I started it cold based on business needs mixed with a basic product offer of training. This helps it appeal to those people with strategic or tactical needs. Their response would determine the direction I would take in the first conversation.

FIGURE B.1 Sample Direct Mail, Telemarketing, and Event Lead Generation Campaign

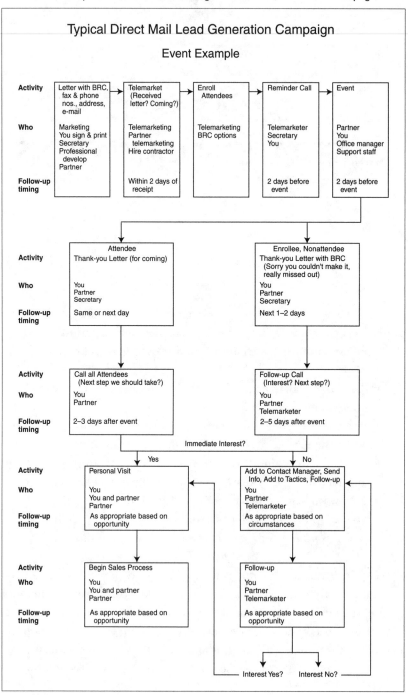

FIGURE B.2 Sample E-mail Lead Generation Campaign

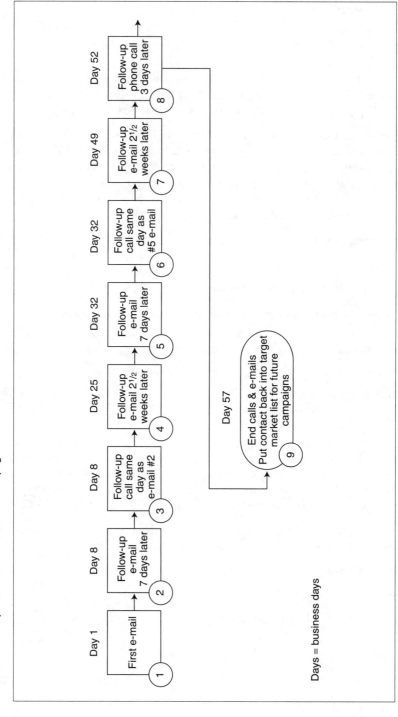

Days = business days

1. First e-mail

Subject: Should we meet?

Hi Jerry,

Several of our clients like yourself are focused on decreasing their overall project costs by improving the skills of their project team members on critical projects. Is this an objective you are focused on as well?

We're running a number of hard-to-find classes such as . . . to help our clients control and reduce project costs. We have several of these classes and others running next quarter. I wanted to touch base with you to see if these might be of interest to you as well. Can we meet in person or over the phone later this week to discuss this or other objectives you have that we might be able to assist with?

Best regards,

Sally

Tag line, including phone number, fax, and Web address

Include hotlinks within the course descriptions mentioned in the body of the e-mail.

2.   Follow-up e-mail five days later
Forward e-mail #1 below this e-mail as a reminder.

Subject: Should we get together?

Hi Jerry,

I just wanted to follow up to see if we should meet either in person or over the phone to discuss your project and people development objectives, and where we might be able to work together to help you achieve them. I'd be very interested in talking with you about it. How does your schedule look for the next two weeks?

I'll leave you a quick voice mail as well in the event you are traveling and that it is easier for you to schedule that way.

Best regards,

Sally .

Tag line, including phone number, fax, and Web address

3. Follow-up call the same day (leave this as voice mail if there is no answer)

Hi Jerry! This is Sally Jones with ABC Company. I just wanted to give you a quick call and follow up on my e-mail to you to see if we should meet either in person or over the phone to discuss your project and people development objectives, and where we might be able to work together to help you achieve them. I'd be very interested in talking with you about it. Is there a time on your schedule over the next two weeks that might work for you? Please give me a call at 524-555-0123 or e-mail me at sally@abccompany.com. I look forward to talking with you, Jerry!

4. Follow-up e-mail 2½ weeks later

Forward e-mails #1 and #2 below this e-mail as a reminder.

Subject: Planning for next quarter

Hi Jerry,

As summertime and vacations draw near next quarter, you might see your project load lightening, and it could be a good time to do some development of your people. Several of our clients are focused on decreasing their overall project costs by improving the skills of their project team members on critical projects. Other clients are looking at outsourcing critical skills and how they can ensure they retain the right skills. I'd enjoy the opportunity to talk with you about how you are controlling project costs, if outsourcing is something you are looking at, and where we might be able to assist you.

Can we meet in person or over the phone later this week to discuss this and other objectives you have that we might be able to assist with?

Best regards,

Sally

Tag line, including phone number, fax, and Web address

5. Follow-up e-mail five days later

Forward e-mails #1,#2, and #3 below this e-mail as a reminder.

Subject: Can we talk next Wednesday at 2:00?

Hi Jerry,

Several of our clients are focused on decreasing their overall project costs by improving the skills of their project team members on critical projects. Other clients are looking at outsourcing critical skills and how they can ensure they retain the right skills. I wanted to check in to see if we can discuss how we might assist you with controlling project costs.

Do you have availability for us to meet by phone next week? Would either next Wednesday at 2:00 your time or next Friday at 9:30 your time work for you? I'll hold both times on my calendar until I hear from you. I'll leave you a quick voice mail as well in the event you are traveling and that it is easier for you to schedule that way.

Best regards,

Sally

Tag line, including phone number, fax, and Web address

6. Follow-up call the same day (leave this as voice mail if there is no answer)

Hi Jerry! This is Sally Jones with ABC Company. We have been working with a number of clients who are focused on controlling project costs through people development or ensuring they retain the right skills as they move to outsourcing. I'd be very interested in talking with you to see if these are areas where we might work together. Would you be available either next Wednesday at 2:00 your time or next Friday at 9:30 your time? I'll hold both times on my calendar until I hear from you. I've also sent you an e-mail in case that is an easier way for you to respond. Let me know. I can be reached at 524-555-0123 or e-mail me at sally@abccompany.com. I look forward to talking with you next week, Jerry!

7. Follow-up e-mail 2½ weeks later if the holiday pricing is announced
Forward only e-mail #5 requesting the meeting

Subject: Special pricing update

Hi Jerry,

I'm sorry we weren't able to connect on Wednesday or Friday. I wanted to check in to see if we should discuss some summer people development for any of your people who might have a lightened workload due to the season, or if we can discuss how we might assist you with controlling project costs. Should we talk?

Best regards,

Sally

Tag line, including phone number, fax, and Web address

8. Follow-up phone call two to three days later (leave this as voice mail if there is no answer)

Hi Jerry! This is Sally Jones with ABC Company. I'm sorry we weren't able to connect last Wednesday or Friday. I look forward to talking with you. I was just calling to follow up on my e-mail to see if we should discuss some summer people development for any of your people who might have a lightened workload due to the season, or if we can discuss how we might assist you with controlling project costs. Should we talk? Let me know. I can be reached at 524-555-0123, or e-mail me at sally@abccompany.com. I look forward to talking with you next week, Jerry!

9. Stop pursuing Jerry and put his name back into your general target marketing list for the next lead generation campaign.

WRITING ACTION PLAN

Date: _____ Edit Date: _____ Proof Date: _____

Who is my target reader?	Target Market: Target Title(s): _____ E-mail or _____ Letter
Why am I writing?	
What do I want to say?	

What do I want to accomplish with this communication?	
What action do I want my reader to take as soon as he finishes reading this communication?	
What action will I take with the reader after this communication is received?	
What unique features does my solution have that will be of interest to my reader?	
What are the benefits to my reader of my solution? List three.	1. 2. 3.
Proofing	Is the communication easy to read? Does it convey what you want it to convey? Did you eliminate the fluff stuff?

LISTS OF TOPICS FOR LEAD GENERATION ACTIVITIES

Following are lists of topics you can use for lead generation campaigns by type of activity. Some ideas work for campaigns targeted to a larger audience. Others work best for campaigns targeted to smaller audiences. Many can be combined into lead generation campaigns.

Telephone Topics

- Call all your competitors' accounts and do a blind survey to determine their satisfaction. Those that show a degree of dissatisfaction should be on your target prospect list.
- Call all the people in your territory who attended any event held by your company in the past two years.
- Call all the high-growth companies in your territory; they may be small today, but if they are growing, so will your opportunity with them.
- Call all the customers in your territory just to say hello, and ask what you could do better; is there anything you can assist them with today?

- Precall before doing any mailings to ensure you have the correct name, address, and title and that the person still works there or the company is still in business.
- Follow up with all event attendees to determine the next step and to find new opportunities.
- Facilitate networking between a client and prospect, two prospects, a prospect or client, and a user group or association to add value and be more than just a salesperson.
- Network with alternative channels to find out which companies are out looking and making decisions.
- Survey to better define your target market and the companies that are a part of it, calling to ask three or four opinion questions. The prospect may become interested in why you are asking, and suddenly you have a lead.
- Call as you do with a customer satisfaction survey. Limit these to no more than one or two per year.

Mailing Topics

- Create a direct mail brochure based on current business issues relevant to your top target markets.
- Send a new product brochure or announcement or a product update letter that marketing has prepared. Handwrite a brief note to each prospect. Or preview new product announcements to build excitement, even if the solutions won't be available for several months.
- Offer a product or technical white paper as a follow-up to an event or direct mailing.
- Send a personal letter, note, or e-mail. If you are new to a part of your territory or to your target market, send a letter of introduction. If you are visiting a city, send a note saying you will be there and request a meeting.
- Update a set of prospects on a recent, successful project similar to one that might be of interest to their companies.
- Send holiday cards, especially for more unusual holidays, such as Thanksgiving, spring, summer, 4th of July, or Halloween.
- Include gifts or small trinkets, if appropriate.

- Send a newspaper or magazine article of interest to your target market.
- Every week, send five letters to potential customers. Address each one to the highest-ranking person in the company and give a valuable business reason for that person to meet you. Include a date and time that you will either personally visit or call the person. Keep the appointment despite the possibility that the prospect will not. Whether or not you get the meeting, try to find out the best time to call your prospect, names of key associates or colleagues, and more general information about the company.
- Send press reviews about your company.
- Take advantage of your competition's downfalls or bad luck and send a direct mail piece that lets your prospects know how you can help them address an important business issue. Do not mention your competition. Rather, focus on your own strengths and let your competition's bad press address their issues.
- Send a reprint of a magazine article pertinent to their industry or your industry.

Event Topics

- Host executive breakfasts that include a customer speaker, special industry speaker from their industry, or special industry speaker from your industry. Always focus on a topic of current interest and limit the breakfast to 90 minutes or less.
- Bring in a key industry speaker and invite your top executive prospects and customers.
- Pick one or two hot industry topics and put together a first-class event complete with customer references, a knowledgeable and motivating speaker from your company, and perhaps a recognized industry leader as another speaker. Limit the event to two hours.
- Host new product or services announcements or new product demonstrations. If possible, include a sample new service giveaway, such as one hour of free consulting.
- Host seminars focusing on a specific aspect of, or department within, their business.
- Host a "Meet the Executives" happy hour, bringing in prospects to meet your company's executives.

- Throw a holiday party at your location, at a special restaurant, or at some other fun, exciting place.
- Host an anniversary party celebrating the anniversary of the installation of your product at a top customer account.
- Host a party celebrating the start or completion of a significant project you are involved with at a client's company in a top customer account you are working to penetrate more deeply. Invite new contacts you are trying to reach.
- Cohost partner events where you team your product and your partner's product or services to offer a specialized solution.
- Take advantage of sporting or cultural events your company may sponsor.
- Throw a customer appreciation dinner or luncheon for your top ten customers to which you invite your top ten prospects as a networking opportunity for them.

Newsletter Topics

- A preview or announcement of new solutions. Keep it brief and business focused. Be sure to include availability information.
- Because companies are always looking for ways to improve their business performance, a brief article about how customers have done so using one of your solutions
- New company information to be included in your newsletter; for example, your company is now ISO 9000 compliant, has won a special award, or has added a new organization.
- Significant press announcements and other coverage
- Factual features and benefits about your product line in relation to your prospects' business needs to combat your competition
- A brief article about your product and company differentiators from a business perspective that catches readers' interest
- A current schedule if your organization does regular training or events
- Invitations to upcoming special events or recently past events. Be sure to include the topic, date, time, location, and how to enroll or where to call for additional information. If the event was recorded, include information on how to get a copy.

- Events to highlight could include user groups, associations, or other pertinent organizations your target market might be interested in and that you plan to attend. Let the readers know you will be there and would look forward to meeting for coffee at a break before or after the event.

- In each issue, focus on a reference account. Cover items such as why the reference chose your company's solutions and the positive results it has experienced. Make it a mini case study that will resonate with your target audience.

- With each release, create a base newsletter with several topics for your top target markets. Have a space to include one or two items tailored specifically to your target market.

- To always ensure your customers can respond easily to you, include four ways to respond.

- Include a FAX BACK section where customers or prospects can check a box and fax you for additional information, to sign up for an event or training, or to receive a technical white paper.

- Include a phone number and e-mail address where customers or prospects can call or e-mail you for the same FAX BACK information.

- Create a format that is easy to replicate each time you want to publish a newsletter with similar topics covered each time—for example, a brief overview of an upcoming event, an interview with a current customer, or a review of a recent article, trade show, or conference.

SAMPLE STRATEGIC TERRITORY PLAN

**Sample Strategic Territory Plan
For Current Year: _____**

Kendra Lee

Territory Profile
Current Year: ____

Territory Description (by assigned geography, industry, or other breakdown)

Target Markets

Top Target Markets by industry

Top Target Markets by your company's key product offerings

Top Target Market by other pertinent breakdown (annual revenue, strategic account, line of business within an industry, number of employees, geography, etc.)

Territory Profile
(continued)

Total number of existing customer accounts: 200+

Top Ten Strategic Customers	Target Market(s)	Projected Opportunity
1. EYR Manufacturing	Manufacturing, replication consulting services, connectivity	$200K
2.		
3.		
4.		
5		
6.		
7.		
8.		
9.		
10.		

Definition of a Strategic Customer or Prospect:

- May or may not have an immediate sales opportunity for the current year
- An account in which the potential to purchase large amounts of your solutions exists
- May require a resource investment to realize the full potential over the next several years

Territory Profile
(continued)

Top Ten Strategic Prospects	Target Market(s)	Projected Opportunity
1. Growing Energy Co., Inc.	Utilities, consulting services, computer server, security software	$250K
2.		
3.		
4.		
5		
6.		
7.		
8.		
9.		
10.		

Definition of a Strategic Customer or Prospect:

- May or may not have an immediate sales opportunity for the current year
- An account in which the potential to purchase large amounts of your solutions exists
- May require a resource investment to realize the full potential over the next several years

Historical Performance
Past Year: ___

Previous Year's Quota	Target Markets	Attainment by Target Market	Variance	Rationale for Variance
$250K	Insurance	$350K	$100K	Overachieved! Won big deal
$750K	Manufacturing	$400K	$350K	No good manufacturing solutions or business partners
$1.5M	Total Annual Quota	$1.6M	$100K	Overachieved!!

Target markets can be aligned by industry, solution, geography, or other pertinent company breakdown.

Personal Goals
Current Year: ___

Goal	Priority	Deadline Date for Achievement

Examples might include:
- Exceed revenue quota by z%.
- Make your top business partners and resources successful.
- Achieve top company award.
- Improve your qualified close rate by x%.
- Grow market share by y%.
- Grow revenue by m% year to year.
- Maintain a sales funnel value of $$w$ all times.

Territory Partners and Resources Quota Projections
Current Year: ___

Partner Contact Name	Target Markets/ Accounts to Use With	Annual Number of Leads You'd Like	Annual Number of Leads Jointly Agreed On	Realistic Number of Leads Annually	Deadline for Buy-in	Realistic Total Revenue Contribution to Your Sales Funnel
Total Partner Quota						

Territory Quota Goals: Number of Leads Required
Current Year: ___

	Best-Case Scenario	Worst-Case Scenario
Realistic Total Revenue Contribution to Your Sales Funnel	_____ / 12 months = _____	$_____ × 50% = $_____
Total Dollar Amount You Need to Maintain in Your Funnel per Year	Less ( )	_____ × 1.25% = Less ( )
Overage/ Underage	= ($)	= ($)

Marketing Strategy by Top Target Markets

1. Target Market: _____

Partners & Resources to Utilize			
1.		8.	
2.		9.	
3.		10.	
4.		11.	
5.		12.	
6.		13.	
7.		14.	

Key Target Market Strengths	
1.	
2.	
3.	
Key Target Market Weaknesses	
1.	
2.	
3.	

Marketing Strategy
Lead Generation Campaign Overview

1. Target Market: _____

Campaigns and Activities to Execute	Planned Start Date	Planned Duration
Hire an aggressive telemarketer with previous software sales experience to find new prospects	1/17	2/13
Health care industry seminar	4/15	6/1
Meet with top five partners to plan one event for this year with each	1/31	2/28

Insert current annual forecast here including projections of where you see your quota coming from by account and target market.

Territory Resource Requirements

Requirement	Assigned To	Due Date